CONSUMER
FRAUD

A Reference Handbook

Other Titles in ABC-CLIO's
CONTEMPORARY
WORLD ISSUES
Series

Books in the Contemporary World Issues series address vital issues in today's society such as terrorism, sexual harassment, homelessness, AIDS, gambling, animal rights, and air pollution. Written by professional writers, scholars, and nonacademic experts, these books are authoritative, clearly written, up-to-date, and objective. They provide a good starting point for research by high school and college students, scholars, and general readers, as well as by legislators, businesspeople, activists, and others.

Each book, carefully organized and easy to use, contains an overview of the subject; a detailed chronology; biographical sketches; facts and data and/or documents and other primary-source material; a directory of organizations and agencies; annotated lists of print and nonprint resources; a glossary; and an index.

Readers of books in the Contemporary World Issues series will find the information they need in order to better understand the social, political, environmental, and economic issues facing the world today.

CONSUMER
F R A U D

A Reference Handbook

Lee E. Norrgard and Julia M. Norrgard

**CONTEMPORARY
WORLD ISSUES**

ABC-CLIO

Santa Barbara, California
Denver, Colorado
Oxford, England

Library of Congress Cataloging-in-Publication Data

Norrgard, Lee E.

   Consumer fraud : a reference handbook / Lee E. Norrgard and Julia M. Norrgard.
      p.   cm. — (Contemporary world issues)
   Includes bibliographical references (p.) and index.
   ISBN 0-87436-991-6 (alk. paper)
      1. Fraud—United States. 2. Consumer protection—United States.
   I. Norrgard, Julia M. II. Title. III. Series.
   HV6695.N67   1998
   364.16'3—dc21   94-42276
                                                                          CIP

02 01 00 99 98   10 9 8 7 6 5 4 3 2 1

ABC-CLIO, Inc.
130 Cremona Drive, P.O. Box 1911
Santa Barbara, California 93116-1911

This book is printed on acid-free paper ∞ .

Manufactured in the United States of America

Contents

Preface

Consumer fraud can touch almost anyone. The poor and vulnerable are particularly targeted, but the rich are not spared. The elderly are swindled by fast-talking telephone crooks, car owners are overcharged for repairs, the health of our families can be threatened by unsafe or misbranded foods, and individuals lose millions of dollars to investment fraud. Even if you are savvy enough to avoid being taken, you may pay for consumer fraud in the increased prices charged by businesses to recoup their loses. Nevertheless, many people have a limited understanding of their own vulnerability to fraud.

This book is an introduction to the vast and ubiquitous topic of consumer fraud. It will provide a basic grounding for students or other interested individuals to begin in-depth research. Besides describing a wide variety of common illegal practices, it places the subject in historical perspective and acquaints the reader with a selection of key personalities who have had an impact on this area of law, including both the heroes and the villains.

There is an extensive collection of relevant consumer statutes and documents, some in full text, and a bibliography of print and nonprint sources, most of which are available in public and university libraries. Particularly valuable to the researcher is the listing of state and federal agencies and private organizations, many of which are accessible via the Internet.

We wish to acknowledge the assistance (and gracious patience) of our editor, Kristi Ward. We dedicate this book to our children, Elayne and Jacob.

A Survey of Consumer Fraud Issues

1

"We are for private enterprise with all its ingenuity, thrift and contrivance, and we believe it can flourish best within a strict and well-understood system of prevention and correction of abuses."
—Winston Churchill

The television cameras snapped to attention as Attorney General Janet Reno opened a news conference in the FBI's Las Vegas office. She was there to announce the results of a two-year undercover operation, dubbed *Senior Sentinel* by the FBI, against illegal telemarketing (U.S. Department of Justice, 1995). "Telephone pitches from illicit boiler room operations cost Americans $40 billion a year," declared the attorney general. Kathryn Landreth, United States attorney for Nevada, charged that the illegal telemarketers arrested that day were responsible for ruining the financial security of many older Americans. Victim losses from just one medium-sized Las Vegas boiler room totaled $23 million, according to the FBI (Owens, 1996). Law enforcement officials, including the FBI, postal inspectors, attorneys from the Federal Trade Commission, state attorneys general, and local police all cooperated in the *takedown* that arrested 400 individuals and permanently closed boiler rooms in cities like

Las Vegas and San Diego. To date, the Justice Department has charged almost 1,000 illegal telemarketers with wire fraud, mail fraud, and other offenses under *Operation Senior Sentinel.*

The practice of telemarketing is not, in and of itself, a consumer fraud. It is a sales device employed by many legitimate companies. L.L. Bean and JC Penney use inbound telemarketing with their catalog sales, for example. Newspapers and magazines sell subscriptions over the phone, local charities solicit funds, and stock brokers sell investments with outbound telemarketing. Although consumers consider the uninvited ring of a telemarketing call a "serious violation of their privacy" (Yankelovich, 1997), legitimate telemarketing is a money-making industry with receipts exceeding $500 billion a year (FBI, 1995). It is also a major source of consumer fraud that often targets the most vulnerable. Unfortunately, for the many consumers who cannot recognize fraudulent calls, there is no bright line distinguishing the two. Both legal and illegal telemarketers use some of the same sales tactics. The real difference becomes apparent only after consumers pay. With legitimate telemarketers, consumers receive something of value. With illegal telemarketers, they receive nothing.

Fraudulent telemarketing is one of the nation's largest consumer frauds, but it is but one of hundreds of devices used against consumers. This reference book is about consumer fraud, a term commonly used to describe the schemes that deceive or defraud consumers. Chapter 1 presents an overview. It discusses the costs of the problem to consumers and describes some of the typical victims. It illustrates selected schemes that defraud and the laws drafted to protect consumers. Subsequent chapters provide: an annotated chronology, brief biographies of some key players (both consumer activists and scammers), a selection of critical documents, a current listing of federal, state, and local consumer protection agencies along with business and consumer groups, a bibliography of print and nonprint materials, and a glossary of terms.

The Nature of the Problem

In 1995, American family household income totaled $4.5 trillion dollars (Hacker, 1997). These dollars were used to purchase food, housing, health care, transportation, clothing, and other necessities. They were used for savings and investments and to satisfy the nation's love affair with material gratification (Alexis de Tocqueville, author of *Democracy in America*, commented early in the nation's history about its passion for satisfying "the least wants of the body and to provide the little conveniences of life. . . .") What do consumers want for their money? They want value and to be treated fairly.

Although most sales are fair and honest, far too often the consumer is at risk. Consumer fraud can be a profitable enterprise. The average household spends more than $32,000 a year and there are more than 260 million consumers in the United States. These figures reflect an enormous amount of disposable income and a powerful temptation to unscrupulous sellers. With the right scheme, often assisted by modern technology, perpetrators are able to target victims, collect the cash, and quickly move elsewhere. Unfortunately, at the same time that technology is enhancing the scammer's craft, government consumer agencies and other organizations that combat fraud face shrinking budgets.

Some critical questions are:

- How big is the problem?
- What are consumer losses?
- How many victims are there?
- What are the most prevalent schemes?
- Which consumers are most vulnerable?

Government findings provide one method to evaluate consumer fraud. Both the U.S. attorney general and the Congress report that telemarketing fraud alone steals $40 billion a year from consumers. But, in truth, this sum is just an estimate of the problem. Consumer fraud is part of the nation's underground economy that never appears in the business statistics collected by the U.S. Department of Commerce. Without hard numbers, any analysis must rely on less exact tools, such as estimates, survey research, anecdotal information, and related indicators.

One of the most comprehensive economic estimates of consumer fraud was released by the U.S. Office of Consumer Affairs in 1993. This office indicated that "Fraud steals at least $100 billion a year from consumers' pockets, every year." The seven most problematic areas listed by this agency were:

- Telemarketing/direct marketing, including mail order (estimated loss $10 billion to $40 billion)
- Credit, including credit card fraud and credit "repair" (estimated loss $3 billion)

- Health care (estimated loss $50 billion to $80 billion)[1]
- Insurance (estimated loss $10 billion)
- Investments (estimated loss $10 billion)
- Home improvement and maintenance (no estimates available)
- Auto repair and sales (no estimates available).

This list, however, is incomplete. It does not include consumer losses from false advertising claims, telephone slamming and cramming, Internet fraud, identity theft, price fixing, or predatory financial practices that particularly affect low-income communities, just to mention a few.

The numbers also do not take into account the full financial impact on the victims. For example, older consumers who lose their nest eggs to a telemarketing scheme are unlikely to be able to replace these funds. Similarly, homeowners saddled with a second mortgage bearing a 24 percent interest rate and a five-year balloon payment will likely not only lose their home equity, built up over time, but the home itself.

A second way of looking at consumer fraud is to survey research of consumer behavior. Again, there are limitations regarding the data. The number of studies available is small, somewhat dated, and the findings can be contradictory at times. Further, in some surveys, the questions asked assumed the consumers' understanding of legal terminology for deception and fraud, for example, "Were you defrauded?" What an individual believes to be consumer fraud may or may not meet the legal standard for a deceptive or fraudulent act.

According to a 1993 survey of adult consumers aged 18 and older conducted for the American Association of Retired Persons (AARP), three-fourths of all consumers claim that they had at least one bad buying experience in the last year in which they were deceived, defrauded, or ripped off (AARP, 1994). The most common complaints were about products that didn't work, late deliveries, false or misleading claims, and repair bills that far exceeded written estimates. One in seven respondents reported that at some point in their lifetimes they had more than just a bad buying experience and were the victims of a major fraud. Projecting that percentage to the entire adult population means that more than 28 million adults believed they were victimized by a major consumer fraud.

Another study (Titus, 1995), funded by the U.S. Department of Justice, asked a different but similar question about major frauds. Thirty-one percent of the respondents reported that someone made a *personal fraud attempt* against them. A *personal fraud attempt* was defined as "someone cheating you or attempting to cheat you . . . by deliberately lying to you or giving you false information or phony promises about a product or service . . . or getting you to pay for something that you never received, or swindling you in some other way." Half of these *personal fraud attempts* succeeded, according to the study, or, in other words, 15 percent of the respondents say they were victimized by some form of *personal fraud*.

Many consumers are wary of particular businesses, according to AARP's survey, and believe these companies try to mislead or take advantage of buyers. For example, over 72 percent of the respondents believe companies selling over the phone take advantage of consumers. Next highest in suspicion were car repair shops (71 percent), followed by door-to-door sales companies (66 percent), insurance companies (63 percent), and home repair contractors (56 percent). From the list provided, consumers were least wary of drug stores (26 percent).

Even though they may be wary of the telemarketers' calls, only a little over half (54 percent) of adult consumers "would hang up the phone when someone they didn't know presented them with a fabulous opportunity to make an investment," according to the findings of a 1992 Lou Harris survey. Law enforcement authorities agree that staying on the phone to listen to a fraudulent telemarketer's high-pressure tactics is dangerous. Nearly two-thirds (62 percent) of respondents surveyed in the same study indicated that they "would not know where to call to find out if a telephone offer or promotion is legitimate."

Some researchers theorize that certain demographic groups are "at a disadvantage in exchange relationships" (Hunt, 1991). These consumer groups include children,[2] older consumers, the uneducated, the poor, the disabled, those with language problems, and racial and ethnic groups. Researchers describe these consumers as vulnerable consumers.

The previously cited AARP survey concluded that older Americans are particularly vulnerable to consumer fraud because they are less familiar with sources of consumer information and have less knowledge of consumer rights. They tend to be more open to direct appeals from sellers like telemarketers and less wary of misleading sales presentations. One-third of people aged 75 and older were classified in the high-vulnerability category as compared to 7 percent for younger people.

It appears that the perpetrators of consumer fraud target different schemes to distinct vulnerable consumer groups. For example, according to the FBI, "the repeated victimization of the elderly is the cornerstone of illegal telemarketing" (Owens, 1996). Survey research on telemarketing fraud victims seems to confirm the FBI's investigative finding. Using mooch lists [victims' lists] secured by law enforcement from illegal telemarketers, an AARP study (AARP, 1996) found that more than 50 percent of telemarketing victims were over the age of 50. That percentage is disproportionate to the percentage of the total population who are 50 and older.

In another instance, immigrants were targeted for consumer frauds involving citizenship issues. The district attorney's office in San Francisco reported complaints from Spanish-speaking immigrants who were allegedly bilked out of thousands of dollars by a woman posing as an immigration and naturalization official. She promised to expedite citizenship applications for money.

The previously mentioned Titus study, however, disputes in part the concept of vulnerable consumers. Specifically, their findings indicate that: "No demographic indicator . . . [predicts] whether a fraud attempt, if received, will be successful. The key factor in victimization by personal fraud appears to be whether one receives an attempt" (Titus, 1995, p. 60). In other words, every consumer is potentially vulnerable to a personal fraud attempt if contacted, not just certain groups.

A third window on consumer fraud in the marketplace is individual consumer complaints. The nation's airwaves, newspapers, and other forms of mass communication provide a steady stream of stories about the marketplace experiences of the public, including the latest consumer frauds, law enforcement investigations, victims' woes, and tips on how consumers can protect themselves. Not only are these stories watched and read with interest, they serve an important role in alerting consumers to new schemes and threats.

How do journalists and law enforcement learn of the latest deceptions and frauds? Through consumer complaints, the lifeblood of consumer protection. Without complaints, government agencies cannot take steps to control current abuses and journalists cannot inform consumers of the dangers to watch for in the marketplace.

Most consumers know to complain to sellers for restitution and redress,[3] but few take the next step and complain to agencies like the Federal Trade Commission, Better Business Bureaus, the media, state attorneys general, or state or local consumer protection agencies. One market researcher concludes that "the most common response to unsatisfactory products is to do nothing" (East, 1997, p. 207). Other research indicates that many consumers don't know where to complain or how to file a complaint under consumer protection laws. Given that there is a general lack of information about where and how to seek redress, consumer complaints cannot be considered a statistically valid indication of the extent of the problems. Because so few consumers take action, the complaints of those who do are often considered to be the tip of the iceberg. Complaints are a limited but tangible indicator of marketplace problems for law enforcement, policy makers, consumers themselves, and competing businesses.

One national index of consumer fraud is the annual complaint survey of the National Association of Consumer Agency Administrators (NACAA). NACAA is an international association of state and local consumer protection agencies that compiles and releases a combined total of complaints from its members in the United States and Canada. In their most recent survey, November 1997, the top five categories for 162,000 complaints from 42 state and local agencies were:

- Auto sales (new and used cars): 20 percent
- Home improvement: 18 percent
- Auto repair: 17 percent
- Retail sales: 11 percent
- Mail order/telemarketing: 5 percent (NACAA, 1997).

Overall, complaints were up by nearly one-third from the previous year, even though consumer protection budgets for these agencies declined. Once again, cars, home improvement, and sales issues (retail, telemarketing, and mail order) were among the most frequent complaints. Although Internet fraud did not appear among the top five categories in the 1997 survey, NACAA staff indicate that "problems with the Internet are growing almost as rapidly as the medium itself" (NACAA, 1997).

One final source of information on consumer fraud is the number of arrests for fraud, published in the FBI's annual report, *Crime in the United States*. The FBI reports that in 1995, local police departments arrested 320,000 individuals for fraud. Unfortunately, there is neither a breakdown as to what kinds of fraud were involved nor what happened to the perpetrators—were they charged, convicted, or released? One demographic measure worth noting, however, is the fact that the perpetrators of fraud tend to be older (ages 25–44) than those arrested for violent crimes like murder, rape, and robbery.

Definition of Consumer Fraud

Consumer fraud is an expansive term that includes a seemingly endless variety of unfair and deceptive acts. It usually involves some form of trickery used to achieve an unfair advantage in a retail sale. In popular usage, many consider any bad buying experience to be a consumer fraud.

For many years, consumer fraud was narrowly construed as a subset in the larger category of frauds, such as tax fraud, bank fraud, and filing false claims with the government. There are a number of federal and state statutes that prohibit specific fraudulent acts that are irrelevant to and have no direct impact on consumers. When one enterprise cheats another or an employee embezzles company funds, such actions may be considered fraudulent, but this is not consumer fraud. There are, however, other antifraud statutes targeting consumer fraud. For example, the Justice Department charged the Las Vegas telemarketers mentioned earlier with violating federal laws against mail fraud, wire fraud (using electronic communications), and criminal conspiracy. Besides the Mail and Wire Fraud statutes, other laws protect consumers against fraud in health care, the securities industry, and the sale of adulterated and unsafe foods and drugs, to name a few.

Under criminal, civil, and common law, fraud is considered to be a scheme or knowing deception to obtain money by means of false pretenses, representations, or promises. To prosecute fraud an attorney must show there was a clear intent to defraud. This could be demonstrated by "deeds, acts, or artifices calculated to deceive . . . as well as words or positive assertions" (*Kestner v. Jakobe*, 446 S.W.2d 188, 193), "proved through the defendant's non-action or non-disclosure of material facts . . ." (*U.S. v. O'Malley* , 707 F.2d, 1240, 1247 (1983)), or exemplified by a refusal to provide "the intangible right of honest services" (18 U.S.C. § 1346).

The requirement of proving intent was often a barrier to prosecuting consumer fraud. That barrier was lifted with the passage of the Federal Trade Commission Act, as amended (15 U.S.C.

§§ 41 through 57), and its focus on the effect of an act or practice. This law, which became the foundation for all state consumer protection laws, prohibits deceptive and unfair acts and practices as well as unfair means of competition. It is a civil, not criminal, enforcement act that permits the Federal Trade Commission (FTC) and, under their respective state laws, the state attorneys general to enjoin, fine, and seek restitution. Unlike the federal act, most of these state laws do permit consumers to bring actions on their own behalf. This is called a private right of action.

The FTC Act does not, like many fraud statutes, contain a laundry list of specifically prohibited acts and practices. According to one legal scholar, judges and legislatures "have been loath to be too specific about what is prohibited for fear of not covering some new form of consumer fraud . . ." (Pridgen, 1997). Instead, there are the broad areas of prohibited activities mentioned above.

For many years, the agency's standard for deception was the "tendency or capacity to deceive." In 1983, the FTC weakened this by adopting a new standard of "likely to mislead the consumer acting reasonably under the circumstances" (FTC Policy Statement, 1983b). This key change is a move away from a focus on the most vulnerable purchaser to what a "reasonable person" would do under the circumstances.

The Commission and the courts have interpreted the "unfairness" provision of the act to focus on consumer injury with or without any deception. In *Orkin v. Federal Trade Commission*, the 11th Circuit Court of Appeals declared the FTC was well within its authority to declare a contract breach an "unfair practice" even without any deception and with no intention to deceive (849 F.2d 1354, 1367-68 (1988)).

Based on federal and state case law, unfair acts and practices that injure consumers would include:

- Certain sales practices such as high-pressure sales
- Targeting vulnerable consumers
- Withholding material information, and
- Unconscionable costs associated with certain purchases or loans.

Such practices, although not deceptive, do give rise to consumer injuries.

The FTC Act also empowered the Commission to "prohibit unfair methods of competition." When Congress established this agency in 1914, it was seeking to restrain monopolization in business that had the effect of reducing competition. For example, with some industries a handful of corporations owns all or virtually all the elements connected with a product or market. Here the potential exists for these companies to reach agreements setting prices (price fixing), market share, or to collude in other practices that reduce competition and injure consumers. Statutes that address these problems are known as antitrust laws. Along with the FTC Act, the U.S. Department of Justice enforces other federal antitrust laws such as the Sherman Antitrust Act. Many state attorneys general also have antitrust authority under their state's laws.

Survey research indicates most consumers regularly encounter bad buying experiences or rip-offs. These could include paying too much for a used car, buying unneeded life insurance, being pressured to buy at a "home sales' party," or giving in to telemarketers selling unwanted magazine subscriptions. While a purchase may be a bad deal, it is not necessarily consumer fraud. It is important to remember that buyers have a responsibility to shop wisely. These purchases may represent a loss to the consumer, but unless they are fraudulent, deceptive, or unfair, they are not consumer fraud and violate no laws.

A Fair Marketplace

Adam Smith, the economist and proponent of laissez-faire capitalism, introduced the concept of consumer sovereignty. In a perfectly competitive world, he reasoned, the consumer would be king. Consumer demand would call the tune to which businesses danced and the marketplace would self-correct abusive behavior. Unfortunately, neither the U.S. nor the global economy is a perfectly competitive world. Hence, the consumer is not king.

Throughout this book, the reader will note the many references to federal and state consumer protection laws. To correct our imperfect world and bring balance and fairness, the nation has chosen to regulate abuses in the marketplace. It is these laws that protect consumers.

Other tools, including education and self-regulation, also provide balance. Consumer education is teaching the knowledge and skills needed for decision making in the marketplace. There is a compelling need to provide this kind of education in schools and elsewhere. Consumers regularly fail tests examining their fundamental knowledge of the marketplace and of their rights. Education alone, however, will not make the consumer sovereign.

It is important to recognize that legitimate businesses are also injured by frauds. Too often, in the consumer's eye, these establishments are tarred with the same brush as fraudulent enterprises. To promote good business practices and avoid government regulation, trade associations set standards for an industry and draft codes of conduct for their members. Since at least the turn of the twentieth century, legitimate businesses have banded together to form Better Business Bureaus (BBBs). These organizations promote ethical standards for advertising and sales, mediate consumer complaints, and provide consumer information. Chapter 5 contains an extensive listing of BBBs throughout the country.

Business, however, recognizes that self-regulation has its limits. During the Reagan era, the then chair of the Federal Trade Commission (FTC) moved to lift agency controls over advertising. *Advertising Age*, an industry publication, editorialized that advertisers want "to be protected from irresponsible FTC behavior, but they also know from 67 years of experience that the marketplace becomes a jungle in the absence of a strong FTC" (*Advertising Age*, 1982, p. 16). *Only* government has the power to police the marketplace.

Consumer protection is not a new concept. Hammurabi's code from the eighteenth century B.C. included investment protections and the Bible exhorted merchants to use *just weights* because "a false balance is an abomination to the Lord" (Proverbs 11:1). *Caveat emptor* or "buyer beware" may be a Latin phrase, but there is no evidence a Roman wrote these words. On the contrary, Roman law (Justinian Code) mandated full disclosure in the sale of beasts of burden and other items. In medieval times, the church played a significant role in overseeing the marketplace. In his *Summa Theologica*, the twelfth-century scholar and theologian, Thomas Aquinas, discussed the sins connected with buying and selling. He wrote, "if the seller be aware of a fault in the thing he is selling, he is guilty of a fraudulent sale." But if the seller "knows nothing about [the fault] . . . [he] does not sin." If a fault later "comes to his knowledge," however, the seller, "is bound to compensate the buyer." Aquinas set the standard for what is called today an implied warranty of merchantability, or a guarantee that a product performs to a certain standard of quality.

Medieval religious strictures also evolved the concept of a "just price for a sound commodity." This was a form of economic price regulation, based on a community standard of what was fair. Merchants were not to realize an undue profit beyond the cost of materials and a reasonable charge for their time and effort in producing the item. The just price was not based on supply and demand. In part, this concept was designed to protect the community from price gouging in times of scarcity and famine. The just price standard lived on and can be found in court decisions as late as the early 1800s in the United States (Horowitz, 1974).

With increasing economic activity and the coming of the Industrial Revolution, *caveat emptor*, which served the needs of a burgeoning products market, supplanted the older "just price" standard. Business was to be free of all governmental restraints. Contracts were supreme, and the parties to a contract (sale) were responsible for the soundness of their purchase. Prior to 1817, the Supreme Court alluded to *caveat emptor* in a number of decisions involving certain kinds of property. According to legal scholars (Horowitz, 1974), however, it did not fully embrace the concept until the case of *Laidlaw v. Organ* (15 U.S. 178). Here one party to a contract for the purchase of tobacco had advanced knowledge that the War of 1812 had ended. He withheld that knowledge, even when asked about any information that would affect the tobacco sale. In fact, the end of the war and the lifting of the English blockade increased the value of this commodity by 30 to 50 percent. Chief Justice Marshall, in delivering the Court's opinion, declared there was no duty to disclose such information (15 U.S. 178, 195). Some 50 years later, the Supreme Court declared that "caveat emptor is of such universal acceptance that with a single exception, the courts of all the states in the Union . . . sanction it" (*Barnard v. Kellogg*, 77 U.S. 383, 388 (1870)).

The pendulum began to swing back in 1872, with the passage of the federal Mail Fraud statute. This was the nation's first consumer protection law. Lotteries, swindles, and medical quackery were widely sold through the mails at that time. This law was drafted to prevent the use of the mails to facilitate such schemes. A Postal Inspection Service was also created to enforce the statute. The appearance of additional, more expansive protections came later, in three major waves: the so-called Progressive Era (from the late 19th century to the First World War), during the 1920s and 1930s, and during the 1960s and 1970s.

Scholars debate both the source and goals of the period called the Progressive Era. What is clear is that it was a period of unprecedented government intervention in the workings of the market. New agencies were created and empowered to regulate and police business. Two of the largest corporations (Standard Oil and American Tobacco) were broken up under new antitrust laws. Packing plants came under federal inspection after muckraker and author, Upton Sinclair, stirred public outrage over fetid conditions in the meat industry. Sinclair's work also helped push through legislation banning adulteration in food and drugs. The Federal Trade Commission was created to prohibit unfair competition. Later, through judicial decisions and subsequent amendments to the act, the agency's mission was expanded to include consumers. On the state level, many legislatures enacted investor protection laws called *blue sky laws*. This period of regulatory activity ended with the coming of the First World War.

The 1920s were a time of unprecedented economic prosperity and growth for most of the country. Personal income soared, as did the purchase of consumer goods like automobiles, appliances, and cosmetics. The stock market boomed until the crash of 1929, and the Great Depression began. Fraud and abuses on Wall Street inspired congressional investigations and the enactment of investor protections in the form of federal securities laws. In 1938, cosmetics were added to a new Food and Drug Act, which also required that new drugs would have to be proved safe before they were sold. Finally, the Federal Trade Commission Act was amended to give this agency clear authority to protect consumers against "unfair and deceptive acts and practices."

Much of what we take for granted today as consumer protection was enacted in the late 1960s and early 1970s. John Kennedy initiated the third wave of government activism by introducing consumer protection as an issue in his 1960 presidential campaign. Assassination cut short his administration's legislative efforts, but Kennedy's message to Congress on what he called the Consumer Bill of Rights was a clear message that the era of *caveat emptor* had ended. The consumer rights he articulated in that message were the right to safety, the right to be informed, the right to choose, and the right to be heard (Kennedy, 1962). (See Chapter 4 for the full text.)

Under the administrations of Presidents Johnson and Nixon, consumer protection was greatly enhanced. Some of the protections included: truth in labeling requirements, truth in lending and fair credit reporting, motor vehicle and consumer product safety standards, an enhanced Food and Drug Administration with drug effectiveness standards, warranty protections, privacy laws, and the regulation of door-to-door salespersons. On the state level, many legislatures adopted consumer protection laws modeled on the FTC Act, enhancing protection at the state and local levels.

Where is consumer protection in the 1990s? Consumer fraud remains, as mentioned earlier, at least a $100 billion dollar problem. Encouraging signs include a Justice Department and FBI war on white-collar crimes like telemarketing and investment fraud, but as *Money Magazine* commented in March 1966, "Gaps in the consumer-protection safety net . . . are widening every day" (Simon, 1996).

Spending cuts are eliminating staff and hours of service at all levels. Fewer complaints are investigated, and 30 agencies or branch offices closed their doors in the 1990s—including the U.S. Office of Consumer Affairs. The magazine article also asserts that consumer protections have failed to keep up with new dangers like abuses in the managed health care industry and E-coli bacteria in meatpacking.

On the horizon are increased Internet commerce and the growth of the global economy. Canada is currently the source of much of the telemarketing fraud perpetrated on victims in the United States. It's quick and easy to call Iowa from Vancouver or Montreal, but to prosecute means law enforcement must navigate through at least two different court systems.

Caveat emptor may be dead, but "buyer beware" remain the watchwords as we turn to the next century.

Consumer Frauds

Advertising

When hearing aid manufacturers aired television commercials for a new kind of device that "suppress[es]" or "automatically reduces background noise," product sales increased. Most devices amplify all sounds, including the background noise, which makes it difficult to distinguish conversation from the sound of an air conditioner or the buzz of a cocktail party. These new devices promised a solution to this long-standing user complaint. One consumer who spent $1,500 for two new units said, "I heard all the wonderful commercials and thought I would go for it." Only later did he conclude, these "aids are not any better than previous aids and highly exaggerated in their advertisements" (AARP, 1993).

Both the FTC and the Food and Drug Administration (FDA)

agreed with the consumer, declaring the ads to be deceptive and misleading. The FDA issued what was, in effect, "cease and desist" orders to six manufacturers. Miracle-Ear, the largest advertiser, while not admitting to any law violation, ultimately paid a $2.5 million civil penalty to settle a government lawsuit (Federal Trade Commission, 1995). Another company, Beltone, settled with the FTC before going to trial.

The modern consumer faces a bewildering array of goods and services. Making rational purchase decisions is a time-consuming and an increasingly difficult task—particularly with new technologies. Like the hearing aid buyer, many consumers learn about products from advertising. The best ads are truthful and provide essential information, such as what the product does, who manufactures it, its size and shape, cost (including any discounts), and where to buy it. The worst ads are those that provide nothing but false and misleading information. Still others are designed to appeal to emotions or provide imagery without substance.

Advertisers flood the media with commercial messages. In one day, an average TV watcher sees almost 100 commercials. The same individual may hear or see 200–300 more advertisements on the radio or in newspapers and magazines (Pratkanis, 1991). The latest platform for advertising is the Internet (Jupiter, 1997). To be sure, consumers are usually not consciously aware of watching, reading, or hearing these commercial messages. The public lives in what some advertisers call a *message-dense*, impersonal world of ads.

Why did sellers spend almost $175 billion dollars in 1996 to publicize their wares? Advertising works. Hearing-impaired consumers purchased expensive new hearing aids based solely on advertising claims. On average, an advertising campaign increases purchases of brand-name products by approximately 6 percent a year (Pratkanis 1991)—a percentage that could represent millions of dollars in revenue for Coke, Crest, or Wendy's.

It wasn't always this way. Promotion and persuasion in one form or another have always played a role in the marketplace, but before the nineteenth century, there were no national markets, brand names, or standardized products (Pope, 1991). The Industrial Revolution and the growth of big business gave rise to advertising, with expenditures increasing rapidly around the turn of the century (estimated at $250,000 to $500,000 in 1900) (Pope, 1991) and tripling by the 1920s ($1.5 billion in 1927) (Allen, 1931).

Advertising was not an issue for reformers during much of the Progressive Era. Muckrakers focused their attention on the adulteration of the products, not their advertising. The Pure Food and Drug Act of 1906, for example, said nothing about false advertising. One muckraker commented, "We who fought to get the law passed aimed at the wrong side of the bottle. We should have attacked the advertisements in the newspapers" (as quoted in Pope, 1991, p. 45). A 1912 amendment to the Pure Food and Drug Act did ban false labeling claims.

The first attempt to control this new juggernaut was targeted at the states. *Printers Ink*, a leading trade publication, drafted a model state law, first enacted in Ohio in 1913, to ban dishonest advertising. By 1921, 22 additional states had approved this law, which remains on the books in most places. The FTC Act and state consumer protection laws have supplanted it.

What is deceptive advertising? The FTC defines it as "a deceptive representation, omission, or practice that is likely to mislead consumers acting reasonably." Some of the more common deceptions include unsubstantiated claims, visual deceptions, and deceptive pricing. Many such practices are illegal, but not all.

The FTC requires that all factual or objective claims in an ad be substantiated before it is aired or published. "Rather than impose a burden upon the consumer to test, investigate, or experiment for himself . . . [he/she] is entitled . . . to rely upon the manufacturer to have a reasonable basis for making claims" (*In Re* Pfizer, Inc., 81 F.T.C. 23 (1972)).

Substantiation goes to the heart of the hearing aid buyer's complaint. He believed the advertising claims he saw on television to be truthful. Like many consumers, he believed the manufacturers couldn't say it if it were not true. The FTC's position is that consumers should be able to rely on claims made about a product. Making an objective claim implies that the advertiser has a reasonable basis to support it (Federal Trade Commission, 1983a). Making claims without supporting information is considered an unfair and deceptive act.

At a minimum, advertisers are expected to have the level of support actually claimed in the ad. That is, if the ad says "studies show," the advertiser must have more than one study. Other factors considered by the FTC in determining whether an ad is deceptive include the kind of claim made, the type of product, the consequences of a false claim, the degree of reliance by the consumer, and the kind of evidence provided. Health and safety claims, for instance, afford a greater potential for consumer harm. They require more substantiation than is needed for other products.

A major exception to the substantiation requirement is for *puffery* or claims that are incapable of measurement (*In Re* Bristol-Myers Co., 102 F.T.C. 21 (1983)). Puffery includes opinions, whether from experts, celebrities, or common consumers. It includes subjective or nonfactual claims such as "none better" or "no product does more for your wash." Puffing claims do not objectively state that Brand X does better or does more. Rather, their assertion is, "we're just as good as the others." Such a statement need not be substantiated, even though the artful phrasing has impact at first glance.

Lastly, puffery includes emotional and psychological appeals. Many advertisers try to associate their product with desirable qualities—motherhood, friendship, patriotism—that are completely unrelated to the product. Cars and sex appeal have been married to each other for decades. A sports car is not likely to improve a consumer's sex appeal, but the image is a tried-and-tested tool for selling cars. Other nonobjective claims include "You meet the nicest people on a Honda," or "Join the Pepsi Generation."

The FTC reasons that consumers don't take these nonfactual claims seriously. Critics disagree. They have charged that such claims bypass consumers' rational decision making and do have an impact on buying. To date, the FTC has not changed its position.

In the television age, visuals are sometimes more important to a truthful presentation than the copy. The FTC scrutinizes both for "the impression made by the advertisement as a whole" (*American Home Products Corp. v. FTC*, 695 F.2d 681 (3rd Cir. 1982)). For example, a 1970s ad for the aspirin Anacin included "technical graphs and chemical formulas." The FTC reasoned that even though the copy made no claim of scientific proof, the visual image implied that Anacin was "scientifically proven superior to its competitors."

Visual exaggerations are also considered deceptive. In the 1970s, Chevron advertised a gasoline that purportedly reduced air pollutants. The visual in the ad was black smoke coming from a car not using this brand of gasoline, contrasted with another car with no visible pollutants after six tankfuls of Chevron with F-310. The courts held that this representation "simply was not true." Many pollutants are invisible, and the disappearing black smoke was not a clear indication they were all eliminated (*Standard Oil Co. v. FTC*, 577 F.2d 653 (9th Cir. 1978)).

Probably the most commonly experienced problem with

advertising is what is called *deceptive pricing*. This includes such tactics as *bait-and-switch* and *false bargains*. These tactics are not frequently targeted by the FTC, but many state attorneys are filling the void.

Bait-and-switch is a tactic known to most consumers. The seller advertises a product at a special attractive price but does not stock the item. Instead, the seller steers customers to another product, or possibly just enjoys the increased foot traffic created by the advertised special. In the 1970s, the FTC enacted a trade rule, known as the unavailability rule, that required grocery stores (but not other types of stores) to have a sufficient supply of advertised specials to meet expected demand. In 1989, the Commission weakened the rule to permit sellers to advertise terms with a caveat of "limited supplies available," or to offer other kinds of compensation, such as rain checks.

A variation on the typical bait-and-switch tactic is to mix name brand and house brands in the same ad. For example, an advertised name brand window at a home improvement store may be but one item or an odd-sized product in a large line. There is also, however, a large line of house brand windows on sale at the same time. When customers come in, they are steered to the house brand.

Deceptive pricing also includes false bargains. The regular price of an item is inflated, only to be marked down in an advertised super sale. Under some state laws, a product must actually be sold at the higher price before it can be sold at the discount price. The Minnesota attorney general's office filed suit against a clothing chain with 140 stores that advertised big discounts on its products. The garments, however, came straight from the factory with inflated prices and the sale price listed on preprinted tags.

Advertising has an undeniable impact on consumers. Ads are attention grabbing, entertaining, and sometimes insulting. They can provide useful information, helping consumers understand complex issues. Because of their reach, they are also one of the most powerful deceptions in the marketplace.

Automobile Purchases and Repair

America's love affair with the automobile began when Henry Ford introduced mass production of cars to the country. In 1919, there were 7 million cars (Allen, 1931). Almost 80 years later, there are approximately 190 million registered cars and light trucks in the United States, according to the Commerce Department.

Automobiles are the second largest investment consumers make in a lifetime, with an average purchase price of almost $20,000 for a new car. Sticker shock has changed the market in three important ways. First, according to *Consumer Reports*, two out of three cars purchased in 1996 were used, not new. Second, roughly one of three new vehicles delivered to consumers is leased, not purchased. Finally, car owners are driving and maintaining cars for more miles. Most cars are accumulating 120,000 miles in their life spans (National Association of Attorneys General, 1995).

Automobile purchases and repairs are a major source of consumer dissatisfaction and fraud. Year after year, auto-related complaints are at the top of both the National Association of Attorneys General's (NAAG) and NAACA's list of consumer complaints. The complaints come from bad experiences in buying a motor vehicle or in auto repairs.

Buying a new or used car can be perilous. It is one of the few products for which bargaining is the norm, not the exception. Although *no-pressure sales* with fixed prices are increasing in the industry, the stereotype of the pushy used car salesman in the loud sports coat remains too real. Sellers frequently pressure buyers to purchase vehicles they can ill afford. Usually this is a rip-off, a bad buying decision, but there are also many tactics that are unfair and deceptive.

A dirty dozen examples of fraudulent sales tactics include:

- Tampering with the odometer to roll back the mileage
- Advertising unavailable vehicles or nonexistent special prices
- Advertising a guaranteed trade-in allowance and then increasing the sales price to cover it
- Failing to post the buyer's guide with a used car
- Failing to disclose that a car was a demonstrator or rental car
- Failing to disclose that a car has safety or material defects
- Failing to disclose that a car was returned as a *lemon*
- Failing to disclose penalties for canceling a sale
- Steering buyers into deceptive leases
- Misstating buyer's income on credit applications
- Steering buyers to finance companies that put a buyer's home at risk with a high-interest home equity loan to finance the car purchase
- Discriminating in sales practices against women and minorities.

For each of these abuses, legal redress is available. Although most of the consumer protections for such sales are at the state level, there are important federal laws. Congress approved the Federal Odometer Act (Federal Motor Vehicle Information and Cost Savings Act, 15 U.S.C. § 1981) in 1986 to stem an estimated $2 billion a year in consumer losses from mileage roll-backs. Either federal or state governments can bring an action in court under this act.

Advertising standards were discussed earlier. They also apply to automobile ads. In January 1998, for example, 20 state attorneys general and the FTC signed consent decrees with ad agencies and a manufacturer regarding the promotion of what were alleged to be deceptive car lease ads. The television commercial had promoted "zero down, short-term leasing," but the *mouse type* (the fine print), which scrolled rapidly down the screen, indicated that the consumer had to pay $600 down and an additional $400 at the end of the lease.

Every used car offered for sale by a business must have a window sticker called a Buyer's Guide under the FTC's *Used Car Rule*. The sticker discloses what, if any, warranty comes with the car or a statement that the vehicle comes *as is*, meaning without any guarantee.

Some states have their own *Used Car Rule* that is stronger than the FTC's, requiring a listing of specific problems with the vehicle. Under state commercial codes, which vary from state to state, there are remedies for the sale of defective goods. The federal Magnuson-Moss Warranty Act may also apply. Every state also has some form of *lemon law*, a special warranty for new car buyers left in the lurch by a new vehicle that will not work and cannot be repaired. Under many state laws, consumers have a private right of action as well. That is, they can sue the seller themselves to enforce the provisions of the law. This is in contrast to other laws that allow only the government agency charged with enforcing the law to bring violators to court.

At both the federal and state levels, consumer credit laws set rules for consumer lending, including the financing of auto purchases. Under the federal Truth in Lending Act, lenders must provide certain key credit disclosures, particularly with certain home equity loans. Some state laws set maximum interest rates for consumer credit.

A new car is one of the most expensive consumer purchases, particularly with the price increases of the last few years. Higher purchase prices require larger down payments and monthly payments that exceed many consumers' ability to pay. Leasing a new car, however, appears to provide an alternative for consumers. The ads tout "no money down" and "low monthly payments." In many instances, these claims are accurate. Leasing has changed the new car market. At this time, approximately one-third of all new cars delivered to consumers are leased, not purchased (Crenshaw, 1997, p. C15).

A car lease is something like an extended car rental, not for just a day or week, but for three to five years. The car dealership, acting on behalf of the finance company of a manufacturer (Ford Credit or General Motors Acceptance Corporation, for example), offers to lease a car to consumers. Similar to a purchase agreement, the consumer trades in his/her old car, and the value of the trade-in usually goes toward the down payment, when a down payment is required. Monthly payments are required for the life of the agreement. At the end of the lease, the consumer may be able to purchase the car for its market value at that time, or he or she can walk away, owing nothing more. With some agreements, however, the person leasing must pay stiff charges for exceeding any mileage limitations in the agreement (48,000 miles with a four-year lease, for example).

Leasing is a financial transaction filled with many new and unfamiliar terms and conditions. Capitalized costs or cap costs, for example, are terms describing the cost of the car. Subventing is a marketing device where the dealer reduces the cost of a lease by subsidizing the sale. In a closed-end lease, the consumer owes nothing more at the end of the lease. In an open-ended lease, however, the consumer must make up any difference between the projected residual value (an estimate of what the car will be worth at the end of the lease) and the actual value of the car.

The confusion surrounding this relatively new financial transaction has allowed some dealers to deceive consumers. After an extensive investigation of car leasing fraud, the attorney general of Florida identified what his office calls 30 separate pockets of profit. Not every pocket of profit was fraudulent, but many were. Some of the fraudulent practices identified include deceptive advertising. The explanations about costs, exclusions, and other important details are written in unreadable mouse type that rapidly scrolls down a TV screen in a 30-second spot. The FTC and several state attorneys general have sued a number of car companies regarding such ads. Other abusive practices have included flipping a consumer into a lease agreement instead of a purchase agreement without informing him or her of the change, misrepresenting cancellation costs, false statements about the costs involved with excess mileage, and not taking into account the trade-in value of the buyer's existing vehicle.

A recent federal disclosure requirement (Regulation M) provides some help for consumers. Sellers are now required to provide a worksheet, at the time of sale, to assist consumers in comparing the costs of a lease with that of a standard purchase contract.

As consumers keep their cars longer and log more miles on them, car maintenance and repairs become more important. In 1994, consumers spent $75 billion on repairs and $15 billion on accessories. Labor costs for the nation's 750,000 technicians constitute 65 percent of the price of a repair, with the remaining 35 percent covering replacement parts. There is wide variety in the types of repair facilities. Service stations perform 27 percent of all repairs; auto dealers 21 percent; discount stores, tire dealers, and chain stores 20 percent, with general and specialty repair shops performing the remainder.

The most frequent consumer complaints about auto repairs relate to unnecessary and unauthorized repairs. Various past state investigations document that unnecessary repairs were conducted at some facilities so that parts could be sold "to meet quotas, qualify for prizes or because [service managers and technicians'] pay was tied to the quantity of merchandise sold and repairs performed" (National Association of Attorneys General, 1995, p. 16).

To curb these abuses, 24 states require auto repair facilities to provide consumers with written estimates for repairs and prohibit repairs that exceed the cost of the estimate, unless the customer approves. These laws also require repair facilities to return all parts replaced in the repair. Some states require repair facilities to be licensed or certified and, in some cases, bonded. Others oblige the service technicians to be licensed or certified. Private certification programs also exist, such as the American Automobile Association's certification of shops or the National Institute for Automotive Service Excellence (ASE seal) certification for technicians.

No estimates of consumer losses to fraud from auto sales and repairs are available, but the problem is clearly pervasive, and even the best corrective legislation will not guarantee customer satisfaction. One consumer plaintively described her experience with auto repair as "the moral equivalent of mugging" ("Auto Repair," 1997).

Credit Issues

It is hard to believe there was a time before credit cards, but the financial revolution of generalized credit is only 30 years old. It began quietly enough when California's largest bank, the Bank of America, mailed out 60,000 preapproved BankAmericards. Before this, there were credit cards for gasoline and retail stores, and Diners had a travel and entertainment card, but this was the first offer for a general credit or bank card (Nocera, 1994). By 1995, according to the Commerce Department, two-thirds of family heads of household held such a card. The outstanding bank card debt nationwide totaled $363 billion dollars in 1996. The credit revolution also spawned new ways of defrauding consumers as well as questions about privacy in, and the accuracy of, a new credit reporting system to keep track of credit payments.

The Lou Harris survey, cited earlier in this chapter, indicates that 14 percent of Americans believe that unauthorized charges have appeared on their credit card. Of those who experienced such a charge, 57 percent believe this was a fraudulent misuse of their account. Of the remainder, 38 percent say it was merely a billing error and 6 percent are unsure.

Visa, which bought out the BankAmericard, indicates that fraud losses cost their member banks almost $500 million in 1997. Losses for all credit cards totaled approximately $1 billion that year. Visa's largest consumer loss categories are:

- Lost and stolen cards—Cards or card numbers lost by or stolen from consumers. Thefts could involve shoulder surfing (capturing an individual's card number by looking over their shoulder), dumpster diving (searching through garbage for the credit card numbers on the carbons of credit card purchases), Internet sales, or simple larceny.
- Cards not received (stolen in the mail)—Similar to the above; however, this practice is becoming less common with new verification procedures.
- Counterfeiting—Fraudulently duplicating a consumers' card number electronically.
- Account takeovers—Taking over the credit identity of an individual (identity theft).

Credit card fraud is not as directly injurious to consumers as other consumer fraud. Under the provisions of the federal Billing

Rights Act (15 U.S.C. § 572) and the Fair Credit Billing Rights Act (15 U.S.C. § 1666), the card holders are liable for only the first $50 of any unauthorized charges, but they must report such losses in writing, within 60 days. Even with relatively small losses, credit card fraud can be a nightmare for consumers trying to straighten out their credit history.

Two areas of growing concern for credit card companies are the increases in counterfeiting card numbers and account take-overs. Counterfeiting involves copying the owner's credit card name and number from the magnetic or mag strip on the back of a card. Sophisticated scammers are beginning to use electronic equipment to duplicate that information. For example, a couple recently paid for a night's lodging at a Vermont bed-and-breakfast with their credit card. The clerk, a local high school student, legitimately swiped their credit card's mag strip on the establishment's verification equipment seeking approval. Unbeknownst to the couple, however, the clerk also swiped their card on a decoding device attached to his laptop computer, capturing the cardholder's name and number off the mag strip.

At the end of his shift, the clerk sold the information to a go-between, who, in turn, forwarded the card information to a confederate in Japan. Before the couple had breakfast at their B & B in Vermont, the Tokyo connection had conducted a criminal shopping spree with their card, racking up thousands of dollars in charges.

Account takeovers are similar to identity theft, discussed elsewhere in this chapter. A scam artist secures personal information about the user. Such information includes the card account number, the user's Social Security number, and his or her mother's maiden name. With that information, the scammer calls the card issuer to report a move, and provides a new address. Two weeks later, the scammer reports a lost card and requests a replacement at the new address. It all seems legitimate, but the real owner and the issuer are left with the bill.

With the development of the general credit card came the rapid expansion of the credit reporting industry. Credit card issuers needed to know if an applicant has been paying bills on time. Credit reporting agencies collect data from all creditors on individual consumers, usually filing such information according to Social Security numbers. This information is then used by creditors to screen applicants.

In the past, consumers frequently complained of false information showing up on their reports without a means to challenge the information. In response to these complaints, the Fair Credit Reporting Act was passed in 1970 to regulate the use of credit reports. It requires credit reporting agencies to provide consumers with the information contained in their reports, and to allow them to challenge inaccurate data. It also provides some privacy protection.

Credit repair clinics, almost always a consumer fraud, have sprouted to prey on those in financial difficulty. Under the Fair Credit Reporting Act, delinquent payments remain on a report for seven years and a bankruptcy for ten. These firms, for a fee, offer the hope of repairing a bad credit report and restoring creditworthiness by challenging delinquent payments and any outstanding claims. They do not, however, tell the consumer that he or she could do the same thing for free.

This scam may be a thing of the past, because in late 1997 the federal Fair Credit Repair Act (15 U.S.C. § 1679) went into effect. This act, along with the FTC Telemarketing Sales Rule (16 CFR 310), states that credit repair clinics must make full disclosures, sign a written contract with the consumer, and that such firms may not receive payment before the "repair" is complete.

A new credit repair scheme, found on the Internet, is the sale of information material on how to establish a new credit file. Creating such a file is fraudulent.

High-Tech Merchandising

Web browsers looking for excitement got more than they bargained for when they double-clicked on www.sexygirls.com. Advertisements on other Internet sites said sexygirls was free, so why not peek. At the site, users were prompted to download a viewer program, which, without the user's knowledge, promptly hijacked his computer. The software disconnected the local telephone connection, and reconnected to the Internet through an international phone call. Long-distance telephone charges to Moldova, in what used to be the Soviet Union, began ticking at $2 per minute. As long as the user stayed on the computer, even after leaving the sexygirls site, the Moldovan phone connection remained with its $2 per minute long-distance charges. More than 38,000 victims were surprised to find a call(s) to Moldova on their next telephone bill. For some who peeked, the charges amounted to thousands of dollars (Federal Trade Commission, 1998).

Some readers may think the thrill seekers got what they deserved. The case, nonetheless, highlights an important fact.

Fraud artists are some of the first to master new technologies, creating audacious schemes to defraud consumers.

It would take a book many times longer than this one to provide a thorough review of the many consumer frauds in merchandising sales. Chapters 6 and 7 list books, articles, and Websites that discuss these schemes. This section, however, highlights the ways in which technology can become a tool to fleece consumers.

Internet scams and telemarketing fraud are remarkably similar. Both use electronic platforms for marketing multiple products directly to consumers. The telephone is the more direct tool. Illegal telemarketers use lists, purchased from legitimate sources or targeted lists of past victims *(mooch list)*, to talk directly with their *mark.* The Internet does not feature direct voice communications with consumers, but it does permit both legitimate and fraudulent sellers to target messages to particular individuals. When consumers visit a Website, they leave "cookie crumbs," or certain information about users. Websites can know users' e-mail addresses and other information. E-mail addresses are compiled in databases, bought and sold to others, for *spamming*, unsolicited commercial e-mail. The messages, costing next to nothing, hype sites similar to ones already visited. The www.sexygirls site may not have sought customers through lists of past user visits to similar sites, but other sellers do.

Of the two technologies, the telephone is the larger market, because 98 percent of U.S. households are connected to the telephone grid. A telemarketer can reach virtually every resident of the country just by dialing his or her number. AARP's consumer behavior survey indicates that telemarketing reaches millions. Two-thirds of the survey respondents reported receiving one or more sales calls in the six months preceding the survey.

At the end of 1997, 62 million Americans and 160 million people worldwide were connected to the Internet, a number that continues to grow at an astounding rate. Marketing, too, is growing, evidenced by the volume of messaging, much of which is unsolicited commercial e-mails. In June 1997, America Online, one of the largest Internet providers, reported processing 15 million electronic messages a day. By September of the same year, that number had jumped to 60 million messages a day (Pitofsky, 1998). Commercial messages may irritate, but most are legitimate. Some, however, are not, and the consumer must distinguish between the two.

Fraud artists, whether on the telephone or the Internet, are peerless in their ability to cloak themselves in the mantle of legitimacy. For example, a sight draft or electronic debit is a means to electronically debit a consumer's bank account. Legitimate sellers use sight drafts to sell products to consumers who do not own or use credit cards. Illegal telemarketers use such transactions to bilk their victims.

One illegal telemarketer explained how he illegally obtained a bank draft this way. After building rapport with a consumer over several telephone calls, he persuaded her to pay an administrative fee to win her big prize. As one of his tools to gain her confidence, the telemarketer advised his victim never to give her credit card number to anyone on the phone. He then suggested that she send a check for the fees, but first he needed to verify her account number. He advises his victim to write void on the face of a blank check, again to "protect her." He next asked that she tell him the account number at the bottom of the check, which she did. After hanging up with the victim, the telemarketer's next call was to the consumer's bank for a quick and illegal withdrawal.

Under the FTC's Telemarketing Sales Rule (see Chapter 4), a financial institution may not debit a customer's bank account(s) without verification of the consumer's approval for such a transaction. Under the rule, an oral verification is acceptable; written approvals, however, should be required.

Both technologies afford anonymity, international connections, and minimal start-up costs. Consumers receiving a telephone call or commercial e-mail don't know the seller or, in most instances, where the seller is located. The www.sexygirl scheme was not created by Moldovans eager to exploit rich North Americans. Fraud artists in the United States hatched this plot and crafted the Moldovan angle. Investigations of such schemes are an enormous challenge to law enforcement. As the FTC commented about www.sexygirls, there was a dual challenge of "mastering the technology and finding the perpetrators in cyberspace."

Sellers can telemarket anywhere. As mentioned earlier, many of the illegal calls coming into the United States are from Canada. Solicitations for foreign lotteries come from Vancouver, sweepstake offers arrive from Montreal, and advance fee loan promotions (offers to secure credit for a fee, paid in advance) are the specialty of illegal telemarketers in Toronto. These sites could change tomorrow, however, moving to a Caribbean island or elsewhere. All the telemarketer needs to begin defrauding is a telephone. The same flexibility is available over the Internet, as anyone can become an international marketer by simply establishing a Website.

Both the telephone and the Internet are facile tools for fraud artists. About half of the illegal telemarketing pitches involve contests and sweepstakes, according to the FBI. Farther down the list are fraudulent charities, investments, and recovery rooms (the telemarketer promises to recover past losses if only the victim pays more money). On the Internet, many of the schemes are not new; they are the same old pitches dressed up in the garments of high-tech clothing. Instead of swampland, the FTC discovered a company called Intellicom Services Inc., selling interests in partnerships to develop a *virtual shopping mall* on the Internet. The deal was a sham, with the perpetrators skimming the proceeds. There are pyramid schemes marketing silver and gold coins, and the National Association of State Security Administrators calls many sites "pump and dump" stock manipulations. That is, Websites hype false or misleading information about the value of penny stocks to pump up stock prices. They then "dump" (sell) the stock at its inflated price before the other investors catch on.

A principal difference between these two platforms is the Internet's ability to teach, even promote, other frauds. For example, computer hackers maintain Websites and newsgroups to share information and brag about their exploits. Several Websites provide instructions on how to steal credit card numbers or create new credit identities.

Consumer advocates also allege that the buying and selling of personal information on the Internet facilitates *identity theft*, taking over the credit identity of an individual. Computers enable private companies to collect a broad spectrum of personal information about individuals. This includes: name, address, names of neighbors, Social Security number, driving records, property records including mortgages and liens, court files such as bankruptcy court, commercial filings, workers' compensation claims, criminal records, professional licenses, military records, and employment verification.

Although many people believe these databases contribute to an invasion of privacy, much of this information was always public record, but what is new is the aggregation of the data and the ease of accessing it, particularly Social Security numbers—the key to individual credit identities. The U.S. Public Interest Research Group (USPIRG) estimates that 40,000 or more consumers lose their identities to fraud artists every year. Criminals take over the credit identities of individual consumers and use their credit and debit cards for shopping sprees and raids on an ATM machine. Some fraud artists, in this age of instant credit, negotiate home equity loans or lines of credit. The abused consumer often does not know of any losses (an address change is filed to forward the bills to a different location) until he or she is dunned for past-due payments. Although the consumer is not liable for the losses, it may take years to straighten out his or her credit history.

In 1997, over 8,000 bills were introduced in the 50 state legislatures regarding privacy. Regulating the Internet through state laws, however, is nothing but a "speed bump on the road to the Information Super Highway," according to Hubert Humphrey III, the attorney general of Minnesota. Federal legislation is pending, but the industry trade association, Individual Reference Services Group, will experiment with a self-regulatory structure, approved by the FTC. Undoubtedly, privacy on the Internet will remain a hot topic for the future.

Many of the existing consumer protection laws already mentioned apply to the deceptive and fraudulent practices found on the Internet and to telemarketing fraud. In addition, the FTC's sales rule on telemarketing fraud prohibits specific fraudulent and abusive practices and requires certain disclosures. There is no specific sales rule that applies to the Internet at this time.

Law enforcement "surfs" the net, seeking to detect fraudulent schemes. These agencies also tape illegal telemarketing calls to prosecute fraud artists. At this time there are no estimates for fraud on the Internet. Telemarketing fraud is estimated to cost $40 billion, and even though this estimate is dated, law enforcement is not signaling victory over the problem. Fraud artists will continue to use these technologies, and others, to defraud in the future.

Investment Frauds

In May 1998, NationsBank, with branches in seven states and the District of Columbia, paid a $6.75 million fine to the federal government. The Securities and Exchange Commission (SEC) charged this firm with "false and misleading sales practices." NationsBank marketed high-risk investments while implying they were as safe as certificates of deposit with the backing of federal deposit insurance. NationsBank referred savers with maturing certificates of deposits to an affiliated securities firm, operating on their premises, selling the investment product. In addition to paying the fine and agreeing to cease and desist from such practices in the future, NationsBank has paid nearly $60 million to settle private law suits (Pae, 1998).

Although this is the first time a major bank has been fined, this is not the first time a financial institution has been charged with mixing insured and uninsured products in a misleading manner. Charles Keating presided over the liquidation of Lincoln Savings & Loan, one of the nation's biggest bank failures. He was convicted of securities fraud in California, although the conviction was subsequently overturned on a technicality. Lincoln's depositors were convinced to switch their insured deposits to highly speculative junk bonds offered by a related Keating corporation. Tellers wore T-shirts with the slogan *Bond for Glory* and won expensive running shoes for referring the most customers for junk bond sales. When Keating's bubble burst, nearly 20,000 investors lost part of their life savings (Campbell, 1998).

The United States is a nation of investors, with more than 40 percent of all Americans owning stocks directly or through mutual funds and 401(k) retirement plans (Dutt, 1997). Mutual fund assets now exceed bank deposits for the first time in the nation's history. Security investments, however, are not the only ventures available for risking hard-earned dollars. There is real estate, or multilevel marketing plans, or business opportunities for consumers to become their own bosses, just to take a few examples. The charges leveled against Keating and NationsBank are apt because they highlight the key concepts, a duty to inform and disclose risk. Federal and state securities laws are grounded in the responsibility of the seller to inform the buyer of all relevant facts in a truthful manner. Even with truthful disclosures, however, the buyer must understand that there are risks in all areas of the investment market.

One of the larger areas of investment fraud perpetrated today is telecommunications scams using licenses auctioned or sold by the Federal Communications Commission (FCC). The government is selling the right to use the airwaves (radio spectrum) to private investors for cellular telephone networks, pagers, and similar devices. These licenses are available to anyone and application fees are minimal, yet fraud artists charge thousands of dollars to investors to apply for such licenses on their behalf.

Another airwaves licensing scheme is the sale of licenses for pagers, wireless cable, personal communications systems, and mobile radios. The fraud artist solicits and acts on behalf of an investor to purchase a license that in itself has no value. The price may be dear, but a license is only useful for those parties who are financially prepared to develop a costly telecommunications system. The unsophisticated investor has the right but not necessarily the means to profit from the license.

Security sales are invading the Internet, where investors can buy and sell through their computers. About 7 million U.S. households are using such investment services (Quinn, 1988). The risks are high. Offers include exotic, "risk-free" investments such as Costa Rican coconut chips that were described as "similar to a CD [certificate of deposit] with a better interest rate" or ethanol plants in the Dominican Republic, promising returns of 50 percent or more. One firm offered investments called prime bank securities, a type of security that doesn't even exist. The seller collected over $3.5 million, while promising to double the values of the investments within four months. Needless to say, a deal that was too good to be true, was not—at least not for the defrauded investor.

Many of the frauds are what is called pump and dump. E-mails and Websites advertise a security that is supposedly poised for rapid growth. There may be claims of insider information. In reality, the promoters are the only persons who stand to gain by pumping up a new issue and then dumping their shares.

Like the Internet scams, penny stock fraud involves deceptive and misleading claims for security and earnings' potential. Penny stocks are low priced (around $5) and undercapitalized securities that are not sold on any major exchanges. Instead, they are commonly sold over the counter (OTC) by brokers.

Penny stock quotations are available to brokers from something called the Over the Counter Bulletin Board. The industry self-regulatory body, the National Association of Securities Dealers, has a subsidiary called the Nasdaq Stock Market. While some brokers want consumers to believe penny stocks are listed and regulated like the stocks sold on the Nasdaq Stock Market, they are not. The OTC markets have minimal standards and although Nasdaq does have a listing service for price quotations, it is nothing more than a listing service.

Two classic investment frauds still practiced today are called *Ponzi schemes*, after the original perpetrator, and pyramid schemes. Charles Ponzi, with his charm and confident manner, wove enough facts together in 1920 to make 30,000 investors believe in his unique venture. It was built around differences in currency exchange rates and the buying and selling of postage stamps. There were no shares or dividends. Investors were promised 50 percent interest on a 90-day note. When state and federal officials closed Ponzi down, many had already handed over their money. Of course no stamps were bought and sold in various countries in exchange for money. New investment funds were merely used to pay off earlier investors. Those who got in and out early made money; everyone else lost.

A pyramid scheme is similar to the financial fraud that Ponzi carried out. Chain letters, which instruct the recipient to send $10 to ten people with the expectation of receiving thousands as the chain letter reaches more "investors," are classic examples. Additional investors are needed to expand the base of the pyramid, and, of course, there is a mathematical certainty that it will collapse.

A variation on the pyramid scheme is called a multilevel marketing plan. A product is marketed through distributors. Commissions are paid not only for an individual's sales, but for the sales of other individuals recruited by the distributor to sell the product. The difference between a pyramid scheme and multilevel marketing is the sale of a product. Nonetheless, these plans are illegal in some states.

In the heart of the Great Depression, when Congress was considering reforms in the securities industry, Felix Frankfurter, a trusted advisor to President Franklin Roosevelt and later a member of the U.S. Supreme Court, proposed that when a corporation publicly trades securities, it becomes a public body, with a duty to provide full disclosure. That concept was incorporated into what became the cornerstone of investment protection, the Securities Act of 1933. Companies must register stock offerings made to the public and provide certain kinds of information. With the passage of the companion Securities Act of 1934, the SEC was created to oversee this industry. The 1934 act also prohibits insider trading and other abusive practices. State securities laws, known as blue sky laws, have adopted the principle of disclosure as well.

Predatory Practices

From her hospital bed, Gael Carter told a Senate Committee in 1998 how she was solicited to borrow against her home. The loan was to consolidate her debts, lower her payments, and leave enough money to pay for a daughter's wedding. Carter was paying off a $50,000 mortgage at 6.5 percent interest on a home valued at $194,000 in wealthy Farifax County, Virginia. By the time the mortgage company finished with her, Carter had accumulated more than $300,000 in debt payments, threatening her $150,000 of home equity.

What happened to Carter is called home equity fraud or stealing the equity (the difference between the appraised value and the amount owed) in a home. It is a pervasive, high cost, predatory practice affecting some of the most vulnerable consumers. Massachusetts's Attorney General Scott Harshbarger calls home equity fraud an "insidious form of urban economic violence." It particularly impacts low-income and minority home owners who have, over the years, paid off their mortgage and seen the value of their home increase.

A variation on the scheme used against Gael Carter involves "tin men," or shoddy home repair contractors. Such contractors have abused consumers for years. They prowl the neighborhoods, peddling unnecessary or substandard work through misrepresentations, deception, and high-pressure sales. The work, if performed, is expensive and inferior. What is new is that the tin men are now peddling home equity loans along with their other tricks. They review the mortgages recorded on land records found at the county recorder of deed's office. Here they can deduce which homeowners have built up equity in their homes. The homeowners with small or no mortgages are the target for the tin men, because they have the most equity.

Annie Ruth Bennett, a 70-year-old woman living with her husband in a small frame house in Atlanta, paid a home repair contractor $10,000 for repairs that were later appraised at a value of only $1,250. To start the job, the contractor required Bennett to sign a second mortgage carrying an 18 percent rate of interest. When he quit the job, the contractor left a gaping hole in the Bennett's living room, covered with plastic, and monthly payments for a home loan that are barely affordable given the Bennett's tiny income. Other homeowners, saddled with loans they could not repay, lost their homes.

Some other tactics include:

- Loan flipping, or layering separate financing agreements one on top of another. For example, the first loan may require full payment, what is called a balloon payment, within five years. If the borrower cannot pay the full amount, he or she must refinance, making another loan with a new balloon payment. With each agreement, he or she pays additional charges (points and fees). Eventually the monthly loan payments are unaffordable and the borrower loses the home.
- Packing or adding unnecessary charges like credit life

insurance to the loan. Life insurance premiums for older homeowners are particularly expensive.

• Equity stripping or issuing a loan based on the home equity rather than the owner's ability to pay. On some applications, contractors and/or mortgage lenders have lied about the borrower's job status or annual income. If the homeowner cannot afford to make the monthly payments, the mortgage company forecloses the loan.

The San Francisco office of Consumers Union reports, "Losses caused by home equity fraud and unscrupulous loans run into tens of millions of dollars" (Hudson, 1998). Conditions have gotten so bad in Los Angeles County that the district attorney there has opened a special unit to investigate and prosecute home equity fraud. In Georgia, a 1996 investigation of a mortgage company called Fleet Finance was conducted by the attorney general and the state consumer affairs office. It documented excessive interest rates, possible erroneous disclosures, and a failure to disclose the methods used to calculate finance charges. In response to a separate action in a private lawsuit, Fleet agreed to pay a $120 million settlement that affected 18,000 Georgia homeowners.

Fleet Finance is not a local loan company. It is an affiliate of one of the nation's largest banks. Obviously, not every mortgage company has been accused of lending abuses, but mainstream financial institutions like Fleet and NationsBank, and Fortune 500 companies like Ford (which just sold a large mortgage affiliate), have discovered the $200 billion to $300 billion *subprime* or *downscale* market. The *subprime market* refers to borrowers whose credit reports are below prime, which is the most creditworthy rating.

Targeted for this market are high-risk mortgages, used car loans, lending by finance companies and pawn shops, check-cashing facilities, and rent-to-own stores. Many states have raised caps on usury limits or eliminated them completely for subprime lending. It is not unusual, then, to see mortgage interest rates as high as 60 percent, pawn shop loans ($3 billion in annual loans) at 200 percent, and finance companies lending at 36 percent to 100 percent. Such rates used to be considered usurious. Couple high rates with unscrupulous salespeople interested in a quick buck and the market is ripe for abuse.

How can a subprime market become so large when the country is riding the crest of prosperity? The rising tide of economic prosperity is not lifting all boats equally. Between 1975 and 1995, the average household income for the wealthiest 5 percent in the nation increased by 54 percent. At the same time, the average household income for three out of five families increased less than 10 percent as real wages for many workers declined. Bankruptcies and credit card delinquencies are at an all-time high, and the number of "unbanked" households (those which do not own either a checking or savings account) is growing.

According to one scholar, "All indications are that these [income] disparities will continue in the decades ahead" (Hacker, 1997).

Parallel with the decline in real income for many middle- and lower-income families, banks began charging higher fees for their services and closing branches in less affluent areas (Hudson, 1998). West Oakland, California, had 48,000 lower-income residents but no banks, according to a 1993 Consumers Union study. Oakland's more affluent areas, on the other hand, had one branch for every 2,400 residents. Discriminatory practices also remain. A 1992 Federal Reserve Bank of Boston study of mortgage applications found that when all creditworthy factors were equal, minority applicants were 60 percent more likely to be denied a loan.

To be sure, many people utilizing "fringe" banks like pawn shops and check-cashing facilities use them as mere conveniences. Others lack sufficient education to understand the meaning of terms like "annual percentage rate" (APR) and how to comparison shop. At least one estimate indicates 30 to 40 percent of subprime borrowers could qualify for conventional loans if they knew it or if they were referred there. Still others use fringe banks because there are no alternatives.

To combat abuses in home mortgage lending, Congress approved the Home Ownership and Equity Protection Act in 1994 (15 U.S.C § 1601) to curb abuses in the high-cost lending market. If a loan has an annual percentage rate ten points higher than comparable Treasury bills, or has fees constituting more than 8 percent of the total loan amount, certain abusive practices are prohibited. These include payments from the lender directly to a home improvement contractor, balloon payments (lump sum) on loans of less than five years, and negative amortization loans in which the monthly payments do not cover the interest on the loan.

Other basic consumer protection laws are also applicable. These include the prohibition on false and misleading practices, mandated disclosures under the Truth in Lending Act, and others. There is no federally imposed cap or ceiling, however, on any interest rates. Usury regulations, where they exist at all, are at the state level.

Many states have chosen to raise the ceiling on usury rates to astronomical levels or eliminated them completely. Lenders justify their interest rates arguing their risks are higher with the subprime market and the rate of interest must be balanced with the lenders' risk.

Sociologist David Caplovitz authored a landmark book in the 1960s entitled *The Poor Pay More* (Caplovitz, 1967). He maintained that the marketplace for low-income neighborhoods is one in which both unethical and illegal practices abound. These practices remain because legitimate institutions do not provide the needed services. It appears that Caplovitz's analysis still applies.

Notes

[1]Frequently, there is not a direct consumer loss for health care fraud. This is because third-party payers, like insurance companies or government programs such as Medicare, pay for health care claims. Fraud does, however, raise premiums and challenge the integrity of the system. Some private insurers estimate that losses to health care fraud range from 5 to 10 percent of total health care costs. This puts the top of the range for health care fraud at $100 billion.

[2]"Children are allowed to choose how to spend $15 billion a year and have a say in how their parents spend another $160 billion" (Hamilton, 1997).

[3]Many legitimate businesses encourage consumer complaints. Such information enables them to improve their products.

[4]The FTC does lack jurisdiction, however, over certain businesses and industries. For example, banking, insurance, common carriers (telecommunications and transportation), and others.

References

AARP. 1993. *A Report on Hearing Aids.* Washington, DC: AARP.

———. 1994. *A Report on the 1993 Survey of Older Consumer Behavior.* Washington, DC: AARP.

———. 1996. *Telemarketing Fraud.* Washington, DC: AARP.

Allen, Frederick Lewis. 1931. *Only Yesterday: An Informal History of the 1920s.* New York: Harper & Row.

American Home Products Corp. v. FTC, 695 F.2d 681 (3rd Cir. 1982).

Aquinas, Thomas. 1266. *Summa Theologica.* Website: http://www.ccel. wheaton.edu.

Barnard v. Kellogg, 77 U.S. 383 (1870).

Bristol-Meyers Co., In re, 102 F.T.C. 21 (1983).

Campbell, Charles. 1998. "Keating Off the State's Hook for Now" *Orange County Register* (6 February).

Caplovitz, David. 1967. *The Poor Pay More.* New York: Free Press.

Chandrasekaran, Rajiv. 1998. "U.S., 20 States Sue Microsoft, Allege Abuses." *The Washington Post* (19 May).

Connor, John M. 1997. "The Global Lysine Price-Fixing Conspiracy of 1992–1995." *Review of Agricultural Economics* 19, no. 2: 412–427.

Crenshaw, Albert B. 1997. "Fed, FTC Drive Home Real Cost of Car Leases." *The Washington Post* (10 December).

de Tocqueville, Alexis. 1976. *Democracy in America.* New York: Alfred A. Knopf.

Dutt, Jill. 1997. "For Investors, Dizzying Growth: Shareholders Cautiously Optimistic as Savings Build." *The Washington Post* (16 February).

East, Robert. 1997. *Consumer Behavior: Advances and Applications in Marketing.* New York: Prentice-Hall.

Fair Credit Billing Rights Act, 15 U.S.C. § 1666.

Fair Credit Repair Act, 15 U.S.C. § 1679.

Fair Credit Reporting Act, 15 U.S.C. § 1681.

Federal Billing Rights Act, 15 U.S.C. § 572.

Federal Bureau of Investigation. 1996. *Senior Sentinel* (December): 1–17.

Federal Motor Vehicle Information and Cost Savings Act, 15 U.S.C. § 1981.

Federal Trade Commission. 1983a. *Policy Statement Regarding Advertising Substantiation.* Website: http://www.ftc.gov.

———. 1983b. *FTC Policy Statement on Deception* (14 October).

———. 1995. "FTC Garners $2.75 Million Civil Penalty in Settlement of False Advertising Charges against Maker of "Miracle-Ear" Hearing Aids." News Release (21 November).

———. 1997. *Fighting Consumer Fraud: New Tools of the Trade.* Washington, DC: FTC.

Federal Trade Commission Act, 15 U.S.C. §§ 41–58.

Hacker, Andrew. 1997. *Money: Who Has How Much and Why?* New York: Scribner.

Hamilton, Martha M. 1997. "Persuading Young Minds to Buy." *The Washington Post* (9 September).

Home Ownership and Equity Protection Act, 15 U.S.C. § 1601.

Horowitz, Morton J. 1974. "The Historical Foundations of Modern Contract Law." *Harvard Law Review* 87, no. 5 (March): 917–956.

Hudson, Michael. 1998. *Predatory Financial Practices: How Can Consumers be Protected?* Washington, DC: AARP.

Jupiter Communications. 1997 *Online Advertising Report* (22 August).

Kennedy, President John F. (1962). *Special Message on Protecting the Consumer Interest*, 15 March, Washington, DC: Government Printing Office.

Kestner v. Jakobe, 446 S.W. 2d 188 (1969).

Laidlaw v. Organ, 15 U.S. 178 (1817).

Lou Harris and Associates. 1992. *Telephone-Based Fraud: A Survey of the American Public*, sponsored by the National Consumers League and the Reference Point Foundation.

Magnuson-Moss Warranty Act, 15 U.S.C. §§ 2301–2312.

Mail Fraud Statute, 18 U.S.C. § 1341.

National Association of Attorneys General. 1995. *Auto Repair Task Force Report*. Washington, DC: NAAG.

National Association of Consumer Agency Administrators. 1997. *Sixth Annual NACAA/CFA Consumer Complaint Survey Report*. News Release (25 November).

Nocera, Joseph. 1994. *A Piece of the Action: How the Middle Class Joined the Money Class*. New York: Scribner.

Orkin v. Federal Trade Commission, 849 F2d 1354 (1988).

Owens, Charles L., Chief Financial Crimes Section, Federal Bureau of Investigation. (1996). Testimony before Senate Aging Committee (6 March). Website: http://www.fbi.gov/congress/telefraud/senate.

Pae, Peter. 1998. "NationsBank to Pay Fine for Understating Risk of Funds." *The Washington Post* (5 May).

Pfizer, Inc., In re, 81 F.T.C. 23 (1972).

Pitofsky, Robert, Chairman of the Federal Trade Commission. (1998). Testimony before the Senate Governmental Affairs Committee (10 February). Website: http://www.ftc.gov/speeches/pitofsky.

Pope, Daniel. 1991. "Advertising as a Consumer Issue: An Historical View." *Journal of Social Issues* 47, no. 1 (Spring 1991): 41–46.

Pratkanis, Anthony, and Elliot Aronson. 1991. *Age of Propaganda: The Everyday Use and Abuse of Persuasion*. New York: W. H. Freeman.

Pridgen, Dee. 1986. *Consumer Protection and the Law*. New York: Clark Boardman.

Quinn, Jane Bryant. 1988. "Stock Scams Invading the Internet." *The Washington Post* (19 April).

Regulation M, Consumer Leasing, 12 C.F.R. § 213.

Sherman Antitrust Act, 15 U.S.C. §§ 1–7.

Simon, Ruth. 1996. "Consumers: You Are on Your Own." *Money Magazine* (25 March).

Standard Oil Co. v. FTC, 577 F.2d 653 (9th Cir. 1978).

Telemarketing Sales Rule, 16 C.F.R. § 310.

Titus, Richard M., Fred Heinzelmann, and John M. Boyle. 1995. "Victimization of Persons by Fraud." *Crime & Delinquency* 41, no. (1 January): 54–72.

Truth in Lending Act, 15 U.S.C. § 1601.

Unavailability Rule, 16 C.F.R. § 424.

U.S. Department of Justice. 1995. "Volunteer Retirees Go Undercover to Help Snare Dishonest Telemarketers, More than 400 Arrests Made in 14 States." News Release (7 December).

U.S. Office of Consumer Affairs. 1993. News Release (26 October).

U.S. v. O'Malley, 707 F2d, 1240 (1983).

Used Car Rule, 16 C.F.R. § 16.01.

Washington Consumer Checkbook. 1997. "Auto Repair." Washington, DC: Center for the Study of Services, Summer/Fall.

Yankelovich Partners. 1997. *Yankelovich Monitor: An Annual Study of Consumer Attitudes, Beliefs, and Social Values.* Norwalk, CT: Yankelovich Partners.

Chronology 2

The marketplace has always been a dangerous place for the consumer. From earliest times, the evidence of fraudulent practices, faulty products, deception, and charlatanism has been reflected in the laws and regulations created to protect the public and in the writings of those concerned with their health and security. The following chronology suggests the scope of sharp dealing from investment transactions in the time of Hammurabi (*ca.* 1800 B.C.) to car leasing on the brink of the twenty-first century.

Thomas Aquinas, an eleventh-century religious philosopher, stated the medieval position that there is a "just price," that is, a fair value that can be placed on goods and services. He expressed the prevailing view of his time, and of the Catholic Church, that no one should profit beyond the actual value of the wares sold. This approach is in stark contrast with the frankly acquisitive economic position reflected in the concept of *caveat emptor*—buyer beware—that showed its face most prominently in the burgeoning world commerce of the nineteenth century.

In the twentieth century, scholars usually describe three significant periods of consumer protection activity. The first is the so-called Progressive Era, which began in the late nineteenth century and reached its peak in the administration of Woodrow Wilson. The next period of reform, in the 1920s, was touched off by revelations of unsafe food, drugs, and cosmetics and the lack of accurate information on products. This, combined with the economic reverberations of the Great Depression of 1929, set the stage for a series of innovative and unprecedented programs in which President Franklin D. Roosevelt attempted to use the power of the federal government to return economic balance to the nation and to expand consumer protection. And more recently, the administration of President John F. Kennedy established a vision of consumer rights and an agenda for legislation that was actualized during the Johnson and Nixon eras. This was also a period of heightened consumer awareness under the leadership of such activists as Ralph Nader and Esther Peterson.

In each of these periods, various factors came together to create a political environment conducive to consumer agitation and government response. Dramatic, even sensational exposés by muckraking reporters and best-selling authors disclosed alarming safety hazards and raised public awareness. Social and economic dislocation, fundamental change in marketplace relationships, rapid technological advances, and a perception of inequities—of pitting the "little guy" against the rich and powerful —were all factors in generating a demand for legislation and government action to protect the consumer from fraud and abuses in the marketplace.

This chronology is a sampling of selected problems in the field of consumer fraud and the nature of the response to those problems.

1800 B.C.   Code of Hammurabi is promulgated. Number 102 in the code provides, "If a merchant entrust money to an agent for some investment and the broker suffer a loss in the place to which he goes, he shall make good the capital to the merchant."

600–500 B.C. Old Testament laws regarding ethical marketplace relationships appear in written form. Based on the oral tradition, these laws address such matters as honest weights and measures and fair dealing. They form a recurring theme throughout the Pentateuch (the first five books of the Old Testament) as well as Proverbs and the books of the Prophets.

500 A.D.   Justinian Code (from Digest of classical Roman law) provides that sellers of beasts of burden must declare with proper publicity any disease or defect in any of them, and the beasts must be delivered to buyers in the best trappings in which they were shown for sale.

1202   Assize of Bread is proclaimed by King John of England to prohibit the adulteration of bread.

1266   *Summa Theologica* is written. Thomas Aquinas articulates the concept of fairness in the marketplace and condemns the sale of products with defects known to the seller but not revealed to the buyer.

1789   U.S. Constitution, Article 1, Section 8, gives Congress the power to set fair weights and measures and to regulate and coin money.

1817   In *Laidlaw v. Organ*, 15 U.S. 178 (1817), the U.S. Supreme Court embraces the policy of *caveat emptor* (buyer beware) in a case involving a contract for purchase of tobacco.

1847   Physician licensing by the states is promoted by the American Medical Association. This leads to standardization of medical education and practice, and acts as a control on the quackery that is rampant during this period. It also prompts a move toward professional licensing in other occupations.

1848   Congress passes the Import Drug Act. The United States initiates the inspection of drugs entering the country from foreign lands to curtail the dumping of contaminated, adulterated, fake, and decomposed drugs on U.S. markets.

1850   California passes a pure food and drug law, the first

1850 *cont.*	state law that seeks to ensure the purity of both food and drugs.
1872	England extends prior food adulteration legislation to include protection for drugs in its Adulteration of Food and Drugs Act. This and subsequent English acts were incorporated into reform proposals for U.S. laws.
	Mail fraud statute is enacted as the first federal consumer protection legislation in the United States. It is designed to combat the rise of lotteries, swindles, and medical quackery marketed through the mail following the Civil War.
1879	The U.S. Department of Agriculture begins investigating food adulteration under the leadership of Peter Collier, its chief chemist.
1883	Harvey Wiley, as new chief chemist of the U.S. Department of Agriculture, expands the investigation into adulteration of food. He discloses such practices as the use of cottonseed oil and beef fat in products sold as pure butter, and the use of dangerous chemicals to preserve food products for shipment. His "poison squad" actually ingests chemical preservatives and reports the resulting effects on their bodies.
1887	The Interstate Commerce Act establishes the Interstate Commerce Commission and federal regulation of railroad rates. This is the nation's first major regulatory agency, and its scope ultimately includes most common carriers.
1890	The Sherman Antitrust Act prohibits contracts, combinations, and conspiracies in restraint of trade, including price fixing, formation of monopolies (trusts), and certain other unfair business practices. The act suffers from vagueness and is not vigorously enforced. Trust formation actually accelerates in the two decades after its passage.

1895   The Supreme Court decides *United States v. E. C. Knight Co.*, 156 U.S. 1 (1895), the first case challenging a monopoly under the Sherman Antitrust Act. The Court determines that the law applies only to monopolies in commerce. The defendant, American Sugar Refining Company, was found to be in manufacturing, rather than "commerce." Thus, it was not an illegal monopoly, even though its acquisition of a competitor, the E. C. Knight Company, gave it control of 98 percent of the sugar market. The decision undermines any attempt to use the Sherman Act to control "trusts," as this interpretation of the law exempts most industrial trusts from its provisions. Thousands of mergers and new monopolies follow.

1898   The Pure Food Congress, held in Washington, D.C., draws attention to the growing national movement lead by Dr. Harvey Wiley calling for federal legislation to prevent misbranding and adulteration of foods and drugs.

1899   The National Consumer's League is formed to promote and represent the interests of consumers. It focuses on child labor and the excesses of the sweatshops, and promotes the use of the consumer's buying power to influence the way businesses treat their employees. This organization continues today and is involved in issues such as telemarketing fraud and consumer education.

1901   Presidency of Theodore Roosevelt (1901–1908). Many scholars equate Roosevelt's administration with the Progressive Era, a period in which reformers seek social improvements through government action. At this time, the political environment is more receptive to legislation designed to protect consumers. This changed with the prosperity and new focus brought about by the onset of World War I.

1904   In *Northern Securities v. United States,* 193 U.S. 197 (1904), the U.S. government achieves its first win in a monopoly action. Northern Securities was a holding company formed by two railroad magnates, J. P.

1904 cont.	Morgan and James J. Hill, involved in a conflict with a third railroad over a major market. The Supreme Court finds that Morgan's and Hill's railroads are clearly in commerce and that combining the stock of these two companies, which were previously independent and competitive, is illegal under the Sherman Act.
1906	*The Jungle*, Upton Sinclair's provocative novel about Chicago stockyard workers, exposes the shocking filth and adulteration of meat that exists in the meatpacking industry. The book is an impetus to corrective federal action. The Meat Inspection Act establishes federal inspection of slaughterhouses and packing and canning plants that ship meat interstate. The Pure Food and Drug Act is signed by Theodore Roosevelt. This legislation prohibits interstate commerce in adulterated or misbranded food, drink, or drugs.
1911	Sherley Amendment is passed by Congress to amend the 1906 Pure Food and Drug Act. The legislation is in response to *United States v. Johnson* (221 U.S. 488 (1911)), a case in which the Supreme Court found that the original act did not prohibit drug manufacturers from making false therapeutic claims, only false and misleading statements about the ingredients or the identity of the drugs. The amendment prohibits the use of false therapeutic claims on labels that are intended to defraud the purchaser. *Printer's Ink*, a trade journal of the advertising industry, publishes a model statute for controlling deceptive advertising in publications. Forty states adopt the model statute in some form. It is an early harbinger of consumer protection. The Supreme Court decides *United States v. Standard Oil Company*, 221 U.S. 1 (1911). One of two cornerstone cases in antitrust policy, this decision regarding

the broad Rockefeller oil interests establishes the "rule of reason." The Supreme Court states that Standard Oil's position as a monopoly is not the question, but rather whether it had obtained its position by monopolizing, that is, by methods that were not normal business practices. In this case, Standard Oil's use of price wars, dummy corporations, preferential rates to railroads, and pressure tactics against suppliers is found to be outside normal business practices and therefore to be monopolizing.

In *United States v. American Tobacco*, 221 U.S. 106 (1911), the "rule of reason" is again applied to a company that has obtained a monopoly position in the tobacco business. In this case, American Tobacco is found to be guilty of monopolizing based on its tactics (specifically, noncompetition agreements, mergers to avoid competition, and the purchase of tobacco plants in order to close them), not the fact of its dominant position.

Blue sky laws are initiated when Kansas passes the first state law designed to protect small investors from fraud. The name comes from a description of worthless stock as "so many feet of blue sky."

1912   The first Better Business Bureau (BBB) is founded in Boston. The BBB becomes the first important self-regulatory organization for business. Fearing that deceptive practices by some businesses would erode the confidence of consumers in all commerce, these nonprofit organizations attempt to monitor businesses for the content of their advertising and for honest business practices.

1913   Presidency of Woodrow Wilson (1913–1921). Wilson, like Theodore Roosevelt, is considered a Progressive and advocates passage of the Clayton Act to correct the inadequacies of the Sherman Antitrust Act as well as the establishment of the Federal Trade Commission. The coming of World War I shifts his attention, and that of the public, away from consumer issues.

1914   The Federal Trade Commission Act creates the Federal Trade Commission, an agency with general powers to regulate unfair competition among businesses. It is not a consumer protection law, but rather an attempt to protect smaller businesses from big business practices that threaten to eliminate them.

The Clayton Antitrust Act is adopted to correct the vagueness of the Sherman Antitrust Act. It prohibits certain types of price discriminations, exclusive dealing, total requirements agreements, acquisitions or mergers that tend to substantially lessen competition, and interlocking directorates.

1924   In *United States v. Ninety-five (More or Less) Barrels Alleged Apple Cider Vinegar*, 265 U.S. 438 (1924), the Supreme Court declares that the Pure Food and Drug Act prohibits all statements, designs, or devices that may mislead or deceive purchasers, even when those statements may be technically true.

1927   *Your Money's Worth: A Study in the Waste of the Consumer's Dollar*, by Stuart Chase and Frederick Schlink, is published. This book spurs a demand by the public for accurate information about the content and quality of the products available to them in the market, as well as standardization in sizes, forms, and product descriptions so that the consumer can make an informed purchase.

1928   Acting on the ideas explored in their book, *Your Money's Worth*, Schlink and Chase create Consumers Research, an organization to test brand-name products and to publish the results of their findings in a magazine, *Consumers Research*. It is an independent and nonprofit educational organization that plays a major role in creating public awareness and action. (Consumers Union is an offshoot of this organization and has come to overshadow the older organization's importance in the consumer movement.)

1933   Presidency of Franklin Delano Roosevelt (1933–1945). This long and eventful administration begins in the midst of the economic disaster known as the Great Depression. Roosevelt initiates what he calls the New Deal, a series of bills designed to stabilize the economy and put people back to work. He also pursues investor protection by promoting the Securities Act of 1933 and the Securities and Exchange Act. Other significant consumer legislation includes a reform of the 1906 Pure Food and Drug Act and expansion of the FTC through the Wheeler-Lea Act.

Congress passes the National Industrial Recovery Act. One of Roosevelt's first measures, it establishes advisory committees made up of labor, business, and consumers to help draft codes of fair competition. Consumer representatives are included to prevent business and labor from dominating the planning of what are envisioned as major changes in the economy. The codes are to help stabilize the economy by establishing minimum wages and hours and curtailing cutthroat competition. The act also permits price fixing and suspends the Sherman Antitrust Act. Within two years, the Supreme Court rules the act unconstitutional, yet many of its goals are met and others are made possible, such as elimination of sweatshops and child labor and the provision of collective bargaining.

The Securities Act of 1933 is passed. The essence of this act is disclosure. It requires that public corporations must register their stock and bond offerings with the federal government and provide specific information to buyers, including the names of officers, directors, and principal shareholders of the company and a current profit-and-loss statement.

100,000 Guinea Pigs: Dangers in Everyday Food, Drugs and Cosmetics, Frederick Schlink's second book coauthored with Arthur Kallet, exposes, with scientific verification, the dangerous chemicals and potentially lethal impurities that exist in products on the market. The consumer is shown as an unknowing "guinea pig" for producers of untested products. The book is a significant force influenc-

1933 *cont.*	ing the passage of the 1938 Food, Drug and Cosmetic Act.
1934	The Securities and Exchange Act is passed to regulate the activities of the exchanges. It protects investors from insider manipulation, reduces speculation by increasing the margin requirements for buying stock, and creates the Securities and Exchange Commission to administer this law and the Securities Act of 1933.
1936	Consumers Union, a nonprofit consumer organization, is founded by Arthur Kallet and later led by Colston Warne. Its publication, *Consumer Reports*, provides detailed information regarding products available on the market based on extensive and sophisticated testing. It acts as a national consumer advocate on the federal and local level and supports other consumer groups. It begins as an offshoot of Consumer Research.
	The Robinson-Patman Act becomes law. Wary of the ability of large chain stores to drive smaller competing businesses out of the market by buying in bulk and selling at artificially low prices, the act prohibits price discrimination by sellers that could lead to a monopoly.
1937	A patent medicine known as elixir of sulfanilamide, which contains a poisonous solvent, kills 107 people, mostly children, before it can be recalled. The widespread public outrage at this tragedy pressures Congress to move forward on an embattled revision of the obsolete Pure Food and Drugs Act of 1906.
1938	The Food, Drug and Cosmetic Act expands the 1906 law and adds important new provisions. It defines "adulterated" as any food or drug that contains a substance unsafe for human use and requires testing to prove the safety of new drugs before they can reach the market. The act covers products prepared for interstate commerce and includes both cosmetics and therapeutic devices. Proof of fraud is no longer needed in order to stop

false claims regarding a drug. The use of injunctions is authorized as a remedy.

The Wheeler-Lea Act extends the prohibitions of the Federal Trade Commission Act to "unfair or deceptive acts or practices affecting commerce," including false advertising, and gives the FTC broad powers over an extensive range of harmful business practices.

1940   Legal scholars, seeking to create uniformity in commercial law, publish a proposed Uniform Commercial Code, a model code for state laws regulating sales transactions. This code specifies the seller's and buyer's rights and duties in a sale. Every state adopts this code, in whole or in part.

1943   In *United States v. Dotterweich*, 302 U.S. 277 (1943), the Supreme Court finds that responsible corporate officials, as well as the corporation itself, can be prosecuted for violations of the law without proving that the officials knew of or intended the violations.

1944   In *United States v. South-Eastern Underwriters Association*, 322 U.S. 533 (1944), the Supreme Court finds that the insurance industry is not in interstate commerce and is therefore exempt from antitrust actions.

1949   Edwin Sutherland, noted criminologist, introduces the concept of, and coins the term, "white-collar crime," to describe corporate misconduct, abuses, and financial crimes. Sutherland's book, *White Collar Crime,* addresses the double standard in effect regarding the crimes of corporate officials compared with conventional ideas of criminality. This work initiated a new area of research and theory in criminology.

1950   In *Alberty Food Products Co. v. United States*, 185 F.2d 321 (9 Cir., 1950), a federal court of appeals finds that drug labels must show the purpose for which the product is offered in the directions for use. Sellers of ineffective products cannot, therefore, avoid

1950
cont.

the requirements of the law by not stating the condition the product is alleged to treat.

Cellar-Kefauver Act is passed to remedy weaknesses in the Clayton Act that prevented effective litigation to stop mergers having deleterious effects on competition. This act applies the law to companies that merge through acquisition of assets, as well as the purchase of stock, and prevents those combinations that might lead to monopoly or a reduction in competition.

1953

The Flammable Fabrics Act prohibits the sale in interstate commerce of clothing and bedding products that do not meet federal flammability standards.

1958

The Bank of America begins circulating the first bank credit cards in Fresno, California.

The Food Additives Amendment is passed by Congress. Manufacturers of new food additives must now prove the safety of their products. This amendment includes the "Delaney proviso," which states that any additive shown to cause cancer in animals is prohibited.

The Federal Aviation Administration is created to regulate all areas of airline safety and the air traffic control system. It licenses airlines, approves new airplane designs, and tests pilots.

State antifraud efforts gain support. Louis Lefkowitz, New York attorney general, institutes a campaign against consumer fraud by using the common law power of his office and the state corporation laws, which give him the authority to enjoin business entities (corporations, partnerships, and associations) that operate in a fraudulent manner. In this, Lefkowitz creates the modern role of the state attorneys general in consumer fraud issues.

1960

The Hazardous Substances Act is passed. It regulates the sale of products that present a substantial risk of harm to consumers. Hazardous substances include toxic, radioactive, or flammable products as well as irritants. The Consumer Product Safety Commission administers this act.

1961   Presidency of John F. Kennedy (1961–1963). Kennedy's most significant consumer protection offerings are the creation of the Consumer Bill of Rights and appointment of a Consumer Advisory Council to represent consumer interests. Kennedy campaigned on this issue, and in a special message to Congress in 1962, he identifies various areas he intends to pursue, including expansion of food and drug protections, legislation to end credit abuse, and empowerment of the FTC to issue temporary cease and desist orders against unfair competitive practices. His assassination in November 1963 cuts short these efforts.

1962   The Consumer Bill of Rights, President Kennedy's message to Congress regarding consumers' rights to safety, to be informed, to choose, and to be heard, becomes the "Magna Carta of the consumer movement," according to longtime consumer activist, Esther Peterson.

The Kefauver-Harris Drug Amendment requires drug manufacturers to prove the safety and effectiveness of their products before marketing. This law is, at least in part, a reaction to the discovery that the drug Thalidomide, which was widely used in Europe by pregnant women, causes extreme birth defects. (Distribution of this product was prevented in the United States by the action of Dr. Frances Kelsey, an FDA medical officer.)

1963   Presidency of Lyndon B. Johnson (1963–1968). Many of the consumer issues identified by President Kennedy are enacted under Johnson. Johnson also creates the office of Special Assistant for Consumer Affairs, the first high-ranking consumer position in the White House, and appoints Esther Peterson to the position.

1965   Ralph Nader publishes his exposé of General Motors, *Unsafe at Any Speed*, claiming that GM's Chevrolet Corvair was negligently designed. The book, plus the behavior of GM in attempting to discover damaging personal information about Nader in order to discredit him and to reduce the impact of his possible testimony in civil lawsuits, causes a public reaction that promotes federal legislation on automobile safety.

1966   The National Traffic and Motor Vehicle Safety Act provides for the creation of safety standards for vehicles, parts, and for recall of defective vehicles.

The Fair Packaging and Labeling Act requires that all interstate consumer products have standardized, honest, and informative labels regarding content, net quantity, and, if a number of servings per package is claimed, a statement of the weight of the serving. Use of meaningless terms such as "jumbo ounces" or "giant half-quart" is prohibited.

The Unfair and Deceptive Practices Model Act is unveiled. One of a series of model laws developed at this time, this act, written by the National Conference of Commissioners on Uniform State Law, prohibits 11 specific deceptive practices or acts that create a likelihood of "confusion or misunderstanding." Variations of this and other model laws are eventually adopted by most states.

1967   The Wholesome Meat Act requires inspection of meat according to federal standards. Prior to this legislation, meat sold and consumed within a state was not covered by the federal safety standards set in 1906. (A companion act, the Poultry Products Inspection Act, follows in 1968.)

The Poor Pay More, a book by David Caplovitz, is published. The book exposes the abuse and exploitation of low-income consumers in the nation's ghettos, including fraud, significantly higher prices, deceptive labeling, and inflated credit rates.

The Consumer Federation of America is formed. An umbrella organization of over 240 nonprofit consumer advocacy groups, small and large, it lobbies before Congress and regulatory agencies on consumer issues; publishes reports, periodicals, and books on subjects of interest to consumers; and encourages the growth of small, grassroots groups.

1968   Congress enacts the Truth in Lending Act. Lenders and creditors are required to disclose the costs of credit in installment loans and sales to the consumer in both dollars and annual percentage rates.

1969   The new Toy Safety Act allows government monitoring of children's toys for safety features.

1970   The Credit Card Liability Act sets a limit of $50 per card as the risk to consumers for lost or stolen credit cards, and prohibits distribution of unsolicited credit cards.

The Fair Credit Reporting Act becomes law. Companies that collect credit information must provide accurate data, make a synopsis of credit reports available to the consumer, and notify him or her if a credit report is being prepared.

The Poison Prevention Packaging Act is passed. Administered by the Consumer Product Safety Commission, this federal law regulates the packaging of household substances to protect children from accidental poisoning.

1971   Public Citizen is formed. This is a nonprofit umbrella organization advocating for various consumer health, safety, environmental, and economic issues. Its founder is Ralph Nader

1973   The federal Consumer Product Safety Act establishes the Consumer Product Safety Commission with the authority to set standards of safety for consumer products (excluding automobiles and food, which are covered under other agencies) and to take products with undue risks off the market.

1974   The Fair Credit Billing Act is enacted. If a product purchased by credit card proves to be defective, the purchaser may refuse to pay the credit card issuer until the matter is resolved. The purchaser, however, must make a good-faith effort to resolve the matter with the seller. The law is both a protection for the purchaser and an incentive for the credit card issuer to monitor the retailers who accept their cards.

The federal Equal Credit Opportunity Act prohibits credit discrimination based on age, gender, race, marital status, color, religion, or national origin.

The Door-to-Door Sales Rule is promulgated by the FTC. Under the rule, consumers must be given a three-day "cooling-off" period in which to withdraw from contracts to purchase goods or services from salespersons who appear at their door. The salesperson must inform the buyer, orally and in writing, of the right to rescind the contract and the time allowed.

1975   The Magnuson-Moss Warranty Act amends the FTC Act to require sellers to make clear disclosure, in simple language, of the terms and conditions of written warranties. If warranties are breached, the new law provides buyers with reasonable and effective remedies, including a private right of action to enforce the warranty provisions. This act expands the power of the FTC to issue trade regulations.

1976   The Consumer Leasing Act is passed. It requires clear disclosure, in language an average adult can understand, of the specific terms of a lease for any period of four months or longer. It does not apply to property leased for business purposes.

The National Association of Consumer Agency Administrators is formed. This is an organization of state and local consumer protection agencies.

The Medical Device Amendment is passed. Under it, the FDA must approve the safety and effectiveness of medical devices, including those for diagnostic use. Manufacturers of medical devices must register with the FDA and follow procedures for quality control.

The Hart-Scott-Rodino Act is passed. Large companies seeking to merge are required to give notice to both the Antitrust Division of the Justice Department and the FTC. If, after careful economic analysis, the government determines that the merger would substantially lesson competition or raise prices, the merger will be challenged. State attorneys general can, under this law, bring actions in federal court against companies that engage in price fixing or other practices that lessen competition to the detriment of the citizens of their states.

1977   The Fair Debt Collection Practices Act becomes law. It prohibits abusive collection practices by collection businesses. It controls the communications of a collection company, both with the debtor and any third party. Harassment, threats, false or misleading statements, or publicizing the debtors name in any way are prohibited.

1978   The Electronic Fund Transfer Act is passed. It covers any transfer of funds that takes place without a document, whether it be an automatic deposit or a deduction from a consumer's bank account. Financial institutions are required to disclose costs associated with use of the electronic transfers, provide protection from unauthorized use (PINs, personal identification numbers), and provide receipts to help the consumer keep accurate records of transactions.

The Airline Deregulation Act is passed. Regulations regarding airline prices and routes are removed to promote greater competition. It is the first of a series of deregulations begun under the Carter administration.

1980   Congress passes the Infant Formula Act. It empowers the FDA to take measures to ensure that com-

1980
cont.

mercial infant formulas meet nutritional and safety levels.

The Federal Trade Commission Improvement Act is passed. The act severely restricts the FTC's power to issue and enforce new rules. This reflects a swing back to a more conservative view of government's role in consumer protection under the Reagan administration.

1982

State lemon laws become popular. Created by state statutes, lemon laws are a response to consumer complaints that car dealers fail to fulfill their warranty obligations. A typical lemon law provides a warranty for the purchaser of a new vehicle that is in addition to any preexisting contract law or statute. It spells out the number of repair attempts considered reasonable before a dealer is required to buy back the vehicle, provide a comparable replacement, or return the purchase price.

1984

The Funeral Rule is implemented by the FTC after surviving a court test. It requires disclosure of the actual prices of goods and services to funeral customers and prohibits such practices as embalming without permission.

1987

Congress passes the Prescription Drug Marketing Act to prevent the distribution of mislabeled, adulterated, subpotent, or counterfeit drugs. It bans the diversion of prescription drugs from legitimate commercial channels, and requires drug wholesalers to be licensed by the states.

1988

The Food and Drug Administration Act officially establishes the FDA as an agency of the Department of Health and Human Services, indicating the broad responsibilities of its officials for research, enforcement, education, and information.

Originally passed in 1946, the Lanham Trademark Act is a federal act that provides for the registration of trademarks or trade names and for their protection in federal courts. The 1988 amendment to this act prohibits sellers from making false claims about "the characteristics or qualities" of their own or their competitors' products. This legislation leads to self-regulation as aggrieved sellers are able to sue their competitors for false advertising claims.

1989   American Continental Corporation (ACC) goes bankrupt, setting in motion one of the nation's largest bank failures, costing taxpayers a billion dollars, and wiping out the investments of 20,000 customers of ACC-owned Lincoln Savings & Loan.

1990   Congress passes the Nutrition Labeling and Education Act. Packaged foods must henceforth bear nutritional labeling, and any health claims made must conform with terms defined by the secretary of Health and Human Services.

1991   The Truth in Savings Act is enacted. It requires banks to disclose all fees, rates of interest, minimum balance requirements, and any penalties that might exist for early withdrawal.

1994   The Home Ownership and Equity Protection Act, a federal statute designed to curtail the growth of equity skimming, is passed. It prohibits abusive credit practices in home equity loans for household repairs.

The Telemarketing and Consumer Fraud and Abuse Prevention Act authorizes the FTC to set restrictions regarding practices connected with frauds and abuses in telemarketing. These include prohibiting calls between 9:00 P.M. and 8:00 P.M., calling people who have asked not to be called, charging fees for recovering money lost in other frauds, misrepresenting facts about products being sold, debiting customers' bank accounts without permission, and failing to acknowledge that the call is a sales call.

1998   The FTC implements auto leasing regulations. They require auto dealers to provide clear and complete

1998
cont.

disclosure of costs in leasing. A work sheet developed by the FTC spells out the costs and how they are derived. Dealers do not have to use the sheet, but they must provide the same information.

Biographies 3

"It seems to me that to be a consumer activist these days you have to have a fairly good sense of humor as well as a sense of dedication, because almost everything we propose is met at first with a barrage of ridicule and the implication that we are trying to take the joy out of life. I think we have done a lot to put more joy into life by the laws we have helped enact in the consumer field."
— Esther Peterson

Individuals on both sides of the law have made their mark in the area of consumer fraud. Included in the following biographies are brief sketches of a representative few of the men and women who have worked, some for a lifetime, to ensure that American consumers have protection from unscrupulous sellers and adequate information to make wise marketplace choices.

On the other side, the malefactors tend to be anonymous, hit-and-run artists who even when apprehended and brought to justice rarely impress themselves, individually, on the public mind. The few who do come from the relatively new arena of white-collar crime, where the repercussions of their frauds touch hundreds, even thousands, of victims. Often, these victims are among the most vulnerable of the population.

In addition to those who have made consumer issues a career, three U.S. presidents are included in these biographies because of the critical role they played in government policy and legislation. Whether arising from their own personal viewpoint or the economic imperative of their unique place in history, these men influenced the direction of consumer protection in America.

Charles Keating Jr. (b. 1923)

Junk bonds, leveraged buyouts, hostile takeovers, and the deregulation of the savings and loan (S&L) industry were the business tools of the 1980s. It was a decade of speculation and greed, and the name of Charles Keating Jr. will always be linked to it. A high-flying deal maker, Keating presided over the nation's largest bank failure, which cost taxpayers an estimated $3.4 billion. Worse, Keating's S&L convinced 20,000 mostly older depositors to buy worthless junk bonds issued by his holding company, American Continental Corporation (ACC). Eventually, after a civil fraud suit, they recovered 71 cents on the dollar.

By 1976, Keating and his law firm were already in trouble with the law, having been charged by the Securities and Exchange Commission (SEC) with using "devices, schemes, and articles to defraud." Keating paid a fine to settle those charges and left Cincinnati two years later to open a new business in Phoenix, Arizona. That business became the infamous American Continental Corporation through which Keating later funnelled the money of investors for his own personal gain. At first, American Continental prospered legitimately under Keating's management, becoming the largest home builder in Phoenix. However, the home-building market dried up in the late 1970s and early 1980s when interest rates hit 15 percent. Savings and loan institutions, which were restricted by federal law to loaning money for home purchases, were also failing at an alarming rate. In the early 1980s, Congress offered an answer to the S&L crisis that was popular with the new Reagan administration. Deregulate the industry, argued the reformers. This would modernize S&Ls and make them competitive. In response, Congress granted the S&Ls wide latitude in where and how they could invest their funds, but the federal government continued to insure the safety of depositors' savings accounts.

Deregulation proved to be a disaster for taxpayers when

many S&Ls plunged recklessly into unsecured and imprudent loans, including giving choice perks to their own executives. When these loans went into default, the federal government was required by law to make good on the losses. With few restrictions on self-dealing, some S&Ls also lent or invested federally insured funds with their parent corporations or related affiliates. This was the angle that Keating exploited.

By 1983, his company, American Continental, had left the home-building business and became a holding company with many varied subsidiaries. It bought a small California-based S&L called Lincoln Savings & Loan for $51 million ($17 million more than Lincoln's net worth at the time). Although Keating's name never appeared on Lincoln's list of officers or directors, evidence indicated that he was clearly in control.

Keating had Lincoln conveniently loan him and ACC vast sums, secure in the knowledge that the federal government would make up any losses if the loans were not repaid. According to Henry Gonzalez (D-Texas), then the chair of the House Banking Committee, which investigated the scandal, Lincoln operated as a sort of "cash machine for Keating and ACC—their own personal ATM." Keating and his family drew millions in salaries from the funds funnelled out of Lincoln. ACC provided Keating with corporate aircraft to fly around the world, expense account meals at the world's finest restaurants, and exclusive company hideaways—all funded through Lincoln. Lincoln allowed Keating to make construction loans to ACC's luxury hotel and its real estate developments, provided investment funds for Ivan Boesky and Michael Milken (both later convicted of insider trading), and allowed Keating to gamble in currency trades.

Investigators described the operation as a giant Ponzi scheme. Money for deal making, much of it unsecured and unappraised, was going out the door as fast as it came in. To keep the money flowing to ACC, Lincoln began selling its depositors junk bonds issued by ACC. As depositors' federally insured savings instruments matured, rather than allow them to withdraw their funds, Lincoln's tellers encouraged depositors to talk with on-site salespersons who convinced them to buy junk bonds issued by ACC instead. Bank employees wore T-shirts declaring *Bond for Glory*, and they earned prizes, such as expensive running shoes, for referring depositors to the bond brokers.

Lincoln claimed the bonds were "backed by the resources and stability of a savings and loan that's made California home since 1926" (Binstein and Bowden, 1993, p. 67). In fact, they were based merely on the hope that ACC would prosper. Nearly 20,000 investors lost millions of dollars by converting their federally insured deposits into junk bonds.

To ward off regulators, Keating and ACC contributed heavily to state and federal political candidates. When asked if such contributions were to influence elected officials, Keating answered, "I want to say . . . I certainly hope so." The contributions appear to have succeeded in part, because five U.S. senators (dubbed the Keating Five) did intervene on Keating's behalf with federal banking officials.

In its heyday, ACC made many large charitable contributions. Homeless shelters were recipients, as were right-wing evangelical groups. Mother Teresa's order received more than $1 million as ACC headed toward bankruptcy. At Keating's sentencing, Mother Teresa wrote the judge pleading for leniency. One of the prosecutors answered Mother Teresa by asking the Nobel prizewinner to return the contribution to those who earned it. "Ask yourself," he wrote, "what Jesus would do if he were given the fruits of a crime?"

Keating's Ponzi scheme came to an end in 1989. ACC declared bankruptcy, and federal officials seized Lincoln S&L. Keating was subsequently charged in federal court with 73 counts of conspiracy, fraud, and racketeering and in state court with 17 counts of securities fraud. He was convicted in both trials and served four and one-half years in prison before his convictions were overturned on technicalities in early 1998.

Although his lawyers are muzzling Keating these days, he has always maintained his innocence. The investments were sound, in conformity with all regulations, prudent, and profitable, he claims. Keating says it was overzealous federal regulators who were at fault.

Perhaps Henry Gonzalez, the former chair of the House Banking Committee, best summed up the Keating case when he said, "Keating never made any secret of his plans. He left no doubt that he intended to . . . take on the high-risk ventures—everything from long-shot land developments to Ivan Boesky junk bond deals. Lincoln was the cash machine for Keating and American Continental Corporation" (Binstein and Bowden, 1993, p. 31).

John F. Kennedy (1917–1963)

John Fitzgerald Kennedy, the 35th president of the United States and the country's first Catholic head of state, was the son and grandson of Irish American politicians. Domestically, Kennedy's administration accomplished little. For consumers, however, the Kennedy administration crafted a bill of rights establishing, "a national standard of responsibility toward consumers," as one consumer advocate described it.

As a war hero and the oldest surviving son of a wealthy political family, Kennedy easily won his first election to political office. He entered Congress in 1947 with many other war veterans, including Richard Nixon, his 1960 presidential opponent. Kennedy never lost an election. In 1952, he defeated a popular Republican incumbent to become a U.S. senator, and in 1960 he became president, albeit winning with a margin of only 100,000 votes. Kennedy joked that his father didn't want to pay for a landslide.

During his presidential campaign, Kennedy actively sought the support of consumers by addressing their issues. He said, "The consumer is the only man in our economy without a high-powered lobbyist," and promised to appoint a consumer counsel to the president to represent consumers. This person would lobby for consumers before the executive branch and before the Congress. Kennedy argued that "consumer protections and education are of basic importance to the economic well-being of the country" (Morse, 1993, p. 174).

He began by appointing a consumer advisory council to work with his economic advisors. In the second year of his presidency, Kennedy's staff began drafting a package of consumer protection bills to send to the Congress. Rather than merely list the president's legislative goals, the staff created, and Kennedy approved, a Consumer Bill of Rights (see Chapter 4). In a 1962 message, Kennedy submitted his bill of rights to Congress together with his legislative package. The president not only captured "the spirit of the newborn (consumer) movement," he recognized and legitimized consumer rights (Maynes, 1988, p. 26). These rights were invoked in the 1960s and continue to be invoked today as basic standards for consumer protections.

Kennedy's Consumer Bill of Rights included the right to safety, the right to be informed, the right to choose, and the right to be heard. Other presidents and organizations added additional items to the list, including a right to redress of grievances and a right to consumer education. What is most interesting is that Kennedy's bill of rights was adopted by the International Organization of Consumers' Unions, becoming the basis for the worldwide consumer movement.

Except for the addition to the Food and Drug Act of a scientific standard of efficacy for new drug applications, Kennedy didn't live long enough to see his consumer protection proposals enacted. On 22 November 1963, he was assassinated. His vice-president and successor, Lyndon B. Johnson, enlarged and passed Kennedy's consumer agenda.

Kennedy's legacy to consumers is his vision for "protecting the consumer interest."

Ralph Nader (b. 1934)

For 30 years, Ralph Nader has symbolized consumer advocacy and the consumer movement to the American public. His legislative accomplishments are legion and include: the National Highway Safety Act, the Wholesome Meat Inspection Act, the Environmental Protection Act, the Consumer Product Safety Act, the Freedom of Information Act, campaign finance reforms, and many others. Over time, he founded a conglomerate of consumer organizations such as Public Citizen with its Litigation Group, Health Research Group, and Congress Watch. There is also the Center for the Study of Responsive Law, Public Interest Research Groups (PIRGs) around the country, the Corporate Accountability Research Group, National Insurance Consumer Organization, and the Center for Auto Safety. Rather than merely responding to tragedies, Nader became proactive, looking at "catastrophes in terms of their prevention," as one observer noted. He also brings the "color of his anger," a moral certitude, and the consummate ability to dramatize an issue, thereby focusing public attention on it.

Nader was born to immigrant, Lebanese American parents in Winstead, Connecticut. His father, a restaurateur, was a student of history and an avid newspaper reader who bequeathed to his son a sense of anger over injustices. His mother emphasized the range of human possibility, and both parents communicated a strong belief in education, an area in which Nader excelled. David Halberstam, a Pulitzer Prize–winning journalist, who grew up with Nader in Connecticut, describes him as "disputatious," even at an early age.

From Connecticut, the young Nader attended Princeton University and graduated with honors in 1955. He subsequently earned a law degree from Harvard, practiced law, served in the Army Reserves, and worked as a freelance writer for various magazines. He also managed to travel the world.

Folklore has it that the young attorney hitchhiked to Washington in the 1960s, checked into a YMCA, and began immediately working for consumer rights and participatory democracy. He has not owned a car since college, still lives in a rooming house, and works long hours for low pay. Nader is also a suspicious individual, distrustful of power, and a loner, zealously guarding against what he calls "an invasion of his self" (privacy).

Auto safety was on the top of Nader's Washington agenda. He worked as a consultant for the Department of Labor conducting research on the issue. In 1965, he penned the first of many books, *Unsafe at Any Speed*. It was a detailed attack on faulty car design and, in particular, an attack on General Motors's (GM's) sporty automobile, the Corvair. Nader alleged that GM had committed one of "the greatest acts of industrial irresponsibility in the present century," by marketing a car they knew was unsafe (McCarry, 1972, p. 9). His research convinced him that the Corvair's rear suspension system had a design flaw that created a tendency for the car to overturn or spin out of control. GM maintained the car was as safe as any comparable car on the market.

Even in his first book, as Nader's biographer, Charles McCarry, writes, the "unjaded quality of his anger" comes through (McCarry, 1972, p. 9). It took more than anger, however, to put a nameless, faceless expert, promoting a highly technical issue, on the evening news. The event that made Ralph Nader a household name was a General Motors investigation.

GM responded to Nader's book by hiring a private investigator and former FBI agent, Vincent Gillen, to turn up information on him. Gillen instructed his men to find out "what makes him tick" (Gillen, as quoted in McCarry, 1972, p. 12). They interviewed Nader's associates and friends. They asked about his work on auto safety, but they also inquired about Nader's sexual preferences and whether or not he was anti-Semitic.

At this time, the young consumer advocate was working as an unpaid Senate committee aide drafting an auto safety law. When GM's private investigators came to the Senate itself, Senator Abraham Ribicoff (D-Connecticut and chairman of the subcommittee for which Nader was then working), outraged, summoned the president of General Motors himself to explain the company's investigation. At that hearing, GM publicly apologized to Nader and the Senate.

In Ralph Nader, the media discovered a modern-day David in their midst who could stand up to a corporate Goliath. The

Senate subcommittee enhanced his image by publicly affirming Nader's virtue and incorruptibility. By its indiscreet actions, GM guaranteed the passage of the auto safety legislation Nader drafted. Later, the company settled an invasion of privacy suit, brought by Nader, for $425,000—money he used to create his consumer conglomerate.

This was the first of many Nader campaigns challenging what he calls the "seller-sovereign" corporate economy. According to Nader, corporations are destroying modern life. The nation's economy is one "where enormous skill, artifice, and resources are used in getting consumers to buy what sellers want, notwithstanding the availability of more efficient, safe, economical, durable, and effective alternatives" (Nader, as quoted in McCarry, 1972, p. 140). Any exploitation must by exposed.

Nader has not limited himself, however, to corporate reforms. He has also advocated for enhanced governmental accountability to counter the influence of corporate giants in the political process. Nader's Raiders, student volunteers working with Nader's different consumer organizations, studied Congress and published a widely read book entitled *Who Runs Congress*. Nader has also supported procedural reforms to make government more accountable and to put limitations on campaign contributions.

Another battle for which Nader is famous was the effort to reform the Federal Trade Commission (FTC). Nader's Raiders issued a report in early 1969 attacking an agency that had become, in their words, "sclerotic." The report was scathing, describing the agency as an "aged courtesan ravaged by the pox" (as quoted by McCarry, 1972, pp. 184–185). A year later, the American Bar Association studied the agency and made similar findings. Under its then-new chairman, Caspar Weinberger, the FTC was revitalized, establishing tougher advertising standards, issuing new trade rules, and pursuing enforcement. Many of these changes remain in place today.

In the heyday of the 1970s, more than 30,000 students, including one-third of the enrollment of Harvard Law School, applied for 200 openings to become a Nader's Raider. The hours were long, the pay was miserable, and the issues were dry and complex, but the reward was in making a difference.

Nader is not without his critics, both inside and outside the consumer movement. One senator, anonymously quoted by Nader's biographer, Charles McCarry, accuses the reformer of "being a fanatic, one who always has to have his own way" (McCarry, 1972, p. 161). McCarry himself believes Nader has the attributes of a "genius," as well as the "marks of a crank" (McCarry, 1972, p. 182).

Although Nader's appeal appears to have waned in the 1990s, it is not yet time to write him off. In 1988, he helped pass a major insurance initiative in California and defeated another in the same state in 1992. In 1996, he ran for president on the Green ticket.

Nader's legacy to the nation is broad and deep. Perhaps he will best be remembered for demonstrating that a citizen David, armed with integrity, information, a sense of outrage, and fortitude, can become an effective advocate.

Esther Peterson (1906–1997)

At 87, an age when most people have long since retired, Esther Peterson accepted President Bill Clinton's appointment as a delegate to the United Nations. Her acceptance was typical of Peterson's long life of commitment, both personally and professionally, to consumer protection, women's rights, and the trade union movement. It did not occur to her that she was too old to make a difference.

Peterson was an advisor to four presidents, serving as Special Assistant for Consumer Affairs to both Presidents Johnson and Carter, Assistant Secretary of Labor and Director of the Women's Bureau in the Kennedy administration, and Executive Vice-Chair of the President's Commission on the Status of Women, also during the Kennedy administration. This is in addition to careers as a union organizer, congressional lobbyist, and consumer activist and educator in both the national and international arena. Prior to being appointed a delegate to the United Nations, she was the International Organization of Consumers Unions' (IOCU) representative to that body. Among many honorary degrees and awards, the greatest tribute in her own eyes was the President's Medal of Freedom, presented by President Carter in 1981.

Born Esther Eggertsen in 1906 in Provo, Utah, she grew up in a sheltered community of strong religious faith and firm ideas about the appropriate work ethic. Peterson described herself as a "strict, conservative Mormon Republican and very antiunion" (Peterson, 1995, p. 18).

This conservative worldview was challenged when Esther moved to New York in 1930 to earn a master's degree in education at Columbia University. There she met her future husband,

Oliver Peterson, who introduced her to a different world, one in which workers were exploited, women and children struggled long hours in sweatshops for minimal wages, and the employers had all the power. Peterson's social consciousness was forever stirred. She made a commitment to working for change that lasted for the rest of her life.

While organizing for textile and education unions, Peterson was impressed by the fair labor standards concept promoted by the National Consumers League and became an active member. The League's emphasis on the consumer's purchasing power to pressure employers to provide fair wages and working conditions became a part of her own economic philosophy. She viewed the economy as really a "three-legged stool," composed of the employers, the workers, and the consumers (Peterson, 1995, p. 38).

Union work led to lobbying when Peterson was sent to Washington in 1944 by the Amalgamated Clothing Workers. Esther's union experience was formative and very positive, but she had not been exempt from chauvinist behavior from her male coworkers. In Washington, this took the form of assigning her to a new representative from Boston who was not expected to amount to much. His name was John Kennedy. As Peterson wrote in her memoir, *Restless*, "It was one of the best breaks I ever had." A decade later when Kennedy ran for president, he brought Peterson into his campaign because of her knowledge and contacts, both in unions and in her native Utah.

Peterson entered the Kennedy administration as director of the Women's Bureau in the Department of Labor where she worked on such issues as equal pay and working conditions for women. Later she was appointed assistant secretary for Labor Standards, a position that made her the highest-ranking woman in the administration. At her urging, Kennedy created a President's Commission on the Status of Women, to which she was appointed executive vice-chair under former First Lady Eleanor Roosevelt, a woman for whom Peterson had the greatest respect. The Commission's report addressed a wide range of economic, legal, and social issues confronting women at midcentury.

One issue facing women, the major purchasers in most families, was a marketplace that was not always consumer friendly. Kennedy had campaigned on the need for a high-powered lobbyist to protect the interest of consumers in Congress. In his 1962 consumer message to Congress, Kennedy announced his Consumer Bill of Rights, giving a new focus and importance to marketplace concerns. Peterson called this the "Magna Carta of the consumer movement worldwide" (Peterson, 1995, p. 119).

When Lyndon Johnson assumed the presidency after Kennedy's assassination, he adopted consumer issues into his program and appointed Peterson to a newly created position, special assistant to the president for consumer affairs. Peterson held regional conferences to hear the concerns of the public, developed an agenda, and set about creating a dialogue between consumers and business.

She found that consumers were faced with misleading advertising, credit industry abuses, marked-up prices in low-income areas, deceptive packaging that put less product in a larger box, and unit sizing that made it impossible to determine the amount intended to constitute a serving of the product, much less how much it would cost. Many of these issues were addressed by legislation under Johnson.

Other problems were handled by negotiation between the parties. Peterson had the wonderful ability to get opposing interests to sit down and talk about the problem. When consumers complained about garments destroyed in dry cleaning because no cleaning information was provided, Peterson brought the dry cleaners and the textile businesses together. The simple solution, something we have come to take for granted, was to have cleaning/laundry directions sewn into the garment.

Peterson's skill in finding workable answers to consumer problems led to a career change that caught Peterson by surprise, as it did her union and activists friends. Her position as special assistant to the president had not been a smooth ride as she was never as integrated into the Johnson White House as she had been under Kennedy. As she said, "I was never in LBJ's inner circle." When she left the Johnson administration, Esther found herself again in the role of special consumer advisor to the president, only this time, to the president of Giant Foods, a major East Coast grocery chain.

Peterson's pioneering role in the food business led to innovations in that industry that had a ripple effect throughout the retail market. She developed and extended Kennedy's concept of a consumer bill of rights as a pledge from Giant to the buyer, and then led the way in implementing such features as "sell-by" dates on perishable products, providing lists of product ingredients on the package, offering a company line of recycled paper products, and creating a system of understandable unit pricing. Because Peterson had learned that the best information came from the customer, she persuaded Giant to set up consumer advisory panels. The ideas generated by consumer complaints or suggestions were developed by the panels and passed on for implementation by Giant.

When President Jimmy Carter asked her to resume her White House role of special assistant for consumer affairs, Peterson accepted and immediately became involved in the legislative battle to create a consumer agency. This agency would consolidate 26 duplicative programs that existed in other federal entities, and would have the authority to directly steer policy matters affecting consumers. Although she was able to assist in the passage of several important consumer laws, the failure of the consumer agency bill was a major disappointment to her. The combination of powerful opposition and administration error defeated the effort.

Peterson, by now in her mid-seventies, accepted the IOCU's call to represent them in the United Nations where they were promoting a UN resolution to publish a list of products banned by any country. This information would provide a global warning of dangerous products so that a nation could make an informed decision regarding admitting that product. In spite of the Reagan administration's opposition, Peterson's efforts were successful.

Early in her career, Esther Peterson had adopted a personal acid test for action. "Do what is right, and let the consequences follow" (Peterson, 1995, p. iii). Applying that test led her into many areas where women had not gone before, and often, were not really welcome. She was a tough, persistent advocate for the issues in which she believed, and she made many enemies as well as devoted friends. She understood the political process, however, and often quoted her friend and mentor, Eleanor Roosevelt, on the necessity of compromise, but always to "compromise upward."

As Ralph Nader eulogized in *The Washington Post* (25 January 1995, p. A25), "In the pantheon of the 20th-century American leaders, Esther Peterson occupied a uniquely versatile place."

Charles Ponzi (1882–1949)

The investment fraud described by one judge as "paying the earlier comers out of the contributions of the later comers" seems to be permanently linked to the name of Charles Ponzi. It was not a new scheme when Ponzi practiced his version of what used to be called a *bubble*, in post–World War I Boston. In less than a year, however, Ponzi enticed thousands of investors to buy notes in amounts of $10, $100, or $1000 that, after 90 days, could be redeemed for the principal plus 50 percent interest. By most estimates, Charles Ponzi, a diminutive, twice-convicted felon, was a most unlikely candidate for perpetrating a $10 million fraud, but his tactics go far in explaining the ingenuity of a fraud artist.

Born in Parma, Italy, in 1882, Ponzi studied at the University of Rome. A life of petty crimes, gambling, and, in his words, spendthrift living brought his studies to an end. In 1903, with the aid of his family, he set out to earn his fortune in the New World, arriving almost penniless—having lost everything in card games on the ship over. For his first years in America, Ponzi wandered the East Coast, working as a waiter, bookkeeper, and at odd jobs. In 1908, he traveled to Montreal, where he became involved with a bank scheme to defraud Italian immigrants. Ponzi was convicted of forgery and served 20 months in a Canadian prison. Upon his release, he was caught smuggling illegal aliens into the United States, and served another term in prison.

Ponzi rubbed elbows with some of the most skilled fraud artists in the country while serving time in federal prison. They taught him how to work a scheme, and, as one writer put it, to "find the big idea" (Dunn, 1975, p. 31). He failed at a number of early attempts, but succeeded beyond his wildest expectations in 1919 and 1920.

The nation was in a bull market at the end of the war and citizens were looking forward to a return to normalcy. The troops were coming home, and consumers were buying again even though prices kept rising.

Ponzi's "big idea" arose out of a failed plan to sell advertising in a catalog for international trade. A Spanish trader wrote Ponzi for information, attaching what were called international postal coupons, to prepay the cost of return postage. That is, the Spaniard purchased a fixed-price coupon using Spanish pesetas to buy U.S. stamps. With the strength of the U.S. dollar in 1919, Ponzi reasoned, an investor could purchase far more U.S. postage by purchasing these international coupons in France, Germany, and other European countries. These could then be traded for a profit. Of course, Ponzi never intended to buy the coupons; it would take wheelbarrows full of these instruments to make the profits he promised. They would, however, become the hook of credibility that snared investors and confused law enforcement—three-fourths of the members of Boston's police force invested in Ponzi's scheme.

Starting in late 1919, Ponzi, who was actually broke, offered notes from his so-called Securities Exchange Company to fellow Italian immigrants, primarily factory workers and small shopkeepers. The scheme grew slowly until "Securities Exchange" mailed postcards, after only 45 days, instead of the stated 90 days, advising investors they could now redeem their notes for the principal plus 50 percent interest. Some investors did redeem their notes. Most, impressed by the rapid return, did not. They reinvested the principal and interest in Securities Exchange.

In July 1920, the press began to notice what some called a "financial wizard" (Bulgatz, 1992, p. 16). Press attention only served to expand the operation as investors began mailing a million dollars a week. The press attention also attracted the interest of law enforcement. Ponzi offered evidence on how money could be made trading in postal coupons but declined to answer specifics. When asked how he accomplished the trades, Ponzi answered, "I do not divulge trade secrets" (Dunn, 1975, p. 94).

A run on Securities Exchange began in late July when the company's viability was challenged by three events. The greatest threat came when the district attorney forced Ponzi to reject any further investments until an auditor could study his books. This agreement turned off the spigot, no longer permitting Ponzi to pay Peter with money from Paul. There were also press stories critical of Securities Exchange, and a declaration by the postmaster of New York that the world's supply of postal reply coupons was insufficient to accumulate the earnings touted by Ponzi. These events triggered the run, and police were eventually called to patrol the line of investors trying to get their money out. It seems odd that Ponzi didn't bolt, fleeing with his ill-gotten gains. That is normal behavior with Ponzi schemes. The Italian immigrant apparently trusted his own abilities to the end.

For two weeks Ponzi redeemed every note presented. Without any new investors, the inevitable happened when the first check bounced in early August. Securities Exchange was declared bankrupt in October, bringing down several banks with it, and Ponzi pled guilty to federal charges in November.

How could a convicted felon pull the wool over the eyes of thousands of investors? He was a skilled propagandist who manufactured his own credibility. Ponzi was a most likable individual. News reports from even a critical journal spoke of his "remarkable and winning charm," "smooth and confident tongue," and "bubbling vivacity" (Bulgatz, 1992, p. 25). Other reports indicate he always spoke with a smile in a "soft confident voice" (Dunn, 1975, p. 81).

From the beginning, Ponzi presented the image of a well-to-do businessman. He used a gold-headed walking stick, wore diamond stickpins with his double-breasted suits, and always sported a skimmer, the then-popular straw hat. Securities Exchange also hired well-regarded lawyers and publicists. Even with these trappings of power and respectability, Ponzi never lost the common touch. For example, when his investors lined up for hours to redeem their notes, he served them coffee and hot dogs.

Skilled in self-promotion, Ponzi spoke in the Populist idiom of an earlier era. He charged his enemies with protecting the evil banks, which earn the same kind of money as Ponzi's scheme but never shared their earnings with depositors. Ponzi attracted investors who came from all walks of life.

Inexplicably, he also acted in ways that were clearly contrary to his self-interest. Forced to accept an agreement not to take in more investors, he challenged note holders to come and get their money. This bold gesture enhanced public confidence in him for the many who believed the dream till the bitter end. It was also this gesture that helped bring him down when the funds ran out.

Ponzi served his time, convicted in both federal and state courts, but never repented. While out on bail, he tried to cash in on popular Florida real estate schemes, and was arrested there. He fled prosecution on a boat bound for Italy but was recaptured. Upon his release from prison in 1932, the Immigration Department deported him to Italy. Ponzi died in 1949 in a hospital charity ward in Brazil, where he had lived for almost ten years.

Too often our society looks on swindlers like Ponzi as romantic figures who fleece only those too dull-witted to know that if something sounds too good to be true, it probably is. For whatever reason, large numbers of Americans do not know how to recognize a fraud, particularly when it contains the trappings of respectability. The Ponzis of the world exploit this environment, through study and trial and error. He may not have had an M.B.A. from Harvard, but for a while, Charles Ponzi knew how to market in Boston with the best of them.

Franklin D. Roosevelt (1882–1945)

Many historians rank Franklin Delano Roosevelt with Washington and Lincoln as one of the nation's greatest presidents. He "mobilized democratic energies and faith first against economic collapse and then against military terror," according to the historian Arthur Schlesinger (1998). The Roosevelt administration also helped safeguard future generations of investors and consumers. Although he is not known as a consumer advocate, Roosevelt's presidency included important policy initiatives that significantly expanded consumer protection.

The thirty-second president of the United States, Roosevelt served longer than any other chief executive (1933–1945). Throughout his term of office, he led a nation in crisis, first as president during the Great Depression of the 1930s, and then as commander-in-chief, leading the Allies against the Axis powers during World War II. His presidency included an era of fervent economic and social experimentation as well as government expansion.

In 1933 when Roosevelt was inaugurated, he faced a nation fearful of its future. The Great Depression had begun with the stock market crash of October 1929. Black Friday, as it was called, set in motion a catastrophic national economic decline that cut manufacturing production by almost half and national income by more than half. Total investment was a negative $5 billion. Many businesses and all levels of individual investors were affected. In 1929, 1 million people held stock on margin; that is, they purchased their shares on credit. When the stock market crashed, their stock lost its value. Nonetheless, these shareholders still owed the money borrowed to purchase their shares. When Roosevelt first spoke to the nation as president, one out of four workers was out of work and on relief. In his inaugural address, Roosevelt tried to both calm the nation and prepare it for change. He promised that "the only thing we have to fear, is fear itself," and declared, "This nation asks for action, and action now."

During its first 100 days, the Roosevelt administration made many important policy recommendations. One of the first proposals, the Securities Act of 1933, significantly expanded investor protections. Black Friday, according to many observers, was precipitated by abusive practices on Wall Street itself. In its investigation, the Senate Commerce Committee found that investors were bilked through misrepresentations, insider trading, and stock manipulations. According to Roosevelt in his first inaugural address, the "practices of the unscrupulous money changers stand indicted in the court of public opinion." He proposed to transform the money changers by applying "social values more noble than mere monetary profit" (Roosevelt, 1933).

Felix Frankfurter, one of the members of Roosevelt's so-called brain trust (his advisors), and later a Supreme Court justice, argued that when a corporation seeks funds from the public by offering stocks or bonds, it in effect becomes a public body with a duty to provide full disclosure. The administration's reform proposal was based on this argument. Stock and bond offerings had to be registered with the federal government, and those offering the sale were required to file detailed information, including the names of officers and directors, principal shareholders, and a current profit-and-loss statement. Congress approved this legislation during the first 100 days of the Roosevelt administration.

One year later, Congress passed the Securities and Exchange Act of 1934, a second Roosevelt initiative to regulate the stock exchanges themselves. The act was intended to protect investors against insider manipulation and reduce speculation by increasing the margin requirements for buying stock. It also created the Securities and Exchange Commission to oversee the 1933 and 1934 acts. Roosevelt nominated Joseph Kennedy, a Wall Street investor and the father of the future president, as the Commission's first chairman.

A second consumer protection initiative, the Food, Drug and Cosmetics Act, took more time. The impetus for this reform, according to historian Arthur Schlesinger Jr., was the publication in 1933 of a popular muckraking book entitled *100,000 Guinea Pigs*, by Arthur Kallet and F. J. Schlink. It was an exposé of the perils of dangerous chemicals and potentially lethal impurities in products in the marketplace. The consumer, according to Kallet and Schlink, was a guinea pig for unsafe and untested foods, drugs, and cosmetics.

Shortly after his inauguration, Roosevelt instructed his brain trust to draft reforms to the 1906 legislation. The administration's bill added cosmetics, which many women had begun to use in the socially more liberal "flapper" era of the 1920s. It also established a standard for the scientific premarket testing of drugs. All new drugs had to be proved safe for human use before their introduction onto the market. Finally, the bill created a new regulatory agency, the Food and Drug Administration (FDA), to administer the act, and it prohibited false and misleading labeling.

This measure generated a storm of controversy, with vigorous industry opposition, and Congress delayed passage until 1938. Even then, approval came only in the wake of tragic consumer injury. An untested patent medicine, elixir of sulfanilamide, contained a deadly solvent. The 107 deaths, mostly of children, that were caused by use of the product provided the impetus for passage of the law.

While the FDA would now oversee labeling, deceptive advertising issues fell within the jurisdiction of the Federal Trade Commission (FTC) under an amendment to that agency's 1914 enabling legislation, the third significant expansion of federal consumer protections during the Roosevelt years. This amendment was the Wheeler-Lea Act, which expanded the FTC's authority to regulate "unfair or deceptive acts or practices" along with "unfair methods of competition." This reform overturned a U.S. Supreme Court decision limiting the agency to antitrust enforcement. With this bill, the federal government now had clear authority to protect consumers against false advertising and deceptive sales practices.

A long-term dream for consumerists has been the creation of a federal consumer protection agency, bringing together all antifraud efforts under one roof. In the 1930s, advocates urged Roosevelt to create what they called the Department of the Consumer. Although this proposal went nowhere, the Roosevelt administration did agree to bring consumers to the table with business and labor.

The National Industrial Recovery Act established business, labor, and consumer advisory committees. These committees were to help draft and promote what the National Recovery Administration (NRA) called codes of fair competition. Such codes were to eliminate cutthroat competition, stabilize employment and production, and establish minimum standards for wages and hours. At the same time, the NRA permitted price fixing and suspended the provisions of the Sherman Antitrust Act. Although the NRA was ruled unconstitutional by the Supreme Court in 1935, it produced many positive outcomes, such as the elimination of sweatshops and child labor and the right to collective bargaining (union-management negotiations).

It was the NRA's consumer advisory committee that first challenged price setting and identified the need for quality assurances. Although these issues became moot with the action of the Supreme Court, it was nevertheless significant that the voice of the consumer was heard at the table for the first time.

Theodore Roosevelt (1858–1919)

Theodore Roosevelt's legacy includes the nation's first food safety laws and the modern concept of regulating corporate activity. He expanded the power of the presidency and the federal government in the interest of the public welfare.

The nation's twenty-sixth president, Roosevelt was a soldier, scholar, author, fervent nationalist, moralist, Nobel Peace Prize winner, and what would today be called an environmentalist. He was also a reformer, a progressive who enlarged the power of the federal government because, "[it] alone can deal adequately with the great corporations" (Brands, 1997, p. 543).

Born to a life of privilege, Roosevelt seemed an unlikely candidate to become a reform president. He grew up in an elite New York City neighborhood, summering at a Long Island estate. TR, as he was called, benefited from studies in Europe, private tutors, and the best schools, graduating from Harvard in 1880.

Roosevelt attended Columbia Law School but never graduated, as politics proved to be more exciting than his studies. While studying law, however, Roosevelt began to question existing government policies toward business. At that time he wrote in his journal, "The *caveat emptor* side of the law, like the *caveat emptor* side of business, seemed to me repellent" (Brands, 1997, p. 114).

Serving in different positions, Roosevelt spent more than 30 years in government. In 1881, he was elected to the New York state assembly. There, political power was in the hands of the Republican and Democratic machines, which were often allied with business trusts. This was the era of the infamous Tammany Hall, run by Democrat Boss Tweed in New York City, but the statewide Republican machine was equally powerful and closed to anyone outside the organization. Roosevelt began his career as he would end it, a reformer challenging the power of the antidemocratic order.

President Benjamin Harrison appointed Roosevelt to the federal civil service commission in 1889. Eliminating political patronage was a hot topic for a reformer like Roosevelt in the late 1880s. Later, he helped clean up New York City's "finest" as a police commissioner. Roosevelt's military triumphs as leader of the Rough Riders in the Spanish-American War led directly to the governor's mansion in New York. After a two-year term there, Republican Party leaders took steps to kick the reformer upstairs by nominating him to the vice-presidency. Historically, this position has been an obscure and powerless post, and Republican leaders hoped Roosevelt would quietly fade into obscurity. They never dreamed that President McKinley would be assassinated, elevating Roosevelt to the presidency.

Roosevelt's political success was never based on party power. Experience had taught him that he could build political power through mass publicity, a tool used by many reformers since that time. In his autobiography Roosevelt wrote, "neither the parties nor the public had any realization that publicity was necessary" to dramatize an issue (Morris, 1979, p. 693). If Roosevelt's name also appeared in the resulting publicity, then so much the better.

Muckraking, or the school of journalism focusing on exposing the ills of society, has a long tradition in American policymaking. It began at the turn of the century and rose to prominence during the Roosevelt presidency (1901–1908). After Roosevelt, the early muckrakers faded from public view. Roosevelt was both a critic and a benefactor of these writers. Roosevelt coined the term in a speech criticizing those who never did anything "save of his feats with the muck rake" (quoted in Weinberg, 1964, p. xvii).

Nonetheless, he skillfully took advantage of Upton Sinclair's revelations of putrid and unwholesome meat products in his blockbuster novel, *The Jungle*, to push the Pure Food and Drug Act and the Meat Inspection Act of 1906 through Congress. These acts formed the basis for consumer protection at the federal level.

Roosevelt is also remembered as a "trust buster" whose Justice Department filed more than 40 cases asserting violations of the Sherman Antitrust Act. It was not trusts or bigness, however, that Roosevelt sought to eliminate. Rather, he said, "We were not attacking corporations, but endeavoring to provide for doing away with any evil in them" (Brands, 1997, p. 492). Roosevelt's vision was not the Jeffersonian world of small farmers and yeomen. The Industrial Revolution had changed all that, and according to Roosevelt, the captains of industry had "on the whole, done a great good to our people." Roosevelt's goal was to rid the business world of what he called "crimes of cunning." Corporations "extorting high prices for the commodity it had made artificially scarce" were to be pursued and "suppressed by all the power of government" (Brands, 1997, p. 438), he promised.

To accomplish this goal, Roosevelt instituted a three-step plan. First, the federal government would utilize the power of disclosure against the trusts. Roosevelt created a Bureau of Corporations in the Commerce and Labor Department to collect information and disclose which corporations were doing business in the various states. The Bureau would also determined which were "good" and which were "evil" trusts.

Second, the Justice Department would begin filing antitrust suits. The first such case, involving the Northern Securities Company, called for the breakup of a railroad trust. This trust involved such captains of industry as the financier J. P. Morgan and James J. Hill. The Supreme Court subsequently upheld the Roosevelt administration's position (*Northern Securities Co. v. United States*, 171 U.S. 600 (1904)).

Third, Roosevelt would seek to regulate corporations. In 1906, at his urging, Congress approved new powers for the Interstate Commerce Commission to regulate railroad rates.

Once out of office, Roosevelt continued his campaign to enact even stronger legislation regulating corporations. As Republicans were preparing to renominate his successor, William Howard Taft, Roosevelt proposed the party adopt what he called "The New Nationalism." He argued that corporations conducting interstate commerce should be incorporated at the federal level, an idea Ralph Nader was to propose some 50 years later. In addition, corporate directors should be held liable for any company wrongdoing, and business would be prohibited from contributing to federal political campaigns. In 1912, Roosevelt parted ways with Taft and the Republican Party when they cast aside his New Nationalism. Rejected by the Republicans, Roosevelt ran for president as a candidate of the Progressive, or "Bull Moose," Party (Roosevelt had declared himself fit as a bull moose). He beat Taft in the polls, but the three-way race ensured the election of the Democrat Woodrow Wilson. In 1916, Roosevelt returned to the Republican fold, dreaming of one more run for the presidency, which was never to be. He died in 1919.

Upton Sinclair (1878–1968)

Upton Sinclair was a writer and social reformer who wrote 80 books, including 42 novels and 11 plays, during his long life. He was also a movie producer, reporter, critic, political agitator, and candidate. While still in his twenties, Sinclair penned the novel for which he is best known, *The Jungle*. The book captured the nation's attention with its graphic descriptions of meatpacking in Chicago's stockyards.

Born in 1878 to aristocratic but impoverished parents, Sinclair was a sickly but precocious child who spent hours reading the classics. His father, a wholesale whiskey salesman and failed businessman, frequently imbibed his own wares. It was the young Uppie, as friends called him, who often searched the bars and alleys to bring his father home. Perhaps these experiences, together with his mother's strong religious beliefs, explain the strong Puritan strain evident in Sinclair's writings and personality. Even though he was convinced of the rightness of his positions, Sinclair was not a self-righteous person. Contemporaries described him as an earnest but gentle man who talked, according to silent film star Charlie Chaplin, as though "he were speaking through a smile" (Mitchell, 1992, p. 15).

In 1888, the family moved to New York, a city teeming with immigrants struggling to achieve the American Dream. New York was also home to many of the nation's 4,000 millionaires, and nowhere was the contrast between rich and poor more evident. A single block in a nineteenth-century tenement harbored 700 families, whereas two miles of fashionable Fifth Avenue housed only 400 wealthy families. The young boy became acutely aware of the many poor and the few rich.

Sinclair graduated from City College of New York in 1897 and attended Columbia University, but he gave up his formal education to become a writer. Paid by the word, he started as a hack writer for cheap magazines that were spawned by the new mechanized printing technology of the time. Always a prolific writer, Sinclair generated thousands of words to support his family.

Tiring of hack work, Sinclair turned to more serious writing. His first novels were commercial and artistic failures, but it was during this time that he became a democratic socialist. Sinclair believed that capitalism was ending. Many of his novels, like *King Coal*, *Oil*, and *Boston*, are grounded in socialist themes. In many of Sinclair's novels "the idea and the symbol [come] first and the character last," according to a review in the *New York Times* (Mitchell, 1992, p. 576).

Sinclair is best remembered, however, not for his ideology, but as the muckraking author who exposed the grisly details of meat production. He was part of a group of writers whose publications captured the ills of society. Other reformers included Ida Mae Tarbell, who chronicled the growth of the Standard Oil monopoly, and Lincoln Steffans, who exposed municipal corruption.

In 1904, *Appeal to Reason*, a socialist magazine, hired Sinclair to write about working conditions in Packingtown, Chicago. Sinclair spent almost two months there conducting interviews and observing conditions. His publisher hoped for a story that would become like *Uncle Tom's Cabin*.

Sinclair dedicated his work to "the working men of America," and with meticulous care he chronicled the arrival of a fictional Lithuanian immigrant family in Chicago. The family is exploited, preyed upon, robbed, and eventually crushed by the harsh conditions, but the husband and family leader, Jurgis Rudkus, doesn't die. He is reborn as a socialist, dreaming of the time when "Chicago will be ours."

First serialized in the weekly newspaper *Appeal to Reason*, Sinclair's work was published as a novel in 1906. It was a national sensation, but not in the way the author had hoped. The public focused on the gruesome details of meat production, the casual processing of rodents, refuse, and even workers into meat products.

After reading the book, President Theodore Roosevelt was outraged. Even though Sinclair was a socialist, which Roosevelt disdained, the president called for a federal investigation by his secretary of agriculture, James Wilson. This investigation corroborated Sinclair's findings, and *The Jungle*, with Roosevelt's support, prodded Congress into approving both a meat inspection bill and the Pure Food and Drug Act of 1906. The latter had languished in Congress for some time.

Sinclair, however, judged his work a failure. He wrote, "I wished to frighten the county by a picture of what its industrial masters were doing to their victims; entirely by chance, I stumbled on another discovery—what they were doing to the meat supply of the civilized world. In other words, I aimed at the public's heart, and by accident I hit it in the stomach" (Sinclair, 1981, p. vi).

After *The Jungle*, Sinclair faded from the public eye until 1934. In the interim, he continued to write and edit, joined several utopian communities, moved to California, ran for Congress on the Socialist ticket, became a vegetarian, dabbled in telepathy, was arrested for playing tennis on Sunday, picketed John D. Rockefeller's office, and helped found the southern California branch of the American Civil Liberties Union.

In 1934, Upton Sinclair switched parties to become a Democrat and ran for governor of California. His campaign to End Poverty in California (EPIC) and surprise primary victory, defeating a much better known Democrat, startled the state, the Hollywood movie community, and the White House. The *Los Angles Times* labeled him a "Red" and warned of Sinclair's "maggot-like horde" (Mitchell, 1992, p. 32). Even President Franklin Roosevelt kept his distance from the EPIC campaign.

The movie industry, with some notable exceptions such as Charlie Chaplin, mobilized against Sinclair. MGM's director of production, Irving Thalberg, helped generate movie shorts attacking Sinclair. These shorts were the precursors to today's political attack ads.

Sinclair lost the general election but continued to write books and maintain correspondence with British and American writers and thinkers. In 1943, he won the Pulitzer Prize in literature for his *Lanny Budd* series. Budd was an international art dealer and envoy for Roosevelt who traveled the world. With this series, editorialized the *New York Times*, the "artist in Sinclair gets the better of the old crusader" (Mitchell, 1992, p. 576).

Sinclair lived a long life, mostly in California. President Lyndon Johnson honored Sinclair by inviting him to the White House for the signing of the Wholesome Meat Inspection Act of 1967. This bill strengthened the original legislation prompted by Sinclair's novel. At the White House, Sinclair met a young consumer advocate by the name of Ralph Nader.

Upton Sinclair was never to experience his vision of America. Whether he intended it or not, his legacy was the nation's first food safety laws. One of Sinclair's biographers, Leon Harris, described Uppie as "something of a crank—one of the grand American Cranks who enriched our lives" (Mitchell, 1992, p. xvi).

Colston E. Warne (1900–1987)

Savvy shoppers today routinely check the product ratings in *Consumer Reports* magazine before making a purchase. This highly respected and familiar consumers' tool is available largely as a result of the efforts of Colston Warne. If that had been his only contribution to consumer education it would have been a significant legacy. Fortunately, it is only his most familiar gift.

Colston Estey Warne was born in central New York state in 1900. His undergraduate education was at Cornell University, where he was introduced to the writings of the innovative economist, Thorstein Veblen. In 1925, he completed his doctoral work at the University of Chicago and came under the influence of Paul H. Douglas, noted labor economist, and a future U.S. senator who authored many consumer protection bills. Warne made an early decision to teach in his chosen field of economics. After brief tenures elsewhere, he became professor of economics at Amherst College, where he remained for 40 years. He was never, however, just an academic.

In her 1980 tribute to her father, Dr. Barbara Warne Newell, president of Wellesley College, said, "Basically, the question that Father was asking in the 1920s and 30s was what institutional changes should a society initiate to maximize human welfare" (Newell, 1980, p. 3). In his long and fruitful career, Warne was a prime factor in initiating many such institutional changes and in cultivating others.

Warne was an advocate of the trade union movement in this country and saw it as one of the necessary elements in the redistribution of wealth. Warne was also an active member of the American Civil Liberties Union and chaired their Pittsburgh branch while teaching at the University of Pittsburgh. There, he clashed with the school's administration over issues of academic freedom and left to settle at Amherst. He was also active in advocating for nuclear disarmament and environmental issues.

The institutions on which Warne focused his greatest attention, however, were those that directly affected the consumer's welfare. The most familiar to the general public is Consumers Union, publisher of *Consumer Reports*. Warne was president and guiding force of Consumers Union for 45 years, from the organization's troubled beginning until his retirement in 1980.

Fraud and manipulation in the marketplace was rife in the 1920s. *Your Money's Worth*, a 1927 book by Frederick J. Schlink and Stuart Chase, explained to consumers how they were being cheated and by whom. This guide, based on actual product testing, exposed inferior quality, deception, and swindles in medicines, food products, cosmetics, household appliances, and automobiles. It was a best-seller. The public was clearly interested and the authors were inspired to expand their work into a totally new enterprise, a non-profit organization for product testing, which they named Consumers' Research. Unfortunately, after only a few years, a bitter labor dispute led to the departure from the organization of many staff members who wanted a collective bargaining agreement.

When the disaffected staff formed their own product testing organization, they recruited Colston Warne to lead it, and Consumers Union was born. Over the next four decades, the concept of product testing and reporting was expanded to include political action and consumer protection. Warne shaped the organization into a major resource for consumers and a powerful force to ensure product accountability from businesses.

It took every bit of Warne's imagination and persuasion to nurse the organization through its early stages. He and his colleagues had counted on the financial support of the labor movement to back the production of *Consumer Reports*, but unions were having their own problems. Warne turned to professionals, the engineers, technicians, scientists, health professionals, and, in particular, teachers and school librarians who saw the potential and the need for consumer education.

Surviving the early years was not easy. The testing program, which relied heavily on automobiles and household appliances, suffered a body blow when the onset of World War II halted production of these products. Consumers Union was able to adapt by changing its focus to product repairs, medical issues, and monitoring rationing and the price control effort. After the war, the organization fell victim to McCarthyism and the "red scare," when it appeared on one of the House Un-American Activities Committee lists. Most people did not connect the magazine, *Consumer Reports*, with Consumers Union, the organization, so sales were only partly affected. Warne was able to get Consumers Union off the list, perhaps the only organization to receive a clean bill of health from that infamous committee.

The 1950s brought prosperity and a solid financial base from which Consumers Union could expand its efforts, particularly in the area of consumer education. In addition to *Consumer Reports*, which has subscriptions of over 5 million, it now provides a variety of industry specific publications, the children's magazine, *Zillions*, and consumer education products designed for classroom use, as well as books such as Rachel Carson's environmental warning, *Silent Spring*, which was distributed in paperback by Consumers Union (Newell, 1980, p. 6).

Warne also saw the need for grassroots consumer activities and was a major force in organizing state and local groups. He advised state governments in developing consumer agencies, and was the inspiration for the American Council on Consumer Interests, an organization of consumer educators that publishes the *Journal of Consumer Affairs*. He served on countless boards and advisory committees, including two terms on the Consumer Advisory Council to the President.

The question of what institutional changes a society should initiate to maximize human welfare naturally lead Warne to assert a leadership role in the international consumer protection arena. In 1960, he helped to established the International Organization of Consumer Unions (IOCU), which has over 200 organization members from all over the world and works for social and economic justice.

Harvey Washington Wiley (1844–1930)

Few people today recognize his name, but in the first decades of the twentieth century, Harvey Washington Wiley was almost a household word as a result of his well-publicized efforts to secure a federal food and drug law to protect the American consumer. From his position as chief of the Bureau of Chemistry, a branch of the Department of Agriculture, Wiley lobbied Congress, lectured to both scientific and lay audiences, wrote articles for scholarly and popular journals, and gathered support for his consumer initiatives everywhere he could. His name became inseparable from the long and often bitter campaign, and, in the end, his success was turned upside down by the enemies he made along the way.

Born in a log cabin in Indiana, Wiley was educated at home and in makeshift schoolhouses typical of farm communities in mid-nineteenth-century America. His studies at Hanover College were briefly interrupted by a stint as a Union soldier during the Civil War. After Hanover, he completed a medical degree in Indianapolis, and a bachelor of science degree in chemistry at Harvard. He then became professor of chemistry, first at Butler University and the Medical College of Indiana, and later when he joined the faculty at the opening of Purdue University.

As a young man on his father's farm, Wiley had experimented with growing sorghum as a sugar crop. His interest in the chemical and agricultural aspects of sugar products, combined with a year of study in food adulteration analysis in Germany, sealed his career focus. He was introduced to new scientific technology at the Imperial German Health Office and used this background in his studies of sugar and syrup adulteration commissioned by the state of Indiana. Based on his extensive experimentation and publications, Wiley became a recognized expert in all types of agricultural products connected with sugar production.

This expertise resulted in his being offered the position of chief of the Bureau of Chemistry in 1883. Wiley accepted the appointment and began a 29-year administration that reinvented the Bureau, from a six-man operation in the basement of the Agriculture Building to a highly efficient organization of over 500 employees operating in branches all over the country. He developed numerous lines of practical chemical research, using innovative apparatus and procedures, which earned him and his department an international reputation.

Wiley's earliest allies in his effort to secure legislation for pure food and drugs were food manufacturers who felt threatened by new products made possible by advances in science. Dairy interests wanted laws to squeeze out the emerging oleomargarine industry. Sugar producers feared cheap glucose, a vegetable starch sweetener that could be disguised as "pure table syrup" by adding flavor and coloring or used as an inexpensive filler in "genuine" products.

Other food products were being pumped full of cheap

fillers, substances that were often not even food based (plaster of paris in bread flour), or altered with dyes to improve their appearance. The ultimate, and not uncommon fraud, was products fabricated to look like what the consumer wished to buy, such as "coffee beans" that were actually roasted peas flavored with chickory and rye (Bettman, 1974, p. 118). Altered and adulterated foods were inexpensive to produce and posed a real threat to legitimate businesses. Finally, various preservatives were being added to foods packaged for mass-market distribution. There was concern that these preservatives were a potential danger to the public and were used in place of more sanitary methods of protecting the food from developing toxins.

Many, both in and outside the food industry, believed that only federal legislation could adequately address the broad scope of the problem. In the vacuum, states and local jurisdictions passed regulations that were often overly burdensome and in conflict with each other. They became a minefield for responsible producers who wished to operate within the law.

Endangered businesses sought to inject a health issue into the debate, but Wiley, like many reformers in the Progressive Era, originally saw the issue in terms of morality. It was simply dishonest to sell adulterated or mislabeled foods. The moral fiber of the nation was endangered when people were permitted to defraud their customers. Wiley believed that a federal law that required producers to provide the consumer with accurate information regarding the contents of their products was the answer. It would also provide relief to the manufacturers from the growing complex of state and local regulations. In time, however, his own research converted Wiley to a "pure food" stance. For many in food production, Wiley became an obstacle because many food producers believed that if he was in charge of enforcement of any future law, he would be too rigid for their best interests.

Wiley was politically astute and realized that compromise would be a necessary component of any strategy. He made himself the prime resource for legislators interested in the law, providing scientific data, testimony, and even advice on strategy. He also knew that public awareness was a critical factor and began to develop a coalition of interest groups across the full spectrum of society. His lectures and publications helped professional groups such as the American Medical Association and the various scientific communities to connect their own interests with a federal law.

Wiley also tapped into a budding new resource for social change, the network of women's organizations. He found that many such groups were no longer content with literary and gardening projects and wanted to affect the world in which they raised their children. Women activists from the Women's Christian Temperance Union, the National Consumers League, and the General Federation of Women's Clubs were enlisted in the battle. He urged them to publish, to become speakers, and to use their contacts to lobby for change. One particularly effective tool of women's groups was to run critical telegram campaigns when a bill was before Congress.

A prime force in all reforms of this era was the growing print industry. So-called muckrakers reported deceptions and adulterations involving food and drugs, often in lurid exposés printed in newspapers and magazines.

Less sensational, but also very effective, were articles published in popular magazines such as *Good Housekeeping*, *The Nation*, and the *Ladies' Home Journal*. The public was becoming educated to food and drug issues, and support for reform grew markedly in the early years of the twentieth century.

One of the most successful of all news stories was the coverage of Wiley's Poison Squad. This was a group of young men who volunteered to ingest, under carefully controlled scientific guidelines, increasingly greater quantities of suspect food preservatives. The results of these studies were so startling to Wiley that he was converted from his former opinion that chemical preservatives were innocuous. It was a cub reporter, George Rothwell Brown, who chose the label Poison Squad, and he worked the study for all the humor and drama he could muster. It was highly compelling reading; however, the public was to receive one more startling jolt before a bitterly contested food and drug bill was passed.

Scholars debate whether, without the public pressure arising from publication of *The Jungle*, Theodore Roosevelt would have been drawn into the battle for pure food and drug legislation. Wiley, the effort's chief proponent and the man the public associated with the issue, was not a favorite of the president. Both were robust, self-confidant, highly energetic men of great intelligence and ability, and both were well-known, popular figures. Like their peers, they shared the Progressive Era attitude that these issues were basically questions of morality. It is perhaps surprising that they did not get along, but Wiley had drawn Roosevelt's hostility early in the president's administration by public, albeit unwilling, testimony in opposition to Roosevelt's proposed reduction of Cuban sugar import duties. Subsequent disagreements further estranged the two.

Portions of the food industry had been extremely resistant to the Pure Food and Drug Act because they feared enforcement by Wiley would mean strict interpretation and rigorous implementation. When, shortly after the passage of the act, Wiley published the balance of the Poison Squad studies, these interests reacted strongly to the results that were critical of chemical food preservatives. Roosevelt adopted their view, and used the publication of the studies as an excuse to appoint a Board of Consulting Experts to review the results. This board reversed Wiley's findings, and so began a rapid process of easing Wiley, the architect and proponent of the act, out of any enforcement role. He resigned from the Bureau in 1912, but continued a very public and effective campaign for food and drug purity until his death in 1930.

References

Anderson, Oscar E. 1958. *The Health of a Nation: Harvey W. Wiley and the Fight for Pure Food*. Chicago: University of Chicago Press.

Barton, Babette B. 1976. "Private Redress for Consumers: Redress or Rape." In Robert N. Katz, editor, *Protecting the Consumer Interest: Private Initiative and Response.* Cambridge, MA: Ballinger Publishing.

Bettmann, Otto L. 1974. *The Good Old Days—They Were Terrible.* New York: Random House.

Binstein, Michael, and Charles Bowden. 1993. *Trust Me: Charles Keating and the Missing Billions*. New York: Random House.

Brands, H. W. 1997. *TR: The Last Romantic.* New York: Basic Books.

Brobeck, Stephen, editor. 1997. *Encyclopedia of the Consumer Movement.* Santa Barbara, CA: ABC-CLIO.

Bulgatz, Joseph. 1992. *Ponzi Schemes, Invaders from Mars and More Extraordinary Popular Delusions and the Madness of Crowds.* New York: Harmony Books.

Campbell, Ronald. 1998. "Fame Complicates Keating Case." *Orange County Register* (10 June).

Charles K. Ponzi Website. 1998. http://www.usinternet.com/users/mcknutson.

Dell, Floyd. 1970. *Upton Sinclair: A Study in Social Protest.* New York: AMS Press.

Dunn, Donald H. 1975. *Ponzi: The Boston Swindler*. New York: McGraw-Hill.

Filler, Louis. 1968. *The Muckrakers: Crusaders for American Liberalism.* Chicago: Regnery Company.

Freidel, Frank. 1990. *Franklin D. Roosevelt: A Rendezvous with Destiny.* Boston: Little, Brown.

Gordon, Leland J. 1970. "Colston Estey Warne: Mr. Consumer. *Journal of Consumer Affairs.* Vol. 4. Columbia, MO: American Council on Consumer Interests.

Mayer, Robert N. 1989. *The Consumer Movement: Guardians of the Marketplace.* Boston: Twayne Publishing.

McCarry, Charles. 1972. *Citizen Nader.* New York: Saturday Review Press.

Maynes, E. Scott, and ACCI Research Committee, editors. 1988. *The Frontier of Research in the Consumer Interest.* Columbia, MO: American Council on Consumer Interests.

Mitchell, Greg. 1992. *The Campaign of the Century: Upton Sinclair's Race for Governor of California and the Birth of Media Politics.* New York: Random House.

Mookerjee, R. N. 1988. *Art for Justice: The Major Novels of Upton Sinclair.* Metuchen, NJ: Scarecrow Press.

Morris, Edmund. 1979. *The Rise of Theodore Roosevelt.* New York: Ballantine Books.

Morse, Richard L. D., editor. 1993. *The Consumer Movement: Lectures by Colston E. Warne.* Manhattan, KS: Family Economics Trust Press.

Nader, Ralph. 1965. *Unsafe at Any Speed.* New York: Grossman.

————. "A Lobbyist with a Heart." Washington, DC: *The Washington Post* (25 January 1995).

Newell, Barbara. 1980. "Tribute to Colston E. Warne." *Journal of Consumer Affairs.* Vol. 14, no. 1. Columbia, MO: American Council on Consumer Interests.

Okun, Mitchell. 1986. *Fair Play in the Marketplace: The First Battle for Pure Food and Drugs.* Dekalb, IL: Northern Illinois University Press.

Peterson, Esther. 1989. "The Legacy of Colston Warne." *Journal of Consumer Affairs.* Vol. 23, no. 2. Columbia, MO: American Council on Consumer Interests.

Peterson, Esther, with Winifred Conklin. 1995. *Restless: Memoirs of Labor and Consumer Activist Esther Peterson.* Washington, DC: Caring Publishing.

Roosevelt, Franklin. 1933. "First Inaugural Address." Reprinted in *The Public Papers and Addresses of Franklin D. Roosevelt.* 1938, Vol. 2 (1933). New York: Random House.

Schlesinger, Arthur M., Jr. 1957. *The Crisis of the Old Order, 1919–1933.* New York: Houghton Mifflin.

———. 1988. *The Coming of the New Deal.* Boston: Houghton Mifflin.

———. 1998. "Franklin Delano Roosevelt." *Time* 151, no. 14. (13 April).

Sinclair, Upton. 1981. *The Jungle.* New York: Bantam Books.

Smith, J. Y. 1997. "Consumer Advocate Esther Peterson Dies." Washington, DC: *The Washington Post.*

Sorensen, Theodore C. 1965. *Kennedy.* New York: Harper & Row.

Weinberg, Arthur, and Lila Weinberg, editors. 1964. *The Muckrakers.* New York: Capricorn Books.

Wiley, Harvey Washington. 1930. *An Autobiography.* Indianapolis: Bobbs-Merrill.

Documents, Laws, and Regulations

4

"[I]f the seller be aware of a fault in the thing he is selling, he is guilty of a fraudulent sale, so that the sale is rendered unlawful. . . . Another defect is in respect of quantity which is known by being measured: wherefore if anyone knowingly make use of a faulty measure in selling, he is guilty of fraud and the sale is illicit. . . . [B]ut if any of the foregoing defects be in the thing sold, and he knows nothing about this, the seller does not sin, because he does that which is unjust materially, nor is his deed unjust. . . . Nevertheless he is bound to compensate the buyer, when the defect comes to his knowledge."

—Thomas Aquinas

The Mail Fraud statute of 1872 was the first federal contribution to what has become an extensive body of consumer protection laws in the United States. The Congress and state legislatures drafted these laws to protect consumers from unsafe, fraudulent, and abusive practices in the marketplace.

This chapter reviews selected portions of some of the most important of these laws and regulations together with other relevant documents. It is divided into four parts:

- Part one—background materials together with President Kennedy's statement of consumer rights

- Part two—selected portions of four federal laws protecting consumers' right to safety
- Part three—selected portions of federal and state statutes, together with interpretative policy statements, protecting the consumers' right to be informed, and
- Part four—selected portions of federal laws, together with an interpretative policy statement protecting the consumers' right to choose.

Consumer Fraud and Consumer Rights

The Constitution of the United States

The U.S. Constitution gives Congress the power to establish weights and measures. The intent here was to facilitate trade and commerce, but fairness in the marketplace founders without a standard weight by which to measure products.

Constitution of the United States (Article 1, Section 8)

"The Congress shall have power. . . . To coin money, regulate the value thereof, and of foreign coin, and fix the Standard of weights and measures";

President Kennedy's 1962 Consumer Message to Congress

President Kennedy's 1962 consumer message to Congress captured the spirit of the consumer movement in the 1960s. The message contained two elements: First, it established the consumer legislative agenda for the 1960s and 1970s. Second, and more importantly, Kennedy formulated a Consumer Bill of Rights. The president also insisted that "The Federal Government has a special obligation . . . to advance the consumers' interest," a premise that is not as popular in the 1990s. Below are extracts from Kennedy's message.

Special Message to the Congress on Protecting the Consumer Interest (15 March 1962)

To the Congress of the United States:

Consumers, by definition, include us all. They are the largest economic group in the economy, affecting and affected by almost every public and private economic decision. Two-thirds of all spending in the economy is by consumers. But they are the only important group in the economy who are not effectively organized, whose views are often not heard.

The Federal Government—by nature the highest spokesman for all the people—has a special obligation to be alert to the consumer's needs and to advance the consumer's interests. Ever since legislation was enacted in 1872 to protect the consumer from frauds involving use of the U.S. mail, the Congress and Executive Branch have been increasingly aware of their responsibility to make certain that our Nation's economy fairly and adequately serves consumers' interests. . . .

Fortunate as we are, we nevertheless cannot afford waste in consumption any more than we can afford inefficiency in business or Government. If consumers are offered inferior products, if prices are exorbitant, if drugs are unsafe or worthless, if the consumer is unable to choose on an informed basis, then his dollar is wasted, his health and safety may be threatened, and the national interest suffers. On the other hand, increased efforts to make the best possible use of their incomes can contribute more to the well-being of most families than equivalent efforts to raise their incomes.

The march of technology—affecting for example, the foods we eat, the medicines we take, and the many appliances we use in our homes—has increased the difficulties of the consumer along with his opportunities; and it has outmoded many of the old laws and regulations and made new legislation necessary. The typical supermarket before World War II stocked about 1,500 separate food items—an impressive figure by any standard. But today it carries over 6,000. Ninety percent of the prescriptions written today are for drugs that were unknown 20 years ago. Many of the new products used every day in the home are highly complex. The housewife is called upon to be an amateur electrician, mechanic, chemist, toxicologist, dietitian, and mathematician—but she is rarely furnished the information she needs to perform these tasks proficiently.

Marketing is increasingly impersonal. Consumer choice is influenced by mass advertising utilizing highly developed arts of persuasion. The consumer typically cannot know whether drug preparations meet minimum standards of safety, quality, and efficacy. He usually does not know how much he pays for consumer credit; whether one prepared food has more nutritional value than another; whether the performance of a product will in fact meet his needs; or whether the "large economy size" is really a bargain.

Nearly all of the programs offered by this Administration— e.g., the expansion of world trade, the improvement of medical care, the reduction of passenger taxes, the strengthening of mass transit, the development of conservation and recreation areas and low-cost power—are of direct or inherent importance to consumers. Additional legislative and administrative action is required, however, if the Federal Government is to meet its responsibility to consumers in the exercise of their rights. These rights include:

(1) **The right to safety**—to be protected against the marketing of goods which are hazardous to health or life.

(2) **The right to be informed**—to be protected against fraudulent, deceitful, or grossly misleading information, advertising, labeling, or other practices, and to be given the facts he needs to make an informed choice.

(3) **The right to choose**—to be assured, wherever possible, access to a variety of products and services at competitive prices; and in those industries in which competition is not workable and Government regulation is substituted, an assurance of satisfactory quality and service at fair prices.

(4) **The right to be heard**—to be assured that consumer interests will receive full and sympathetic consideration in the formulation of Government policy, and fair and expeditious treatment in its administrative tribunals. [Emphasis added.]

To promote the fuller realization of these consumer rights, it is necessary that existing Government programs be strengthened, that Government organization be improved, and, in certain areas, that new legislation be enacted. . . .

II. NEW LEGISLATIVE AUTHORITY FOR ADDED CONSUMER PROTECTION

[N]ew legislative authority is also essential to advance and protect the consumer interest.

(A) *Strengthen regulatory authority over foods and drugs*
The successful development of more than 9,000 new drugs in the last 25 years has saved countless lives and relieved millions of victims of acute and chronic illnesses. However, new drugs are being placed on the market with no requirement that there be either advance proof that they will be effective in treating the diseases and conditions for which they are recommended or the prompt reporting of adverse reactions. These new drugs present greater hazards as well as greater potential benefits than ever before—for they are widely used, they are often very potent, and they are promoted by aggressive sales campaigns that may tend to overstate their merits and fail to indicate the risks involved in their use. For example, over 20 percent of the new drugs listed since 1956 in the publication New and Non-Official Drugs were found, upon being tested, to be incapable of sustaining one or more of their sponsor's claims regarding their therapeutic effect. There is no way of measuring the needless suffering, the money innocently squandered, and the protraction of illnesses resulting from the use of such ineffective drugs.

The physician and consumer should have the assurance, from an impartial scientific source, that any drug or therapeutic device on the market today is safe and effective for its intended use; that it has the strength and quality represented; and that the accompanying promotional material tells the full story—its bad effects as well as its good. They should be able to identify the drug by a simple, common name in order to avoid confusion and to enable the purchaser to buy the quality drugs he actually needs at the lowest competitive price.

Existing law gives no such assurance to the consumer—a fact highlighted by the thoroughgoing investigation led by Senator Kefauver. It is time to give American men, women and children the same protection we have been giving hogs, sheep and cattle since 1913, under an act forbidding the marketing of worthless serums and other drugs for the treatment of these animals. . . .

In short, existing laws in the food, drug, and cosmetic area are inadequate to assure the necessary protection the American consumer deserves. . . .

(B) *Require "truth in lending"*

. . . Excessive and untimely use of credit arising out of ignorance of its true cost is harmful both to the stability of the economy and to the welfare of the public. Legislation should therefore be enacted requiring lenders and vendors to disclose to borrowers in advance the actual amounts and rates which they will be paying for credit. Such legislation, similar in this sense to the "Truth-in-Securities" laws of 1933–34, would not control prices or charges. But it would require full disclosure to installment buyers and other prospective credit users, and thus permit consumers to make informed decisions before signing on the dotted line. Inasmuch as the specific credit practices which such a bill would be designed to correct are closely related to and often combined with other types of misleading trade practices which the Federal Trade Commission is already regulating, I recommend that enforcement of the new authority be assigned to the Commission. The Government agencies most concerned in this area have been cooperating with the subcommittee in developing the information necessary to prepare a workable and effective bill; and in view of the exhaustive hearings already held, I hope that the Congress can complete action on this important matter before it adjourns. . . .

(D) *Strengthen laws promoting competition and prohibiting monopoly*
The most basic and long-standing protections for the right of consumers, to a choice at a competitive price, are the various laws designed to assure effective competition and to prevent monopoly. The Sherman Act of 1890, the Clayton Act of 1914, and many related laws are the strongest shields the consumer possesses against the growth of unchecked monopoly power. In addition to the measure now nearing final passage which would provide subpoena powers for civil as well as criminal antitrust investigations, several other improvements are needed. . . .

As all of us are consumers, these actions and proposals in the interest of consumers are in the interest of us all. The budgetary investment required by these programs is very modest—but they can yield rich dividends in strengthening our free competitive economy, our standard of living and health and our traditionally high ethical patterns of business conduct. Fair competition aids both business and consumer.

It is my hope that this Message, and the recommendations and requests it contains, can help alert every agency and branch of government to the needs of our consumers. Their voice is not always as loudly heard in Washington as the voices of smaller and better-organized groups—nor is their point of view always defined and presented. But under our economic as well as our political form of democracy, we share an obligation to protect the common interest in every decision we make. I ask the Congress, and every Department and Agency, to help in the fulfillment of that obligation.

—John F. Kennedy

The Consumers' Right to Safety

Nineteenth-century consumers routinely encountered adulterated, impure, and unsanitary foods and drugs. The publication of The Jungle, *Upton Sinclair's shocking book about the meat processing industry, triggered a government investigation, significant press attention, and political pressure from President Theodore Roosevelt. As a result, Congress approved the nation's first protective acts against dangerous products in 1906, the Pure Food and Drug and the Meat Inspection Acts. Since that time, Congress has expanded the former many times and it now bears the name, Food, Drug and Cosmetic Act. Below are extracts from that act.*

Federal Food, Drug and Cosmetic Act

Food, Drug and Cosmetic Act (21 U.S.C. §§ 301–392)

Section 331. Prohibited acts

The following acts and the causing thereof are prohibited:

(a) The introduction or delivery for introduction into interstate commerce of any food, drug, device, or cosmetic that is adulterated or misbranded.

(b) The adulteration or misbranding of any food, drug, device, or cosmetic in interstate commerce.

(c) The receipt in interstate commerce of any food, drug, device, or cosmetic that is adulterated or misbranded, and the delivery or proffered delivery thereof for pay or otherwise. . . .

(g) The manufacture within any Territory of any food, drug, device, or cosmetic that is adulterated or misbranded. . . .

(i)(1) Forging, counterfeiting, simulating, or falsely representing, or without proper authority using any mark, stamp, tag, label, or other identification device authorized or required by regulations. . . .

(k) The alteration, mutilation, destruction, obliteration, or removal of the whole or any part of the labeling of, or the doing of any other act with respect to, a food, drug, device, or cosmetic, if such act is done while such article is held for sale (whether or not the first sale) after shipment in interstate commerce and results in such article being adulterated or misbranded. . . .

Section 342. Adulterated food
A food shall be deemed to be adulterated—

(a) Poisonous, insanitary, etc., ingredients

   (1) If it bears or contains any poisonous or deleterious substance which may render it injurious to health; but in case the substance is not an added substance such food shall not be considered adulterated under this clause if the quantity of such substance in such food does not ordinarily render it injurious to health.

   (2)(A) if it bears or contains any added poisonous or added deleterious substance (other than one which is

      (i) a pesticide chemical in or on a raw agricultural commodity; (ii) a food additive; (iii) a color additive; or (iv) a new animal drug) which is unsafe within the meaning of section 346 of this title, or (B) if it is a raw agricultural commodity and it bears or contains a pesticide chemical which is unsafe within the meaning of section 346a(a) of this title, or (C) if it is, or if it bears or contains, any food additive which is unsafe. . . .

(b) Absence, substitution, or addition of constituents

   (1) If any valuable constituent has been in whole or in part omitted or abstracted therefrom; or (2) if any substance has been substituted wholly or in part therefor; or (3) if damage or inferiority has been concealed in any manner; or (4) if any

substance has been added thereto or mixed or packed therewith so as to increase its bulk or weight, or reduce its quality or strength, or make it appear better or of greater value than it is.

(c) Color additives

If it is, or it bears or contains, a color additive which is unsafe . . .

Section 351. Adulterated drugs and devices
A drug or device shall be deemed to be adulterated—

(a) Poisonous, insanitary, etc., ingredients; adequate controls in manufacture
 (1) If it consists in whole or in part of any filthy, putrid, or decomposed substance; or (2)(A) if it has been prepared, packed, or held under unsanitary conditions whereby it may have been contaminated with filth, or whereby it may have been rendered injurious to health; or (B) if it is a drug and the methods used in, or the facilities or controls used for, its manufacture, processing, packing, or holding do not conform to or are not operated or administered in conformity with current good manufacturing practice to assure that such drug meets the requirements of this chapter as to safety and has the identity and strength, and meets the quality and purity characteristics, which it purports or is represented to possess; or (3) if its container is composed, in whole or in part, of any poisonous or deleterious substance which may render the contents injurious to health; or (4) if (A) it bears or contains, for purposes of coloring only, a color additive which is unsafe . . . ; or (5) if it is a new animal drug which is unsafe . . . ; or (6) if it is an animal feed bearing or containing a new animal drug, and such animal feed is unsafe. . . .

(b) Strength, quality, or purity differing from official compendium
If it purports to be or is represented as a drug the name of which is recognized in an official compendium, and its strength differs from, or its quality or purity falls below, the standard set forth in such compendium. . . .

(d) Mixture with or substitution of another substance
If it is a drug and any substance has been (1) mixed or packed

therewith so as to reduce its quality or strength or (2) substituted wholly or in part therefor.

(e) Devices not in conformity with performance standards
If it is, or purports to be or is represented as, a device which is subject to a performance standard established under section 360d of this title unless such device is in all respects in conformity with such standard. . . .

(h) Manufacture, packing, storage, or installation of device not in conformity with applicable requirements or conditions.
If it is a device and the methods used in, or the facilities or controls used for, its manufacture, packing, storage, or installation are not in conformity with applicable requirements. . . .

Wholesome Meat Inspection Act (1967)

In 1906, Congress passed a federal inspection law to address findings of putrid, adulterated, and unsanitary meat products. This act was later amended, and the current version, and a companion poultry inspection law (not included here), date to 1967.

Wholesome Meat Inspection Act (21 U.S.C. §§ 601–695. Section 602. Congressional statement of findings)

Meat and meat food products are an important source of the Nation's total supply of food. They are consumed throughout the Nation and the major portion thereof moves in interstate or foreign commerce. It is essential in the public interest that the health and welfare of consumers be protected by assuring that meat and meat food products distributed to them are wholesome, not adulterated, and properly marked, labeled, and packaged. Unwholesome, adulterated, or misbranded meat or meat food products impair the effective regulation of meat and meat food products in interstate or foreign commerce, are injurious to the public welfare, destroy markets for wholesome, not adulterated, and properly labeled and packaged meat and meat food products, and result in sundry losses to livestock producers and processors of meat and meat food products, as well as injury to consumers. The unwholesome, adulterated, mislabeled, or deceptively packaged articles can be sold at lower prices and compete unfairly with the wholesome, not adulterated, and properly labeled and packaged articles, to the detriment of consumers and the public generally. It is hereby found that all articles and animals which are regulated under this chapter are either in interstate or foreign commerce or substantially affect such commerce, and that regulation by the Secretary and cooperation by the States and other jurisdictions as contemplated by this chapter are appropriate to prevent and eliminate burdens upon such commerce, to effectively regulate such commerce, and to protect the health and welfare of consumers.

Section 606. Inspectors of meat food products; marks of inspection; destruction of condemned products; products for export

For the purposes hereinbefore set forth the Secretary shall cause to be made, by inspectors appointed for that purpose, an examination and inspection of all meat food products prepared for commerce in any slaughtering, meat-canning, salting, packing, rendering, or similar establishment, and for the purposes of any examination and inspection and inspectors shall have access at all times, by day or night, whether the establishment be operated or not, to every part of said establishment; and said inspectors shall mark, stamp, tag, or label as "Inspected and passed" all such products found to be not adulterated; and said inspectors shall label, mark, stamp, or tag as "Inspected and condemned" all such products found adulterated, and all such condemned meat food products shall be destroyed for food purposes, as hereinbefore provided, and the Secretary may remove inspectors from any establishment which fails to so destroy such condemned meat food products . . .

Section 608. Sanitary inspection and regulation of slaughtering and packing establishments; rejection of adulterated meat or meat food products

The Secretary shall cause to be made, by experts in sanitation or by other competent inspectors, such inspection of all slaughtering, meat canning, salting, packing, rendering, or similar establishments in which cattle, sheep, swine, goats, horses, mules and other equines are slaughtered and the meat and meat food products thereof are prepared for commerce as may be necessary to inform himself concerning the sanitary conditions of the same, and to prescribe the rules and regulations of sanitation under which such establishments shall be maintained; and where the sanitary conditions of any such establishment are such that the meat or meat food products are rendered adulterated, he shall refuse to allow said meat or meat food products to be labeled, marked, stamped or tagged as "inspected and passed."

The Consumers' Right to Be Informed
Mail Fraud Statute (1872)

The Mail Fraud Statute, the nation's first federal consumer protection, became law in 1872. It prohibits any scheme using the U.S. postal system to fraudulently obtain money or anything of value and is one of the principal fraud statutes used in criminal prosecutions.

Mail Fraud Statute (18 U.S.C. § 1341)

Section 1341. Frauds and swindles
Whoever, having devised or intending to devise any scheme or artifice to defraud, or for obtaining money or property by means of false or fraudulent pretenses, representations, or promises, or to sell, dispose of, loan, exchange, alter, give away, distribute, supply, or furnish or procure for unlawful use any counterfeit or spurious coin, obligation, security, or other article, or anything represented to be or intimated or held out to be such counterfeit or spurious article, for the purpose of executing such scheme or artifice or attempting so to do, places in any post office or authorized depository for mail matter, any matter or thing whatever to be sent or delivered by the Postal Service, or deposits or causes to be deposited any matter or thing whatever to be sent or delivered by any private or commercial interstate carrier, or takes or receives therefrom, any such matter or thing, or knowingly causes to be delivered by mail or such carrier according to the direction thereon, or at the place at which it is directed to be delivered by the person to whom it is addressed, any such matter or thing, shall be fined under this title or imprisoned not more than five years, or both. If the violation affects a financial institution, such person shall be fined not more than $1,000,000 or imprisoned not more than 30 years, or both.

Wire Fraud Statute (1952)

Similar to the Mail Fraud Statute, this law prohibits the use of the telephone (including the Internet), radio, or the television in any scheme to defraud. It, too, is frequently used in the criminal prosecution of fraud.

Wire Fraud Statute (18 U.S.C. §1343)

Section 1343. Fraud by wire, radio, or television
Whoever, having devised or intending to devise any scheme or artifice to defraud, or for obtaining money or property by means of false or fraudulent pretenses, representations, or promises, transmits or causes to be transmitted by means of wire, radio, or television communication in interstate or foreign commerce, any writings, signs, signals, pictures, or sounds for the purpose of executing such scheme or artifice, shall be fined under this title or imprisoned not more than five years, or both. If the violation affects a financial institution, such person shall be fined not more than $1,000,000 or imprisoned not more than 30 years, or both.

Federal Trade Commission Act (1914)

Originally approved in 1914 and later expanded by Congress, this act is the principal federal consumer protection statute. It prohibits unfair methods of competition and unfair or deceptive acts or practices. This law also created the Federal Trade Commission (FTC), an independent regulatory agency, to enforce these provisions. It grants the Commission civil, but not criminal, jurisdiction to pursue unfair and deceptive market practices. Below are extracts from the Federal Trade Commission Act.

Federal Trade Commission Act (15 U.S.C. §§ 41–58)

Section 41. Federal Trade Commission established; membership vacancies; seal
A commission is created and established, to be known as the Federal Trade Commission (hereinafter referred to as the Commission), which shall be composed of five Commissioners, who shall be appointed by the President, by and with the advice and consent of the Senate . . . The President shall choose a chairman from the Commission's membership. No Commissioner shall engage in any other business, vocation, or employment.

Section 45. Unfair methods of competition unlawful; prevention by Commission
(a) Declaration of unlawfulness; power to prohibit unfair practices; inapplicability to foreign trade

> (1) Unfair methods of competition in or affecting commerce, and unfair or deceptive acts or practices in or affecting commerce, are hereby declared unlawful.

> (2) The Commission is hereby empowered and directed to prevent persons, partnerships, or corporations . . . from using unfair methods of competition in or affecting commerce and unfair or deceptive acts or practices in or affecting commerce.

(b) Proceeding by Commission; modifying and setting aside orders
Whenever the Commission shall have reason to believe that any such person, partnership, or corporation has been or is using any unfair method of competition or unfair or deceptive act or practice in or affecting commerce, and if it shall appear to the Commission that a proceeding by it in respect thereof would be to the interest of the public, it shall issue and serve upon such person, partnership, or corporation a complaint stating its charges in that respect and containing a notice of a hearing. . . .

If upon such hearing the Commission shall be of the opinion that the method of competition or the act or practice in question is prohibited by this subchapter, it shall make a report in writing in which it shall state its findings as to the facts and shall issue and cause to be served on such person, partnership, or corporation an order requiring such person, partnership, or corporation to cease and desist from using such method of competition or such act or practice . . .

Section 52. Dissemination of false advertisements
(a) Unlawfulness
It shall be unlawful for any person, partnership, or corporation to disseminate, or cause to be disseminated, any false advertisement—

> (1) By United States mails, or in or having an effect upon commerce, by any means, for the purpose of inducing, or which is likely to induce, directly or indirectly the purchase of food, drugs, devices, services, or cosmetics; or

(2) By any means, for the purpose of inducing, or which is likely to induce, directly or indirectly, the purchase in or having an effect upon commerce, of food, drugs, devices, services, or cosmetics.

(b) Unfair or deceptive act or practice
The dissemination or the causing to be disseminated of any false advertisement within the provisions of subsection (a) of this section shall be an unfair or deceptive act or practice in or affecting commerce within the meaning of section 45 of this title.

Telemarketing Sales Rule (1995)

Congress has granted the FTC authority to issue trade or sales rules. These are regulations that have the force of law, governing a particular industry or sales practice. Such rules include the Door-to-Door Sales Rule, Mail and Telephone Order Rule, and the Funeral Rule. Listed below are excerpts from the Commission's Telemarketing Sales Rule, issued in 1995 to combat fraudulent practices in the telemarketing industry. This rule declares certain telemarketing practices to be deceptive or abusive and provides consumers with specific rights. Below are extracts from this regulation.

Telemarketing Sales Rule (Title 16, Code of Federal Regulations § 310)

Section 310.3 Deceptive telemarketing acts or practices.
(a) Prohibited deceptive telemarketing acts or practices. It is a deceptive telemarketing act or practice and a violation of this Rule for any seller or telemarketer to engage in the following conduct:

(1) Before a customer pays for goods or services offered, failing to disclose, in a clear and conspicuous manner, the following material information:

(i) The total costs to purchase, receive, or use, and the quantity of, any goods or services that are the subject of the sales offer;

(ii) All material restrictions, limitations, or conditions to purchase, receive, or use the goods or services that are the subject of the sales offer;

(iii) If the seller has a policy of not making refunds, cancellations, exchanges, or repurchases, a statement informing the customer that this is the seller's policy; or, if the seller or telemarketer makes a representation about a refund, cancellation, exchange, or repurchase policy, a statement of all material terms and conditions of such policy;

(iv) In any prize promotion, the odds of being able to receive the prize, and if the odds are not calculable in advance, the factors used in calculating the odds; that no purchase or payment is required to win a prize or to participate in a prize promotion; and the no purchase/no payment method of participating in the prize promotion with either instructions on how to participate or an address or local or toll-free telephone number to which customers may write or call for information on how to participate; and

(v) All material costs or conditions to receive or redeem a prize that is the subject of the prize promotion;

(2) Misrepresenting, directly or by implication, any of the following material information:

(i) The total costs to purchase, receive, or use, and the quantity of, any goods or services that are the subject of a sales offer;

(ii) Any material restriction, limitation, or condition to purchase, receive, or use goods or services that are the subject of a sales offer;

(iii) Any material aspect of the performance, efficacy, nature, or central characteristics of goods or services that are the subject of a sales offer;

(iv) Any material aspect of the nature or terms of the seller's refund, cancellation, exchange, or repurchase policies;

(v) Any material aspect of a prize promotion including, but not limited to, the odds of being able to receive a prize, the nature or value of a prize, or that a purchase or payment is required to win a prize or to participate in a prize promotion;

(vi) Any material aspect of an investment opportunity including, but not limited to, risk, liquidity, earnings potential, or profitability; or

(vii) A seller's or telemarketer's affiliation with, or endorsement by, any government or third-party organization;

(3) Obtaining or submitting for payment a check, draft, or other form of negotiable paper drawn on a person's checking, savings, share, or similar account, without that person's express verifiable authorization. Such authorization shall be deemed verifiable if any of the following means are employed:

(i) Express written authorization by the customer, which may include the customer's signature on the negotiable instrument; or

(ii) Express oral authorization which is tape recorded and made available upon request to the customer's bank and which evidences clearly both the customer's authorization of payment for the goods and services that are the subject of the sales offer. . . .

(4) Making a false or misleading statement to induce any person to pay for goods or services.

(b) Assisting and facilitating. It is a deceptive telemarketing act or practice and a violation of this Rule for a person to provide substantial assistance or support to any seller or telemarketer when that person knows or consciously avoids knowing that the seller or telemarketer is engaged in any act or practice that violates §§ 310.3(a) or (c), or § 310.4 of this Rule.

(c) Credit card laundering. Except as expressly permitted by the applicable credit card system, it is a deceptive telemarketing act or practice and a violation of this Rule for:

(1) A merchant to present to or deposit into, or cause another to present to or deposit into, the credit card system for payment, a credit card sales draft generated by a telemarketing transaction that is not the result of a

telemarketing credit card transaction between the cardholder and the merchant;

(2) Any person to employ, solicit, or otherwise cause a merchant or an employee, representative, or agent of the merchant, to present to or deposit into the credit card system for payment, a credit card sales draft generated by a telemarketing transaction that is not the result of a telemarketing credit card transaction between the cardholder and the merchant; or

(3) Any person to obtain access to the credit card system through the use of a business relationship or an affiliation with a merchant, when such access is not authorized by the merchant agreement or the applicable credit card system.

Section 310.4 Abusive telemarketing acts or practices.

(a) Abusive conduct generally. It is an abusive telemarketing act or practice and a violation of this Rule for any seller or telemarketer to engage in the following conduct:

(1) Threats, intimidation, or the use of profane or obscene language;

(2) Requesting or receiving payment of any fee or consideration for goods or services represented to remove derogatory information from, or improve, a person's credit history, credit record, or credit rating until:

(i) The time frame in which the seller has represented all of the goods or services will be provided to that person has expired; and

(ii) The seller has provided the person with documentation in the form of a consumer report from a consumer reporting agency demonstrating that the promised results have been achieved, such report having been issued more than six months after the results were achieved. Nothing in this Rule should be construed to affect the requirement in the Fair Credit Reporting Act, 15 U.S.C. § 1681, that a consumer report may only be obtained for a specified permissible purpose;

(3) Requesting or receiving payment of any fee or consideration from a person, for goods or services represented to recover or otherwise assist in the return of money or any other item of value paid for by, or promised to, that person in a previous telemarketing transaction, until seven (7) business days after such money or other item is delivered to that person. This provision shall not apply to goods or services provided to a person by a licensed attorney; or

(4) Requesting or receiving payment of any fee or consideration in advance of obtaining a loan or other extension of credit when the seller or telemarketer has guaranteed or represented a high likelihood of success in obtaining or arranging a loan or other extension of credit for a person.

(b) Pattern of calls.

(1) It is an abusive telemarketing act or practice and a violation of this Rule for a telemarketer to engage in, or for a seller to cause a telemarketer to engage in, the following conduct:

(i) Causing any telephone to ring, or engaging any person in telephone conversation, repeatedly or continuously with intent to annoy, abuse, or harass any person at the called number; or

(ii) Initiating an outbound telephone call to a person when that person previously has stated that he or she does not wish to receive an outbound telephone call made by or on behalf of the seller whose goods or services are being offered. . . .

(c) Calling time restrictions. Without the prior consent of a person, it is an abusive telemarketing act or practice and a violation of this Rule for a telemarketer to engage in outbound telephone calls to a person's residence at any time other than between 8:00 A.M. and 9:00 P.M. local time at the called person's location.

(d) Required oral disclosures. It is an abusive telemarketing act or practice and a violation of this Rule for a telemarketer in an outbound telephone call to fail to disclose promptly and in a clear and conspicuous manner to the person receiving the call, the following information:

(1) The identity of the seller;

(2) That the purpose of the call is to sell goods or services;

(3) The nature of the goods or services; and

(4) That no purchase or payment is necessary to be able to win a prize or participate in a prize promotion if a prize promotion is offered. This disclosure must be made before or in conjunction with the description of the prize to the person called. If requested by that person, the telemarketer must disclose the no-purchase/no-payment entry method for the prize promotion.

Federal Trade Commission Policy Statement on Unfairness (1980)

The FTC Act bars all "unfair acts or practices in or affecting commerce" but doesn't define what such an act or practice is. The statute was framed in general terms because any list of unfair practices would quickly become outdated, leaving loopholes. Instead, the Commission was assigned the task of determining what constitutes an unfair act or practice. The letter below, addressed to members of Congress, discusses the factors used by the Commission in making that decision. It is one of three Commission policy statements listed here. Below are extracts from this policy statement.

Federal Trade Commission Policy Statement on Unfairness

Federal Trade Commission
Washington, D. C. 20580
December 17, 1980

This letter thus delineates the Commission's views of the boundaries of its consumer unfairness jurisdiction. . . .
*Commission Statement of Policy on the Scope
of the Consumer Unfairness Jurisdiction*

Section 5 of the FTC Act prohibits, in part,
"unfair . . . acts or practices in or affecting commerce." This is commonly referred to as the Commission's consumer

unfairness jurisdiction. The Commission's jurisdiction over "unfair methods of competition" is not discussed in this letter. Although we cannot give an exhaustive treatment of the law of consumer unfairness in this short statement, some relatively concrete conclusions can nonetheless be drawn.

The present understanding of the unfairness standard is the result of an evolutionary process. The statute was deliberately framed in general terms since Congress recognized the impossibility of drafting a complete list of unfair trade practices that would not quickly become outdated or leave loopholes for easy evasion. The task of identifying unfair trade practices was therefore assigned to the Commission, subject to judicial review, in the expectation that the underlying criteria would evolve and develop over time. As the Supreme Court observed as early as 1931, the ban on unfairness "belongs to that class of phrases which do not admit of precise definition, but the meaning and application of which must be arrived at by what this court elsewhere has called 'the gradual process of judicial inclusion and exclusion.'"

By 1964 enough cases had been decided to enable the Commission to identify three factors that it considered when applying the prohibition against consumer unfairness. These were: (1) whether the practice injures consumers; (2) whether it violates established public policy; (3) whether it is unethical or unscrupulous. These factors were later quoted with apparent approval by the Supreme Court in the 1972 case of *Sperry & Hutchinson*. Since then the Commission has continued to refine the standard of unfairness in its cases and rules, and it has now reached a more detailed sense of both the definition and the limits of these criteria.

Consumer injury
Unjustified consumer injury is the primary focus of the FTC Act, and the most important of the three S&H criteria. By itself it can be sufficient to warrant a finding of unfairness. The Commission's ability to rely on an independent criterion of consumer injury is consistent with the intent of the statute, which was to "[make] the consumer who may be injured by an unfair trade practice of equal concern before the law with the merchant injured by the unfair methods of a dishonest competitor."

The independent nature of the consumer injury criterion does not mean that every consumer injury is legally "unfair," however. To justify a finding of unfairness the injury must satisfy three tests. It must be substantial; it must not be outweighed by any countervailing benefits to consumers or competition that the practice produces; and it must be an injury that consumers themselves could not reasonably have avoided.

First of all, the injury must be substantial. The Commission is not concerned with trivial or merely speculative harms. In most cases a substantial injury involves monetary harm, as when sellers coerce consumers into purchasing unwanted goods or services or when consumers buy defective goods or services on credit but are unable to assert against the creditor claims or defenses arising from the transaction.

Unwarranted health and safety risks may also support a finding of unfairness. Emotional impact and other more subjective types of harm, on the other hand, will not ordinarily make a practice unfair. Thus, for example, the Commission will not seek to ban an advertisement merely because it offends the tastes or social beliefs of some viewers, as has been suggested in some of the comments.

Second, the injury must not be outweighed by any offsetting consumer or competitive benefits that the sales practice also produces. Most business practices entail a mixture of economic and other costs and benefits for purchasers. A seller's failure to present complex technical data on his product may lessen a consumer's ability to choose, for example, but may also reduce the initial price he must pay for the article. The Commission is aware of these tradeoffs and will not find that a practice unfairly injures consumers unless it is injurious in its net effects. The Commission also takes account of the various costs that a remedy would entail. These include not only the costs to the parties directly before the agency, but also the burdens on society in general in the form of increased paperwork, increased regulatory burdens on the flow of information, reduced incentives to innovation and capital formation, and similar matters. Finally, the injury must be one which consumers could not reasonably have avoided. Normally we expect the marketplace to be self-correcting, and we rely on consumer choice—the ability of individual consumers to make their own private purchasing decisions without regulatory intervention—to govern the market. We anticipate that consumers will survey the available alternatives, choose those that are most desirable, and avoid those that are inadequate or unsatisfactory. However, it has long been recognized that certain types of sales techniques may prevent consumers from effectively making their own decisions, and that corrective action may then become necessary. . . .

Violation of public policy

The second S&H standard asks whether the conduct violates public policy as it has been established by statute, common law, industry practice, or otherwise. This criterion may be applied in two different ways. It may be used to test the validity and strength of the evidence of consumer injury, or, less often, it may be cited for a dispositive legislative or judicial determination that such injury is present.

Although public policy was listed by the S&H Court as a separate consideration, it is used most frequently by the Commission as a means of providing additional evidence on the degree of consumer injury caused by specific practices. To be sure, most Commission actions are brought to redress relatively clear-cut injuries, and those determinations are based, in large part, on objective economic analysis. As we have indicated before, the Commission believes that considerable attention should be devoted to the analysis of whether substantial net harm has occurred, not only because that is part of the unfairness test, but also because the focus on injury is the best way to ensure that the Commission acts responsibly and uses its resources wisely. Nonetheless, the Commission wishes to emphasize the importance of examining outside statutory policies and established judicial principles for assistance in helping the agency ascertain whether a particular form of conduct does in fact tend to harm consumers. Thus the agency has referred to First Amendment decisions upholding consumers' rights to receive information, for example, to confirm that restrictions on advertising tend unfairly to hinder the informed exercise of consumer choice.

Conversely, statutes or other sources of public policy may affirmatively allow for a practice that the Commission tentatively views as unfair. The existence of such policies will then give the agency reason to reconsider its assessment of whether the practice is actually injurious in its net effects. In other situations there may be no clearly established public policies, or the policies may even be in conflict.

While that does not necessarily preclude the Commission from taking action if there is strong evidence of net consumer injury, it does underscore the desirability of carefully examining public policies in all instances. In any event, whenever objective evidence of consumer injury is difficult to obtain, the need to identify and assess all relevant public policies assumes increased importance. . . .

Unethical or unscrupulous conduct
Finally, the third S&H standard asks whether the conduct was immoral, unethical, oppressive, or unscrupulous. This test was presumably included in order to be sure of reaching all the purposes of the underlying statute, which forbids "unfair" acts or practices. It would therefore allow the Commission to reach conduct that violates generally recognized standards of business ethics. The test has proven, however, to be largely duplicative. Conduct that is truly unethical or unscrupulous will almost always injure consumers or violate public policy as well. The Commission has therefore never relied on the third element of S&H as an independent basis for a finding of unfairness, and it will act in the future only on the basis of the first two.

We hope this letter has given you the information that you require. Please do not hesitate to call if we can be of any further assistance. With best regards,

/s/Michael Pertschuk Chairman
/s/Paul Rand Dixon Commissioner
/s/David A. Clanton Commissioner
/s/Robert Pitofsky Commissioner
/s/Patricia P. Bailey Commissioner
[Footnotes Omitted]

Federal Trade Commission Policy Statement on Deception (1983)

The FTC Act also prohibits "deceptive . . . acts or practices affecting commerce." In this 1983 letter to Congress, the Commission articulated standards for enforcing the prohibition on deceptive acts and practices.

FTC Policy Statement on Deception
Federal Trade Commission
Washington, DC 20580
October 14, 1983

I. SUMMARY
Certain elements undergird all deception cases. First, there must

be a representation, omission or practice that is likely to mislead the consumer. Practices that have been found misleading or deceptive in specific cases include false oral or written representations, misleading price claims, sales of hazardous or systematically defective products or services, without adequate disclosures, failure to disclose information regarding pyramid sales, use of bait and switch techniques, failure to perform promised services, and failure to meet warranty obligations.

Second, we examine the practice from the perspective of a consumer acting reasonably in the circumstances. If the representation or practice affects or is directed primarily to a particular group, the Commission examines reasonableness from the perspective of that group.

Third, the representation, omission, or practice must be a "material" one. The basic question is whether the act or practice is likely to affect the consumer's conduct or decision with regard to a product or service. If so, the practice is material, and consumer injury is likely, because consumers are likely to have chosen differently but for the deception. In many instances, materiality, and hence injury, can be presumed from the nature of the practice. In other instances, evidence of materiality may be necessary.

Thus, the Commission will find deception if there is a representation, omission or practice that is likely to mislead the consumer acting reasonably in the circumstances, to the consumer's detriment. We discuss each of these elements below.

II. THERE MUST BE A REPRESENTATION, OMISSION, OR PRACTICE THAT IS LIKELY TO MISLEAD THE CONSUMER.

Most deception involves written or oral misrepresentations, or omissions of material information. Deception may also occur in other forms of conduct associated with a sales transaction. The entire advertisement, transaction or course of dealing will be considered. The issue is whether the act or practice is likely to mislead, rather than whether it causes actual deceptions.

Of course, the Commission must find that a representation, omission, or practice occurred. In cases of express claims, the representation itself establishes the meaning. In cases of implied claims, the Commission will often be able to determine meaning through an examination of the representation itself, including an evaluation of such factors as the entire document, the juxtaposition of various phrases in the document, the nature of the claim, and the nature of the transactions. In other situations, the Commission will require extrinsic evidence that reasonable consumers reach the implied claims. In all instances, the Commission will carefully consider any extrinsic evidence that is introduced.

Some cases involve omission of material information, the disclosure of which is necessary to prevent the claim, practice, or sale from being misleading. Information may be omitted from written or oral representations or from the commercial transaction.

In some circumstances, the Commission can presume that consumers are likely to reach false beliefs about the product or service because of an omission. At other times, however, the Commission may require evidence on consumers' expectations.

Marketing and point-of-sales practices that are likely to mislead consumers are also deceptive. For instance, in bait and switch cases, a violation occurs when the offer to sell the product is not a bona fide offer. The Commission has also found deception where a sales representative misrepresented the purpose of the initial contact with customers. When a product is sold, there is an implied representation that the product is fit for the purposes for which it is sold. When it is not, deception occurs. There may be a concern about the way a product or service is marketed, such as where inaccurate or incomplete information is provided. A failure to perform services promised under a warranty or by contract can also be deceptive.

III. THE ACT OR PRACTICE MUST BE CONSIDERED FROM THE PERSPECTIVE OF THE REASONABLE CONSUMER

The Commission believes that to be deceptive the representation, omission or practice must be likely to mislead reasonable consumers under the circumstances. The test is whether the consumer's interpretation or reaction is reasonable. When representations or sales practices are targeted to a specific audience, the Commission determines the effect of the practice on a reasonable member of that group. In evaluating a particular practice, the Commission considers the totality of the practice in determining how reasonable consumers are likely to respond.

A company is not liable for every interpretation or action

by a consumer. In an advertising context, this principle has been well-stated:

> An advertiser cannot be charged with liability with respect to every conceivable misconception, however outlandish, to which his representations might be subject among the foolish or feeble-minded.

> Some people, because of ignorance or incomprehension, may be misled by even a scrupulously honest claim. Perhaps a few misguided souls believe, for example, that all "Danish pastry" is made in Denmark. Is it therefore an actionable deception to advertise "Danish pastry" when it is made in this country? Of course not. A representation does not become "false and deceptive" merely because it will be unreasonably misunderstood by an insignificant and unrepresentative segment of the class of persons to whom the representation is addressed. Heinz W. Kirchner, 63 F.T.C. 1282, 1290 (1963).

To be considered reasonable, the interpretation or reaction does not have to be the only one. A seller's representation conveys more than one meaning to reasonable consumers, one of which is false, the seller is liable for the misleading interpretation. An interpretation will be presumed reasonable if it is the one the respondent intended to convey. . . .

Finally, as a matter of policy, when consumers can easily evaluate the product or service, it is inexpensive, and it is frequently purchased, the Commission will examine the practice closely before issuing a complaint based on deception. There is little incentive for sellers to misrepresent (either by an explicit false statement or a deliberate false implied statement) in these circumstances since they normally would seek to encourage repeat purchases. There, as here, market incentives place strong constraints on the likelihood of deception, the Commission will examine a practice closely before proceeding.

In sum, the Commission will consider many factors in determining the reaction of the ordinary consumer to a claim or practice. As would any trier of fact, the Commission will evaluate the totality of the ad or the practice and ask questions such as: how clear is the representation? how conspicuous is any qualifying information? how important is the omitted information? do other sources for the omitted information exist? how familiar is the public with the product or service?

IV. THE REPRESENTATION, OMISSION OR PRACTICE MUST BE MATERIAL

The third element of deception is materiality. That is, a representation, omission or practice must be a material one for deception to occur. A "material" misrepresentation or practice is one which is likely to affect a consumer's choice of or conduct regarding a product. In other words, it is information that is important to consumers. If inaccurate or omitted information is material, injury is likely.

The Commission considers certain categories of information presumptively material. First, the Commission presumes that express claims are material. As the Supreme Court stated recently, "[i]n the absence of factors that would distort the decision to advertise, we may assume that the willingness of a business to promote its products reflects a belief that consumers are interested in the advertising." Where the seller knew, or should have known, that an ordinary consumer would need omitted information to evaluate the product or service, or that the claim was false, materiality will be presumed because the manufacturer intended the information or omission to have an effect. Similarly, when evidence exists that a seller intended to make an implied claim, the Commission will infer materiality. . . .

V. CONCLUSION

The Commission will find an act or practice deceptive if there is a misrepresentation, omission, or other practice, that misleads the consumer acting reasonably in the circumstances, to the consumer's detriment. The Commission will not generally require extrinsic evidence concerning the representations understood by reasonable consumers or the materiality of a challenged claim, but in some instances extrinsic evidence will be necessary.

The Commission intends to enforce the FTC Act vigorously. We will investigate, and prosecute where appropriate, acts or practices that are deceptive. We hope this letter will help provide you and the public with a greater sense of certainty concerning how the Commission will exercise its jurisdiction over deception. Please do not hesitate to call if we can be of any further assistance.

By direction of the Commission, Commissioners Pertschuk and Bailey dissenting, with separate statements attached and with separate response to the Committee's request for a legal analysis to follow.

/s/James C. Miller III
Chairman
[Footnotes Omitted]

Federal Trade Commission Policy Statement Regarding Advertising Substantiation (1984)

With its authority to prohibit deceptive and unfair acts and practices, the FTC plays a major role in regulating advertising claims. Advertisers must have a reasonable basis for making an objective claim. In this statement, the Commission articulates its criteria for what is needed to substantiate an objective advertising claim. Below are extracts from this policy statement.

Policy Statement Regarding Advertising Substantiation

Introduction
On March 11, 1983, the Commission published a notice requesting comments on its advertising substantiation program. To facilitate analysis of the program, the notice posed a number of questions concerning the program's procedures, standards, benefits, and costs, and solicited suggestions for making the program more effective. Based on the public comments and the staff's review, the Commission has drawn certain conclusions about how the program is being implemented and how it might be refined to serve better the objective of maintaining a marketplace free of unfair and deceptive acts or practices. This statement articulates the Commission's policy with respect to advertising substantiation.

The Reasonable Basis Requirement
First, we reaffirm our commitment to the underlying legal requirement of advertising substantiation—that advertisers and ad agencies have a reasonable basis for advertising claims before they are disseminated. The Commission intends to continue vigorous enforcement of this existing legal requirement that advertisers substantiate express and implied claims, however conveyed, that make objective assertions about

the item or service advertised. Objective claims for products or services represent explicitly or by implication that the advertiser has a reasonable basis supporting these claims. These representations of substantiation are material to consumers. That is, consumers would be less likely to rely on claims for products and services if they knew the advertiser did not have a reasonable basis for believing them to be true. Therefore, a firm's failure to possess and rely upon a reasonable basis for objective claims constitutes an unfair and deceptive act or practice in violation of Section 5 of the Federal Trade Commission Act.

Standards for Prior Substantiation

Many ads contain express or implied statements regarding the amount of support the advertiser has for the product claim. ᐧ When the substantiation claim is express (e.g., "tests prove," "doctors recommend," and "studies show"), the Commission expects the firm to have at least the advertised level of substantiation. Of course, an ad may imply more substantiation than it expressly claims or may imply to consumers that the firm has a certain type of support; in such cases, the advertiser must possess the amount and type of substantiation the ad actually communicates to consumers.

Absent an express or implied reference to a certain level of support, and absent other evidence indicating what consumer expectations would be, the Commission assumes that consumers expect a "reasonable basis" for claims. The Commission's determination of what constitutes a reasonable basis depends, as it does in an unfairness analysis, on a number of factors relevant to the benefits and costs of substantiating a particular claim. These factors include: the type of claim, the product, the consequences of a false claim, the benefits of a truthful claim, the cost of developing substantiation for the claim, and the amount of substantiation experts in the field believe is reasonable. Extrinsic evidence, such as expert testimony or consumer surveys, is useful to determine what level of substantiation consumers expect to support a particular product claim and the adequacy of evidence an advertiser possesses. . . .

Procedures for Obtaining Substantiation

In the past, the Commission has sought substantiation from firms in two different ways: through industry-wide "rounds" that involved publicized inquiries with identical or substantially similar demands to a number of firms within a targeted industry or to firms in different industries making the same type of claim; and on a case-by-case basis, by sending specific requests to individual companies under investigation. The Commission's review indicates that "rounds" have been costly to both the recipient and to the agency and have produced little or no law enforcement benefit over a case-by-case approach.

The Commission's traditional investigatory procedures allow the staff to investigate a number of firms within an industry at the same time, to develop necessary expertise within the area of investigation, and to announce our activities publicly in circumstances where public notice or comment is desirable. The Commission intends to continue undertaking such law enforcement efforts when appropriate. However, since substantiation is principally a law enforcement tool and the Commission's concern in such investigations is with the substantiation in the advertiser's possession, there is little, if any, information that the public could contribute in such investigations. Therefore, the Commission anticipates that substantiation investigations will rarely be made public before they are completed. . . .

Truth in Lending Act (1969)

Truth in Lending, part of the legislative package recommended by President Kennedy in his message quoted earlier, is a credit disclosure law. It standardizes information to enable "apples to apples" comparisons of finance charges and annual percentage rates. In addition, it provides a three-day right of recision for credit agreements. Truth in Lending was enacted in 1969 to correct abuses in the credit industry, particularly regarding home improvement loans and auto loans. Below are extracts from this act.

Truth in Lending Act
15 U.S.C. § 1601

Section 1601. Congressional findings and declaration of purpose

(a) Informed use of credit

The Congress finds that economic stabilization would be enhanced and the competition among the various financial institutions and other firms engaged in the extension of consumer credit would be strengthened by the informed use of credit. The informed use of credit results from an awareness of the cost thereof by consumers. It is the purpose of this subchapter to assure a meaningful disclosure of credit terms so that the consumer will be able to compare more readily the various credit terms available to him and avoid the uninformed use of credit, and to protect the consumer against inaccurate and unfair credit billing and credit card practices. . . .

Section 1604. Disclosure guidelines
(a) Promulgation, contents, etc., of regulations
The Board [Federal Reserve Board] shall prescribe regulations to carry out the purposes of this subchapter. . . .

(b) Model disclosure forms and clauses; publication, criteria, compliance, etc.
The Board shall publish model disclosure forms and clauses for common transactions to facilitate compliance with the disclosure requirements of this subchapter and to aid the borrower or lessee in understanding the transaction by utilizing readily understandable language to simplify the technical nature of the disclosures. In devising such forms, the Board shall consider the use by creditors or lessors of data processing or similar automated equipment. . . .

Section 1605. Determination of finance charge
(a) "Finance charge" defined
Except as otherwise provided in this section, the amount of the finance charge in connection with any consumer credit transaction shall be determined as the sum of all charges, payable directly or indirectly by the person to whom the credit is extended, and imposed directly or indirectly by the creditor as an incident to the extension of credit . . .

Examples of charges which are included in the finance charge include any of the following types of charges which are applicable:

(1) Interest, time price differential, and any amount payable under a point, discount, or other system or additional charges.

(2) Service or carrying charge.

(3) Loan fee, finder's fee, or similar charge.

(4) Fee for an investigation or credit report.

(5) Premium or other charge for any guarantee or insurance protecting the creditor against the obligor's default or other credit loss.

(6) Borrower-paid mortgage broker fees, including fees paid directly to the broker or the lender (for delivery to the broker) whether such fees are paid in cash or financed.

(b) Life, accident, or health insurance premiums included in finance charge
Charges or premiums for credit life, accident, or health insurance written in connection with any consumer credit transaction shall be included in the finance charges unless

(1) the coverage of the debtor by the insurance is not a factor in the approval by the creditor of the extension of credit, and this fact is clearly disclosed in writing to the person applying for or obtaining the extension of credit; and

(2) in order to obtain the insurance in connection with the extension of credit, the person to whom the credit is extended must give specific affirmative written indication of his desire to do so after written disclosure to him of the cost thereof. . . .

Section 1606. Determination of annual percentage rate
(a) "Annual percentage rate" defined
The annual percentage rate applicable to any extension of consumer credit shall be determined, in accordance with the regulations of the Board,

(1) in the case of any extension of credit other than under an open end credit plan, as

(A) that nominal annual percentage rate which will yield a sum equal to the amount of the finance charge when it is applied to the unpaid balances of the amount financed, calculated according to the actuarial method of allocating payments made on a debt between the amount financed and the amount of the finance charge, pursuant to which a payment is applied first to the accumulated finance charge and the balance is applied to the unpaid amount financed; or

(B) the rate determined by any method prescribed by the Board as a method which materially simplifies computation while retaining reasonable accuracy as compared with the rate determined under subparagraph (A).

(2) in the case of any extension of credit under an open end credit plan, as the quotient (expressed as a percentage) of the total finance charge for the period to which it relates divided by the amount upon which the finance charge for that period is based, multiplied by the number of such periods in a year.

(b) Computation of rate of finance charges for balances within a specified range
Where a creditor imposes the same finance charge for balances within a specified range, the annual percentage rate shall be computed on the median balance within the range, except that if the Board determines that a rate so computed would not be meaningful, or would be materially misleading, the annual percentage rate shall be computed on such other basis as the Board may by regulation require.

(c) Allowable tolerances for purposes of compliance with disclosure requirements
The disclosure of an annual percentage rate is accurate for the purpose of this subchapter if the rate disclosed is within a tolerance not greater than one-eighth of 1 per centum more or less than the actual rate or rounded to the nearest one-fourth of 1 per centum. The Board may allow a greater tolerance to simplify compliance where irregular payments are involved. . . .

Fair Credit Reporting Act (1970)

This federal statute, approved in 1970, regulates credit reporting agencies and the use of credit reports. Congress approved this act in response to the growth of credit bureaus and reports of unfairness and inaccuracy in records. It was the first major privacy law protecting personal information in the computer age. Below are extracts from this statute.

Fair Credit Reporting Act (15 U.S.C. 1681)

Section 1681. Congressional findings and statement of purpose
(a) Accuracy and fairness of credit reporting
The Congress makes the following findings:

> (1) The banking system is dependent upon fair and accurate credit reporting. Inaccurate credit reports directly impair the efficiency of the banking system, and unfair credit reporting methods undermine the public confidence which is essential to the continued functioning of the banking system.

> (2) An elaborate mechanism has been developed for investigating and evaluating the credit worthiness, credit standing, credit capacity, character, and general reputation of consumers.

> (3) Consumer reporting agencies have assumed a vital role in assembling and evaluating consumer credit and other information on consumers.

> (4) There is a need to insure that consumer reporting agencies exercise their grave responsibilities with fairness, impartiality, and a respect for the consumer's right to privacy.

(b) Reasonable procedures
It is the purpose of this subchapter to require that consumer reporting agencies adopt reasonable procedures for meeting the needs of commerce for consumer credit, personnel, insurance, and other information in a manner which is fair and equitable to the consumer, with regard to the confidentiality, accuracy, relevancy, and proper utilization of such information in accordance with the requirements of this subchapter.

Section 1681b. Permissible purposes of consumer reports
A consumer reporting agency may furnish a consumer report under the following circumstances and no other:

> (1) In response to the order of a court having jurisdiction to issue such an order, or a subpoena issued in connection with proceedings before a Federal grand jury.

> (2) In accordance with the written instructions of the consumer to whom it relates.

(3) To a person which it has reason to believe—

(A) intends to use the information in connection with a credit transaction involving the consumer on whom the information is to be furnished and involving the extension of credit to, or review or collection of an account of, the consumer; or

(B) intends to use the information for employment purposes; or

(C) intends to use the information in connection with the underwriting of insurance involving the consumer; or

(D) intends to use the information in connection with a determination of the consumer's eligibility for a license or other benefit granted by a governmental instrumentality required by law to consider an applicant's financial responsibility or status; or

(E) otherwise has a legitimate business need for the information in connection with a business transaction involving the consumer.

Section 1681c. Reporting of obsolete information prohibited
(a) Prohibited items . . .
[N]o consumer reporting agency may make any consumer report containing any of the following items of information:

(1) cases under Title 11 or under the Bankruptcy Act that, from the date of entry of the order for relief or the date of adjudication, as the case may be, antedate the report by more than 10 years.

(2) Suits and judgments which, from date of entry, antedate the report by more than seven years or until the governing statute of limitations has expired, whichever is the longer period.

(3) Paid tax liens which, from date of payment, antedate the report by more than seven years.

(4) Accounts placed for collection or charged to profit and loss which antedate the report by more than seven years.

(5) Records of arrest, indictment, or conviction of crime which, from date of disposition, release, or parole, antedate the report by more than seven years.

(6) Any other adverse item of information which antedates the report by more than seven years. . . .

Section 1681g. Disclosures to consumers
(a) Information on file; sources; report recipients
Every consumer reporting agency shall, upon request and proper identification of any consumer, clearly and accurately disclose to the consumer:

(1) The nature and substance of all information (except medical information) in its files on the consumer at the time of the request.

(2) The sources of the information; except that the sources of information acquired solely for use in preparing an investigative consumer report and actually used for no other purpose need not be disclosed: Provided, That in the event an action is brought under this subchapter, such sources shall be available to the plaintiff under appropriate discovery procedures in the court in which the action is brought.

(3) The recipients of any consumer report on the consumer which it has furnished—

(A) for employment purposes within the two-year period preceding the request, and

(B) for any other purpose within the six-month period preceding the request. . . .

Section 1681i. Procedure in case of disputed accuracy
(a) Dispute; reinvestigation
If the completeness or accuracy of any item of information contained in his file is disputed by a consumer, and such dispute is directly conveyed to the consumer reporting agency by the consumer, the consumer reporting agency shall within a reasonable period of time reinvestigate and record the current status of that information unless it has reasonable grounds to believe that the dispute by the consumer is frivolous or

irrelevant. If after such reinvestigation such information is found to be inaccurate or can no longer be verified, the consumer reporting agency shall promptly delete such information. The presence of contradictory information in the consumer's file does not in and of itself constitute reasonable grounds for believing the dispute is frivolous or irrelevant.

(b) Statement of dispute
If the reinvestigation does not resolve the dispute, the consumer may file a brief statement setting forth the nature of the dispute. The consumer reporting agency may limit such statements to not more than one hundred words if it provides the consumer with assistance in writing a clear summary of the dispute.

(c) Notification of consumer dispute in subsequent consumer reports
Whenever a statement of a dispute is filed, unless there is reasonable grounds to believe that it is frivolous or irrelevant, the consumer reporting agency shall, in any subsequent consumer report containing the information in question, clearly note that it is disputed by the consumer and provide either the consumer's statement or a clear and accurate codification or summary thereof. . . .

Magnuson-Moss Warranty Act (1975)

In response to consumer problems with warranties, particularly automobile and home appliance guarantees, Congress approved this legislation in 1975. It sets standards for product warranties, expands the authority of the FTC to regulate such guarantees, and grants the Commission authority to issue sales rules. Below are extracts from this law.

Magnuson-Moss Warranty Act (15 U.S.C. §§ 2301–2312)

Section 2302. Rules governing contents of warranties
(a) Full and conspicuous disclosure of terms and conditions; additional requirements for contents
In order to improve the adequacy of information available to consumers, prevent deception, and improve competition in the marketing of consumer products, any warrantor warranting a consumer product to a consumer by means of a written warranty shall, to the extent required by rules of the Commission, fully and conspicuously disclose in simple and

readily understood language the terms and conditions of such warranty. Such rules may require inclusion in the written warranty of any of the following items among others:

(1) The clear identification of the names and addresses of the warrantors.

(2) The identity of the party or parties to whom the warranty is extended.

(3) The products or parts covered.

(4) A statement of what the warrantor will do in the event of a defect, malfunction, or failure to conform with such written warranty—at whose expense—and for what period of time.

(5) A statement of what the consumer must do and expenses he must bear.

(6) Exceptions and exclusions from the terms of the warranty.

(7) The step-by-step procedure which the consumer should take in order to obtain performance of any obligation under the warranty, including the identification of any person or class of persons authorized to perform the obligations set forth in the warranty.

(8) Information respecting the availability of any informal dispute settlement procedure offered by the warrantor and a recital, where the warranty so provides, that the purchaser may be required to resort to such procedure before pursuing any legal remedies in the courts.

(9) A brief, general description of the legal remedies available to the consumer.

(10) The time at which the warrantor will perform any obligations under the warranty.

(11) The period of time within which, after notice of a defect, malfunction, or failure to conform with the warranty, the warrantor will perform any obligations under the warranty.

(12) The characteristics or properties of the products, or parts thereof, that are not covered by the warranty.

(13) The elements of the warranty in words or phrases which would not mislead a reasonable, average consumer. . . .

Section 2304. Federal minimum standards for warranties
(a) Remedies under written warranty; duration of implied warranty; exclusion or limitation on consequential damages for breach of written or implied warranty; election of refund or replacement

In order for a warrantor warranting a consumer product by means of a written warranty to meet the Federal minimum standards for warranty—

(1) such warrantor must as a minimum remedy such consumer product within a reasonable time and without charge, in the case of a defect, malfunction, or failure to conform with such written warranty;

(2) notwithstanding section 2308(b) of this title, such warrantor may not impose any limitation on the duration of any implied warranty on the product;

(3) such warrantor may not exclude or limit consequential damages for breach of any written or implied warranty on such product, unless such exclusion or limitation conspicuously appears on the face of the warranty; and

(4) if the product (or a component part thereof) contains a defect or malfunction after a reasonable number of attempts by the warrantor to remedy defects or malfunctions in such product, such warrantor must permit the consumer to elect either a refund for, or replacement without charge of, such product or part (as the case may be). The Commission may by rule specify for purposes of this paragraph, what constitutes a reasonable number of attempts to remedy particular kinds of defects or malfunctions under different circumstances. If the warrantor replaces a component part of a consumer product, such replacement shall include installing the part in the product without charge.

(b) Duties and conditions imposed on consumer by warrantor

(1) In fulfilling the duties under subsection (a) of this section respecting a written warranty, the warrantor shall not impose any duty other than notification upon any consumer as a condition of securing remedy of any consumer product which malfunctions, is defective, or does not conform to the written warranty, unless the warrantor has demonstrated in a rulemaking proceeding, or can demonstrate in an administrative or judicial enforcement proceeding (including private enforcement), or in an informal dispute settlement proceeding, that such a duty is reasonable.

(2) Notwithstanding paragraph (1), a warrantor may require, as a condition to replacement of, or refund for, any consumer product under subsection (a) of this section, that such consumer product shall be made available to the warrantor free and clear of liens and other encumbrances, except as otherwise provided by rule or order of the Commission in cases in which such a requirement would not be practicable.

(3) The Commission may, by rule define in detail the duties set forth in subsection (a) of this section and the applicability of such duties to warrantors of different categories of consumer products with "full (statement of duration)" warranties.

(4) The duties under subsection (a) of this section extend from the warrantor to each person who is a consumer with respect to the consumer product. . . .

Securities Act of 1933

This act is one in a series of investor protection laws approved in the early 1930s. Reformers called for regulations to control fraud and other schemes in the wake of the stock market crash of 1929. It requires the registration of all securities and the regular disclosure of key information. A companion act, the Securities Exchange Act of 1934, created the Securities and Exchange Commission to regulate securities, exchanges, brokers, and over-the-counter sales. Below are extracts from this law.

Securities Act of 1933 (15 U.S.C. § 77)

Section 77e. Prohibitions relating to interstate commerce and the mails
(a) Sale or delivery after sale of unregistered securities
Unless a registration statement is in effect as to a security, it shall be unlawful for any person, directly or indirectly—

> (1) to make use of any means or instruments of transportation or communication in interstate commerce or of the mails to sell such security through the use or medium of any prospectus or otherwise; or

> (2) to carry or cause to be carried through the mails or in interstate commerce, by any means or instruments of transportation, any such security for the purpose of sale or for delivery after sale. . . .

(c) Necessity of filing registration statement

It shall be unlawful for any person, directly or indirectly, to make use of any means or instruments of transportation or communication in interstate commerce or of the mails to offer to sell or offer to buy through the use or medium of any prospectus or otherwise any security, unless a registration statement has been filed as to such security. . . .

Section 77q. Fraudulent interstate transactions
(a) Use of interstate commerce for purpose of fraud or deceit
It shall be unlawful for any person in the offer or sale of any securities by the use of any means or instruments of transportation or communication in interstate commerce or by the use of the mails, directly or indirectly—

> (1) to employ any device, scheme, or artifice to defraud, or

> (2) to obtain money or property by means of any untrue statement of a material fact or any omission to state a material fact necessary in order to make the statements made, in the light of the circumstances under which they were made, not misleading, or

> (3) to engage in any transaction, practice, or course of business which operates or would operate as a fraud or deceit upon the purchaser.

(b) Use of interstate commerce for purpose of offering for sale
It shall be unlawful for any person, by the use of any means or
instruments of transportation or communication in interstate
commerce or by the use of the mails, to publish, give publicity
to, or circulate any notice, circular, advertisement, newspaper,
article, letter, investment service, or communication which,
though not purporting to offer a security for sale, describes
such security for a consideration received or to be received,
directly or indirectly, from an issuer, underwriter, or dealer,
without fully disclosing the receipt, whether past or
prospective, of such consideration and the amount thereof.

**Section 77aa. Schedule of information required in registration
statement**
SCHEDULE A
(1) The name under which the issuer is doing or intends to do
business;

(2) the name of the State . . . under which the issue is organized;

(3) the location of the issuer's principal business office . . . ;

(4) the names and addresses of the directors or persons
performing similar functions, and the chief executive, financial
and accounting officers . . . ;

(5) the names and addresses of the underwriters;

(6) the names and addresses of all persons, if any, owning of
record or beneficially, if known, more than 10 per centum of any
class of stock of the issuer . . . ;

(7) the amount of securities of the issuer held by any person
specified in paragraphs (4), (5), and (6) of this schedule . . . ;

(8) the general character of the business actually transacted or to
be transacted by the issuer;

(9) a statement of the capitalization of the issuer . . . ;

(10) a statement of the securities, if any, covered by options
outstanding or to be created in connection with the security to
be offered . . . ;

(11) the amount of capital stock of each class issued or included in the shares of stock to be offered;

(12) the amount of the funded debt outstanding and to be created by the security to be offered . . . ;

(13) the specific purposes in detail and the approximate amounts to be devoted to such purposes, so far as determinable, for which the security to be offered is to supply funds . . . ;

(14) the remuneration, paid or estimated to be paid, by the issuer or its predecessor, directly or indirectly, during the past year and ensuing year to (a) the directors or persons performing similar functions, and (b) its officers and other persons, naming them wherever such remuneration exceeded $25,000 during any such year;

(15) the estimated net proceeds to be derived from the security to be offered;

(16) the price at which it is proposed that the security shall be offered to the public or the method by which such price is computed . . . ;

(17) all commissions or discounts paid or to be paid, directly or indirectly, by the issuer to the underwriters in respect of the sale of the security to be offered . . . ;

(18) the amount or estimated amounts, itemized in reasonable detail, of expenses, other than commissions . . . ;

(19) the net proceeds derived from any security sold by the issuer during the two years preceding the filing of the registration statement. . . ;

(20) any amount paid within two years preceding the filing of the registration statement or intended to be paid to any promoter and the consideration for any such payment;

(21) the names and addresses of the vendors and the purchase price of any property, or good will, acquired or to be acquired, not in the ordinary course of business, which is to be defrayed

in whole or in part from the proceeds of the security to be offered . . . ;

(22) full particulars of the nature and extent of the interest, if any, of every director, principal executive officer, and of every stockholder holding more than 10 per centum of any class of stock . . . ;

(23) the names and addresses of counsel who have passed on the legality of the issue;

(24) dates of and parties to, and the general effect concisely stated of every material contract made, not in the ordinary course of business . . . ;

(25) a balance sheet as of a date not more than ninety days prior to the date of the filing of the registration statement showing all of the assets of the issuer, the nature and cost thereof, whenever determinable, in such detail and in such form as the Commission shall prescribe (with intangible items segregated), including any loan in excess of $20,000 to any officer, director, stockholder or person directly or indirectly controlling or controlled by the issuer, or person under direct or indirect common control with the issuer. All the liabilities of the issuer in such detail and such form as the Commission shall prescribe . . . ;

(26) a profit and loss statement of the issuer showing earnings and income, the nature and source thereof, and the expenses and fixed charges in such detail and such form as the Commission shall prescribe . . . ;

(27) if the proceeds, or any part of the proceeds, of the security to be issued is to be applied directly or indirectly to the purchase of any business, a profit and loss statement of such business certified by an independent public or certified accountant . . . ;

(28) a copy of any agreement or agreements (or, if identical agreements are used, the forms thereof) made with any underwriter . . . ;

(29) a copy of the opinion or opinions of counsel in respect to the legality of the issue . . . ;

(30) a copy of all material contracts referred to in paragraph (24) of this schedule . . . ;

(31) unless previously filed . . . (a) a copy of its articles of incorporation, with all amendments thereof and of its existing bylaws or instruments corresponding thereto, whatever the name, if the issuer be a corporation . . . and

(32) a copy of the underlying agreements or indentures affecting any stock, bonds, or debentures offered or to be offered. . . .

An Example of an Unfair and Deceptive Practices Law

By the end of the 1970s, almost every state had adopted what are commonly referred to as UDAP (unfair and deceptive acts and practices) or mini-FTC laws. These are state consumer protection laws based, in many cases, on the federal FTC Act. They prohibit unfair and deceptive acts or practices, unfair means of competition, false or misleading acts or practices, and include an itemized list of prohibited practices. Included here is Colorado's consumer protection act. It is but one example of a UDAP statute. Below are extracts from this state statute.

Colorado Revised Statutes: Colorado Consumer Protection Act. §§ 6-1-101 to 6-1-305 (1969)

PART 1. CONSUMER PROTECTION—GENERAL
6-1-103. Attorney general and district attorneys concurrently responsible for enforcement. The attorney general and the district attorneys of the several judicial districts of this state are concurrently responsible for the enforcement of this article. Until the Colorado supreme court adopts a venue provision relating to this article, actions instituted pursuant to this article may be brought in the county where an alleged deceptive trade practice occurred or where any portion of a transaction involving an alleged deceptive trade practice occurred, or in the county where the principal place of business of any defendant is located, or in the county in which any defendant resides.

6-1-105. Deceptive trade practices. (1) A person engages in a deceptive trade practice when, in the course of such person's business, vocation, or occupation, such person:

(a) Knowingly passes off goods, services, or property as those of another;

(b) Knowingly makes a false representation as to the source, sponsorship, approval, or certification of goods, services, or property;

(c) Knowingly makes a false representation as to affiliation, connection, or association with or certification by another;

(d) Uses deceptive representations or designations of geographic origin in connection with goods or services;

(e) Knowingly makes a false representation as to the characteristics, ingredients, uses, benefits, alterations, or quantities of goods, food, services, or property or a false representation . . . ;

(f) Represents that goods are original or new if he knows or should know that they are deteriorated, altered, reconditioned, reclaimed, used, or secondhand;

(g) Represents that goods, food, services, or property are of a particular standard, quality, or grade, or that goods are of a particular style or model, if he knows or should know that they are of another;

(h) Disparages the goods, services, property, or business of another by false or misleading representation of fact;

(i) Advertises goods, services, or property with intent not to sell them as advertised;

(j) Advertises goods or services with intent not to supply reasonably expectable public demand, unless the advertisement discloses a limitation of quantity;

(k) Advertises under the guise of obtaining sales personnel when in fact the purpose is to first sell a product or service to the sales personnel applicant;

(l) Makes false or misleading statements of fact concerning the price of goods, services, or property or the reasons for, existence of, or amounts of price reductions;

(m) Fails to deliver to the customer at the time of an installment sale of goods or services a written order, contract, or receipt setting forth the name and address of the seller, the name and address of the organization which he represents, and all of the terms and conditions of the sale, including a description of the goods or services, stated in readable, clear, and unambiguous language;

(n) Employs "bait and switch" advertising, which is advertising accompanied by an effort to sell goods, services, or property other than those advertised or on terms other than those advertised and which is also accompanied by one or more of the following practices:

(I) Refusal to show the goods or property advertised or to offer the services advertised;

(II) Disparagement in any respect of the advertised goods, property, or services or the terms of sale;

(III) Requiring tie-in sales or other undisclosed conditions to be met prior to selling the advertised goods, property, or services;

(IV) Refusal to take orders for the goods, property, or services advertised for delivery within a reasonable time;

(V) Showing or demonstrating defective goods, property, or services which are unusable or impractical for the purposes set forth in the advertisement;

(VI) Accepting a deposit for the goods, property, or services and subsequently switching the purchase order to higher-priced goods, property, or services; or

(VII) Failure to make deliveries of the goods, property, or services within a reasonable time or to make a refund therefor;

(o) Knowingly fails to identify flood-damaged or water-damaged goods as to such damages;

(p) Solicits door-to-door as a seller, unless the seller, within thirty seconds after beginning the conversation, identifies himself or herself, whom he or she represents, and the purpose of the call;

(p.3) (I) Solicits a consumer residing in Colorado by telephone as a seller, unless the seller, within one minute after beginning the conversation, identifies himself or herself, whom he or she represents, and the purpose of the call or repeatedly causes any telephone to ring or engages any person in a telephone conversation repeatedly or continuously with the intent to annoy, abuse, or harass any person at the telephone number called.

(II) The provisions of this paragraph (p.3) shall not apply to a telephone solicitation between a seller and a consumer if there is an existing business relationship between the seller and the consumer at the time of the telephone solicitation or if the call is initiated by the consumer.

(q) Contrives, prepares, sets up, operates, publicizes by means of advertisements, or promotes any pyramid promotional scheme.

(r) Advertises or otherwise represents that goods or services are guaranteed without clearly and conspicuously disclosing the nature and extent of the guarantee, any material conditions or limitations in the guarantee which are imposed by the guarantor, the manner in which the guarantor will perform, and the identity of such guarantor. Any representation that goods or services are "guaranteed for life" or have a "lifetime guarantee" shall contain, in addition to the other requirements of this paragraph (r), a conspicuous disclosure of the meaning of "life" or "lifetime" as used in such representation (whether that of the purchaser, the goods or services, or otherwise). Guarantees shall not be used which under normal conditions could not be practically fulfilled or which are for such a period of time or are otherwise of such a nature as to have the capacity and tendency of misleading purchasers or prospective purchasers into believing that the goods or services so guaranteed have a greater degree of serviceability, durability, or performance capability in actual use than is true in fact. The provisions of this paragraph (r) apply not only to guarantees but also to warranties, to disclaimer of warranties, to purported guarantees and warranties, and to any promise or representation in the nature of a guarantee or warranty; however, such provisions do not apply to any reference to a guarantee in a slogan or advertisement so long as there is no guarantee or warranty of specific merchandise or other property. . . .

(u) Fails to disclose material information concerning goods, services, or property which information was known at the time of an advertisement or sale if such failure to disclose such information was intended to induce the consumer to enter into a transaction. . . .

An Example of a Blue Sky Law

Almost every state now has what are called blue sky laws, or state statutes protecting investors. These laws require the registration of securities' dealers to conduct business in that state. Kansas was the first state to pass such an investor protection law in 1911. These state laws were the only investor protections available until the 1930s when federal legislation was passed. Below are excerpts from this state statute.

Virginia Code, §§ 13.1-501 to 13.1-527.3 (1950)

Section 13.1-502
Unlawful offers and sales

It shall be unlawful for any person in the offer or sale of any securities, directly or indirectly,

(1) To employ any device, scheme or artifice to defraud, or

(2) To obtain money or property by means of any untrue statement of a material fact or any omission to state a material fact necessary in order to make the statements made, in the light of the circumstances under which they were made, not misleading, or

(3) To engage in any transaction, practice or course of business which operates or would operate as a fraud or deceit upon the purchaser.

Section 13.1-503
Unlawful advice

A. It shall be unlawful for any person who receives directly or indirectly any consideration from another person primarily for advising such other person as to the value of securities or their purchase or sale, whether through the issuance of analyses or reports or otherwise,

1. To employ any device, scheme, or artifice to defraud such other person,

2. To engage in any transaction, practice, or course of business which operates or would operate as a fraud or deceit upon such other person,

3. Acting as principal for his own account, knowingly to sell any security to or purchase any security from a client, or acting as broker for a person other than such client, knowingly to effect any sale or purchase of any security for the account of such client, without disclosing to such client in writing before the completion of such transaction the capacity in which he is acting and obtaining the consent of the client to such transaction. The prohibitions of this subdivision shall not apply to any transaction with a customer of a broker-dealer if such broker-dealer is not acting as an investment advisor in relation to such transaction, or

4. To engage in dishonest or unethical practices as the [State Corporation] Commission may define by rule.

B. In the solicitation of advisory clients, it shall be unlawful for any person to make any untrue statement of a material fact, or omit to state a material fact necessary in order to make the statements made, in light of the circumstances under which they were made, not misleading.

C. Except as may be permitted by rule or order of the Commission, it shall be unlawful for any investment advisor to enter into, extend, or renew any investment advisory contract unless it provides in writing:

1. That the investment advisor shall not be compensated on the basis of a share of capital gains upon or capital appreciation of the funds or any portion of the funds of the client;

2. That no assignment of the contract may be made by the investment advisor without the consent of the other party to the contract; and

3. That the investment advisor, if a partnership, shall notify the other party to the contract of any change in the membership of the partnership within a reasonable time after the change. . . .

Section 13.1-504
Registration

A. It shall be unlawful for any person to transact business in this Commonwealth as (i) a broker-dealer or an agent, except in transactions exempted by subsection B of Section 13.1-514, unless he is so registered under this chapter; or (ii) an investment advisor or investment advisor representative unless he is so registered under this chapter. Notwithstanding the exclusion provided by subdivision (vi) of Section 13.1-501 in the definition of "investment advisor," for the period ending three years from October 11, 1996, the Commission may require the registration as an investment advisor of any federal covered advisor who fails or refuses to pay a fee required by this chapter or rule promulgated pursuant to this chapter; provided, that a delay in payment or an underpayment of a fee that is remedied within fifteen days after receipt of notice from the Commission shall not constitute a failure or refusal to pay the fee.

B. The registration of an agent shall be deemed effective only so long as he is connected with a specified broker-dealer registered under this chapter or a specified issuer. When an agent begins or terminates a connection with a broker-dealer or issuer, both the agent and the broker-dealer or issuer shall promptly notify the Commission. An agent who changes his connection from one broker-dealer or issuer to another shall be required to file a new application for registration and pay the necessary fee in accordance with § 13.1-505. It shall be unlawful for any broker-dealer or issuer to employ an unregistered agent. No agent shall be employed by more than one broker-dealer or issuer. . . .

Section 13.1-516
Misleading filings

It shall be unlawful for any person willfully to make or cause to be made, in any document filed with the Commission or in any proceeding under this chapter, any statement which is, at the time and in the light of the circumstances in which it is made, false or misleading in any material respect.

Section 13.1-520
Crimes

A. Any person who shall knowingly and willfully make, or cause to be made, any false statement in any book of account or other paper of any person subject to the provisions of this chapter, or knowingly and willfully exhibit any false paper to the Commission, or who shall knowingly and willfully commit any act declared unlawful by this chapter, with the intent to defraud any purchaser of securities or user of investment advisory services or with intent to deceive the Commission as to any material fact for the purpose of inducing the Commission to take any action or refrain from taking any action pursuant to this chapter, shall be guilty of a Class 4 felony.

B. Any person who shall knowingly make or cause to be made any false statement in any book of account or other paper of any person subject to the provisions of this chapter or exhibit any false paper to the Commission or who shall commit any act declared unlawful by this chapter shall be guilty of a Class 1 misdemeanor.

C. Prosecutions under this section shall be instituted by indictments in the courts of record having jurisdiction of felonies within three years from the date of the offense.

An Example of a Lemon Law

Consumers expect their new automobiles to work. Nonetheless, there are cars that seem immune to corrective measures. Such cars are called "lemons." There are legal remedies for correcting defective products such as "lemons" but many consumers do not want to pay the expense or endure a lengthy wait for a court case. Instead, many state legislatures have approved super warranties to protect car buyers against "lemons." Below are extracts from one such law.

Florida Statutes, Annotated §§ 681.10–108

681.10 Short title.
This chapter shall be known and may be cited as the "Motor Vehicle Warranty Enforcement Act."

681.101 Legislative intent.
The Legislature recognizes that a motor vehicle is a major consumer purchase and that a defective motor vehicle undoubtedly creates a hardship for the consumer. The Legislature further recognizes that a duly franchised motor vehicle dealer is an authorized service agent of the manufacturer. It is the intent of the Legislature that a good faith motor vehicle warranty complaint by a consumer be resolved by the manufacturer within a specified period of time. It is further the intent of the Legislature to provide the statutory procedures whereby a consumer may receive a replacement motor vehicle, or a full refund, for a motor vehicle which cannot be brought into conformity with the warranty provided for in this chapter. However, nothing in this chapter shall in any way limit or expand the rights or remedies which are otherwise available to a consumer under any other law.

681.103 Duty of manufacturer to conform a motor vehicle to the warranty.
(1)
(a) If a motor vehicle does not conform to the warranty and the consumer first reports the problem to the manufacturer or its authorized service agent during the first 12 months or 12,000 miles, whichever occurs first, of the Lemon Law rights period, the manufacturer or its authorized service agent shall, at no cost to the consumer, make such repairs as are necessary to conform the vehicle to the warranty, irrespective of whether such repairs are made after the expiration of the Lemon Law rights period.

(b) If a motor vehicle does not conform to the warranty and the consumer first reports the problem to the manufacturer or its authorized service agent after the first 12 months or 12,000 miles, whichever occurs first, of the Lemon Law rights period, the manufacturer or its authorized service agent shall make such repairs as are necessary to conform the vehicle to the warranty, irrespective of whether such repairs are made after the expiration of the Lemon Law rights period. The manufacturer may charge for such repairs if the warranty so provides.

(2) Each manufacturer shall provide to its consumers conspicuous notice of the address and phone number for its zone, district, or regional office for this state in the written warranty or owner's manual. By January 1 of each year, each manufacturer shall forward to the Department of Legal Affairs a copy of the owner's manual and any written warranty for each make and model of motor vehicle that it sells in this state.

(3) At the time of acquisition, the manufacturer shall inform the consumer clearly and conspicuously in writing how and where to file a claim with a certified procedure if such procedure has been established by the manufacturer pursuant to s. 681.108 and shall provide to the consumer a written statement that explains the consumer's rights under this chapter. The written statement shall be prepared by the Department of Legal Affairs and shall contain a toll-free number for the division that the consumer can contact to obtain information regarding the consumer's rights and obligations under this chapter or to commence arbitration.

(4) A manufacturer, through its authorized service agent, shall provide to the consumer, each time the consumer's motor vehicle is returned after being examined or repaired under the warranty, a fully itemized, legible statement or repair order indicating any test drive performed and the approximate length of the test drive, any diagnosis made, and all work performed on the motor vehicle including, but not limited to, a general description of the problem reported by the consumer or an identification of the defect or condition, parts and labor, the date and the odometer reading when the motor vehicle was submitted for examination or repair, and the date when the repair or examination was completed.

681.104 Nonconformity of motor vehicles.
(1)
(a) After three attempts have been made to repair the same nonconformity, the consumer shall give written notification, by registered or express mail to the manufacturer, of the need to repair the nonconformity to allow the manufacturer a final attempt to cure the nonconformity. The manufacturer shall have

10 days, commencing upon receipt of such notification, to respond and give the consumer the opportunity to have the motor vehicle repaired at a reasonably accessible repair facility within a reasonable time after the consumer's receipt of the response. The manufacturer shall have 10 days, commencing upon the delivery of the motor vehicle to the designated repair facility by the consumer, to conform the motor vehicle to the warranty. If the manufacturer fails to respond to the consumer and give the consumer the opportunity to have the motor vehicle repaired at a reasonably accessible repair facility or perform the repairs within the time periods prescribed in this subsection, the requirement that the manufacturer be given a final attempt to cure the nonconformity, or in complete absence of a justiciable issue of either law or fact raised by the consumer, does not apply. . . .

(2)
(a) If the manufacturer, or its authorized service agent, cannot conform the motor vehicle to the warranty by repairing or correcting any nonconformity after a reasonable number of attempts, the manufacturer, within 40 days, shall repurchase the motor vehicle and refund the full purchase price to the consumer, less a reasonable offset for use, or, in consideration of its receipt of payment from the consumer of a reasonable offset for use, replace the motor vehicle with a replacement motor vehicle acceptable to the consumer. The refund or replacement must include all reasonably incurred collateral and incidental charges. However, the consumer has an unconditional right to choose a refund rather than a replacement. Upon receipt of such refund or replacement, the consumer, lienholder, or lessor shall furnish to the manufacturer clear title to and possession of the motor vehicle. . . .

(3)
(a) It is presumed that a reasonable number of attempts have been undertaken to conform a motor vehicle to the warranty if, during the Lemon Law rights period, either: 1. The same nonconformity has been subject to repair at least three times by the manufacturer or its authorized service agent, plus a final attempt by the manufacturer to repair the motor vehicle if undertaken as provided for in paragraph (1)(a), and such nonconformity continues to exist; or 2. The motor vehicle has been out of service by reason of repair of one or more

nonconformities by the manufacturer, or its authorized service agent, for a cumulative total of 30 or more days, exclusive of downtime for routine maintenance prescribed by the owner's manual. The manufacturer or its authorized service agent must have had at least one opportunity to inspect or repair the vehicle following receipt of the notification as provided in paragraph (1)(b). The 30-day period may be extended by any period of time during which repair services are not available to the consumer because of war, invasion, strike, fire, flood, or natural disaster. . . .

The Consumers' Right to Choose

Sherman Antitrust Act (1890)

Consumers living in the decades following the Civil War witnessed an extraordinary concentration of economic power in the hands of the few. By eliminating competition, trusts were able to increase prices for their products and limit marketplace choices. In 1890, Congress responded by passing the Sherman Antitrust Act. It declares illegal "every contract . . . or conspiracy, in restraint of trade." Below are extracts from this act.

Sherman Antitrust Act (15 U.S.C. §§ 1–7)

Section 1. Trusts, etc., in restraint of trade illegal; penalty
Every contract, combination in the form of trust or otherwise, or conspiracy, in restraint of trade or commerce among the several States, or with foreign nations, is declared to be illegal. Every person who shall make any contract or engage in any combination or conspiracy hereby declared to be illegal shall be deemed guilty of a felony, and, on conviction thereof, shall be punished by fine. . . .

Section 2. Monopolizing trade a felony; penalty
Every person who shall monopolize, or attempt to monopolize, or combine or conspire with any other person or persons, to monopolize any part of the trade or commerce among the several States, or with foreign nations, shall be deemed guilty of a felony. . . .

Section 7. "Person" or "persons" defined
The word "person," or "persons," wherever used in sections 1 to 7 of this title shall be deemed to include corporations and

associations existing under or authorized by the laws of either the United States, the laws of any of the Territories, the laws of any State, or the laws of any foreign country.

Clayton Antitrust Act (1914)

Dissatisfaction with the Sherman Act led to the passage of the Clayton Act in 1914. It seeks to prevent monopolies as they arise by prohibiting interlocking directorates, tying arrangements, and corporate mergers. It also permits state attorneys general to bring antitrust actions in federal district courts.Below are extracts from the Clayton Antitrust Act.

Clayton Antitrust Act
(15 U.S.C. §§ 12, 13, 14–19, 20, 21, 22–27)

Section 12. Definitions; short title

(a) . . . "Commerce," as used herein, means trade or commerce among the several States and with foreign nations. . . . The word "person" or "persons" wherever used in this Act shall be deemed to include corporations and associations existing under or authorized by the laws of either the United States, the laws of any of the Territories, the laws of any State, or the laws of any foreign country.

(b) This Act may be cited as the "Clayton Act."

Section 14. Sale, etc., on agreement not to use goods of competitor

It shall be unlawful for any person engaged in commerce, in the course of such commerce, to lease or make a sale or contract for sale of goods, wares, merchandise, machinery, supplies, or other commodities, whether patented or unpatented, for use, consumption, or resale within the United States . . . or fix a price charged therefor, or discount from, or rebate upon, such price, on the condition, agreement, or understanding that the lessee or purchaser thereof shall not use or deal in the goods, wares, merchandise, machinery, supplies, or other commodities of a competitor or competitors of the lessor or seller, where the effect of such lease, sale, or contract for sale or such condition, agreement, or understanding may be to substantially lessen competition or tend to create a monopoly in any line of commerce.

Section 18. Acquisition by one corporation of stock of another
No person engaged in commerce or in any activity affecting commerce shall acquire, directly or indirectly, the whole or any part of the stock or other share capital and no person subject to the jurisdiction of the Federal Trade Commission shall acquire the whole or any part of the assets of another person engaged also in commerce or in any activity affecting commerce, where in any line of commerce or in any activity affecting commerce in any section of the country, the effect of such acquisition may be substantially to lessen competition, or to tend to create a monopoly.

No person shall acquire, directly or indirectly, the whole or any part of the stock or other share capital and no person subject to the jurisdiction of the Federal Trade Commission shall acquire the whole or any part of the assets of one or more persons engaged in commerce or in any activity affecting commerce, where in any line of commerce or in any activity affecting commerce in any section of the country, the effect of such acquisition, of such stocks or assets, or of the use of such stock by the voting or granting of proxies or otherwise, may be substantially to lessen competition, or to tend to create a monopoly. . . .

Section 18a. Premerger notification and waiting period
(a) Filing
Except as exempted pursuant to subsection (c) of this section, no person shall acquire, directly or indirectly, any voting securities or assets of any other person, unless both persons (or in the case of a tender offer, the acquiring person) file notification pursuant to rules under subsection (d)(1) of this section and the waiting period described in subsection (b)(1) of this section has expired, if—

(1) the acquiring person, or the person whose voting securities or assets are being acquired, is engaged in commerce or in any activity affecting commerce;

(2)(A) any voting securities or assets of a person engaged in manufacturing which has annual net sales or total assets of $10,000,000 or more are being acquired by any person which has total assets or annual net sales of $100,000,000 or more;

(B) any voting securities or assets of a person not engaged in manufacturing which has total assets of $10,000,000 or more are being acquired by any person which has total assets or annual net sales of $100,000,000 or more; or

(C) any voting securities or assets of a person with annual net sales or total assets of $100,000,000 or more are being acquired by any person with total assets or annual net sales of $10,000,000 or more; and

(3) as a result of such acquisition, the acquiring person would hold—

(A) 15 per centum or more of the voting securities or assets of the acquired person, or

(B) an aggregate total amount of the voting securities and assets of the acquired person in excess of $15,000,000. In the case of a tender offer, the person whose voting securities are sought to be acquired by a person required to file notification under this subsection shall file notification pursuant to rules under subsection (d) of this section.

Section 19. Interlocking directorates and officers
(a)(1) No person shall, at the same time, serve as a director or officer in any two corporations (other than banks, banking associations, and trust companies) that are—(A) engaged in whole or in part in commerce; and

(B) by virtue of their business and location of operation, competitors, so that the elimination of competition by agreement between them would constitute a violation of any of the antitrust laws; if each of the corporations has capital, surplus, and undivided profits aggregating more than $10,000,000 as adjusted pursuant to paragraph (5) of this subsection. . . .

Section 24. Liability of directors and agents of corporation
Whenever a corporation shall violate any of the penal provisions of the antitrust laws, such violation shall be deemed to be also that of the individual directors, officers, or agents of such corporation who shall have authorized, ordered, or done any of the acts constituting in whole or in part such violation. . . .

Robinson-Patman Act (1938)

An amendment to the Clayton Act, the Robinson-Patman Act of 1938 is often called the "chain store act." It prohibits price cutting, by large chains, that eliminates competition from smaller businesses. Under this law, it is illegal for wholesalers to grant discounts to large chains without providing discounts to smaller stores. Below are extracts from this statute.

Robinson-Patman Act (15 U.S.C. § 13)

Section 13. Discrimination in price, services, or facilities

(a) Price; selection of customers

It shall be unlawful for any person engaged in commerce, in the course of such commerce, either directly or indirectly, to discriminate in price between different purchasers of commodities of like grade and quality, where either or any of the purchases involved in such discrimination are in commerce, where such commodities are sold for use, consumption, or resale within the United States or any Territory thereof or the District of Columbia or any insular possession or other place under the jurisdiction of the United States, and where the effect of such discrimination may be substantially to lessen competition or tend to create a monopoly in any line of commerce, or to injure, destroy, or prevent competition with any person who either grants or knowingly receives the benefit of such discrimination, or with customers of either of them: Provided, That nothing herein contained shall prevent differentials which make only due allowance for differences in the cost of manufacture, sale, or delivery resulting from the differing methods or quantities in which such commodities are to such purchasers sold or delivered: Provided, however, That the Federal Trade Commission may, after due investigation and hearing to all interested parties, fix and establish quantity limits, and revise the same as it finds necessary, as to particular commodities or classes of commodities, where it finds that available purchasers in greater quantities are so few as to render differentials on account thereof unjustly discriminatory or promotive of monopoly in any line of commerce; and the foregoing shall then not be construed to permit differentials based on differences in quantities greater than those so fixed and established: And provided further, That nothing herein contained shall prevent persons engaged in selling goods, wares, or merchandise in commerce from selecting their own customers in bona fide transactions and not in restraint of trade: And provided further, That nothing herein contained shall prevent price changes from time to time here in response to changing conditions affecting the market for or the marketability of the goods concerned, such as but not limited to actual or imminent deterioration of perishable goods, obsolescence of seasonal goods, distress sales under court process, or sales in good faith in discontinuance of business in the goods concerned.

(b) Burden of rebutting prima-facie case of discrimination
Upon proof being made, at any hearing on a complaint under this section, that there has been discrimination in price or services or facilities furnished, the burden of rebutting the prima-facie case thus made by showing justification shall be upon the person charged with a violation of this section, and unless justification shall be affirmatively shown, the Commission is authorized to issue an order terminating the discrimination: Provided, however, That nothing herein contained shall prevent a seller rebutting the prima-facie case thus made by showing that his lower price or the furnishing of services or facilities to any purchaser or purchasers was made in good faith to meet an equally low price of a competitor, or the services or facilities furnished by a competitor.

(c) Payment or acceptance of commission, brokerage, or other compensation
It shall be unlawful for any person engaged in commerce, in the course of such commerce, to pay or grant, or to receive or accept, anything of value as a commission, brokerage, or other compensation, or any allowance or discount in lieu thereof, except for services rendered in connection with the sale or purchase of goods, wares, or merchandise, either to the other party to such transaction or to an agent, representative, or other intermediary therein where such intermediary is acting in fact for or in behalf, or is subject to the direct or indirect control, of any party to such transaction other than the person by whom such compensation is so granted or paid.

(d) Payment for services or facilities for processing or sale
It shall be unlawful for any person engaged in commerce to pay or contract for the payment of anything of value to or for the

benefit of a customer of such person in the course of such
commerce as compensation or in consideration for any services
or facilities furnished by or through such customer in
connection with the processing, handling, sale, or offering for
sale of any products or commodities manufactured, sold, or
offered for sale by such person, unless such payment or
consideration is available on proportionally equal terms to all
other customers competing in the distribution of such products
or commodities.

(e) Furnishing services or facilities for processing, handling, etc.
It shall be unlawful for any person to discriminate in favor of
one purchaser against another purchaser or purchasers of a
commodity bought for resale, with or without processing, by
contracting to furnish or furnishing, or by contributing to the
furnishing of, any services or facilities connected with the
processing, handling, sale, or offering for sale of such
commodity so purchased upon terms not accorded to all
purchasers on proportionally equal terms.

(f) Knowingly inducing or receiving discriminatory price
It shall be unlawful for any person engaged in commerce, in the
course of such commerce, knowingly to induce or receive a
discrimination in price which is prohibited by this section.

Section 13a. Discrimination in rebates, discounts, or advertising service charges; underselling in particular localities; penalties
It shall be unlawful for any person engaged in commerce, in the
course of such commerce, to be a party to, or assist in, any
transaction of sale, or contract to sell, which discriminates to his
knowledge against competitors of the purchaser, in that, any
discount, rebate, allowance, or advertising service charge is
granted to the purchaser over and above any discount, rebate,
allowance, or advertising service charge available at the time of
such transaction to said competitors in respect of a sale of goods
of like grade, quality, and quantity; to sell, or contract to sell,
goods in any part of the United States at prices lower than those
exacted by said person elsewhere in the United States for the
purpose of destroying competition, or eliminating a competitor
in such part of the United States; or, to sell, or contract to sell,
goods at unreasonably low prices for the purpose of destroying
competition or eliminating a competitor.

Any person violating any of the provisions of this section shall, upon conviction thereof, be fined not more than $5,000 or imprisoned not more than one year, or both.

Remarks by Robert Pitofsky, Chairman, Federal Trade Commission

In 1911, the Supreme Court broke up the nation's most notorious trust, Standard Oil, but it also ruled that not every contract "in restraint of trade" is illegal. It is the unreasonable practices that violate antitrust laws. Regulators and the courts are to apply a "rule of reason," to weigh the effects on competition in an antitrust case. In this article, the chair of the Federal Trade Commission discusses two recent mergers and what actions his agency took. In the proposed merger of Staples and Office Depot, the FTC challenged the combination. In the merger of Boeing and McDonnell Douglas, the Commission took no action.

Staples and Boeing: What They Say about Merger Enforcement at the FTC

Prepared Remarks of Robert Pitofsky, chairman, Federal Trade Commission

Presented at Antitrust 1998 (Business Development Associates, The Madison Hotel, Washington, D.C., 23 September 1997)

In the 1990s, the most significant aspect of antitrust enforcement relates to the merger wave and the appropriate response to it.

The merger wave itself is remarkable. In the fiscal year that will end September 30, 1997, there will have been about 3,500 transactions valued at more than $15 million dollars reported to the federal enforcement agencies. That is more than twice as many as just five years ago. One hundred twenty-eight of those transactions were valued at more than $1 billion dollars. By the end of the present calendar year, approximately three quarters of a trillion dollars of assets will have been acquired in mergers and acquisitions reviewed in the United States.

Unlike the conglomerate merger wave of the late 1960s, and the leveraged buyout hostile takeover junk bond activities of the 1980s, this current wave of transactions on the whole does not seem to be motivated nearly as much by financial considerations or stock market manipulation. Rather a larger percentage of these transactions appear to be a response to changes in the world economy. Many are a response to the sharp increase in global competition (pharmaceuticals and auto parts), others to new economic conditions produced by deregulation (telecommunications and electric utilities) and still others to over capacity in some industries and to an effort through mergers to bring supply more in line with demand (defense industries and hospitals).

While a large portion of the mergers in this current wave appear to be motivated by a legitimate response to fast changing business conditions, a larger proportion than in the recent past seem to involve direct competitors. As a result, the threat of increased market power, and abusive effects on consumer welfare, is often present.

As to policy approaches to mergers, the enforcement agencies still rely heavily on the Merger Guidelines first adopted in 1982 and revised several times since. The main difference is that the Guidelines are enforced today more nearly as written, and some of the defenses offered by sponsors of a merger, such as the claim that supply substitution would occur if prices were increased shortly after the merger was completed, are viewed with greater caution. Partly as a result of differences in interpretation of precedent and the guidelines, the antitrust agencies—the Antitrust Division and the Federal Trade Commission—each challenged roughly three times as many mergers in the mid-1990s as each enforcement agency challenged 10 years earlier.

Merger policy was clarified in another respect. The Merger Guidelines were revised in 1997 to make it clear that efficiency claims will be taken into account and, in a close case, may demonstrate that the total competitive effect of a merger will help rather than injure competition. By integrating efficiency analysis more fully into the merger review process, those reviews will be more complicated because of the need to carefully trade off anticompetitive effects derived from increases in market power against procompetitive effects that may result from real and substantial efficiencies. Nevertheless, my view is that by taking both sides of the ledger—the dangers and benefits of a merger—more fully into account, U.S. merger policy overall, despite the costs and increased complexity, is more sensible and balanced.

At the Federal Trade Commission, the two recent merger cases that attracted the most public attention were the challenges to the proposed acquisition by Staples of Office

Depot, and the decision not to challenge Boeing's acquisition of McDonnell Douglas. Merger cases are highly fact intensive and no two cases can really illustrate enforcement approaches; nevertheless, several of the most interesting aspects of current merger review can be discussed in the context of those two proceedings.

1. Staples/Office Depot

The *Staples* case raised a broad range of merger issues, but two of the most important were definition of relevant product market, and how to treat claims of efficiency in defense of a merger. Staples was the second largest office supply super store chain in the United States with approximately 550 retail stores and $4 billion in sales. It proposed to acquire Office Depot, the largest office supply super store chain with over 500 retail outlets and a little over $6 billion in sales. OfficeMax was the only other office supply super store firm in the United States.

a. Relevant Product Market.

The Commission's contention was that the sale of consumable office supplies (i.e. not durables like computers or office furniture) through office supply super stores was a separate relevant product market. The Commission conceded that office supply products like paper, pens, file folders and post-it notes were widely available through many outlets and did not vary in quality depending on the outlet where these supplies were purchased. On the other hand it contended that in appearance, size, format, pricing and range of inventory, these super stores were far different from small independent stationery stores and even large retailers like Wal Mart [sic] and K Mart that carried such supplies but in a different format and inventory. In effect the Commission argued that office supply super stores are to small office supply outlets as super market food chains are to independent groceries and commercial banks are to other sources of credit and financial services and therefore were properly viewed as a separate product market.

The argument about anticompetitive effect in *Staples* turned on a single overwhelming fact: prices of office supplies could be shown on average to be substantially higher in cities where only one office supply super store chain was located than where two super store chains competed, and even higher than in cities where the three super store chains all faced each other in the market place. Several studies indicated that the difference in price between one chain cities and three chain cities was approximately 13%—an extremely large price difference in retailing where profits and profit margins are usually narrow and volume is great.

Moreover, these differences persisted regardless of the presence or absence of other sources of office supplies like mail order, price clubs, large wholesalers, and independent stationers. The Commission's case was aided by the fact that the price differences to some extent were confirmed in the companies' own documents, leading the companies to characterize the cities with a single super store chain as "noncompetitive" zones.

Ordinarily in antitrust analysis, market power is measured by examining the characteristics of a given set of products or markets, defining differences between that set and actual or potential competitors, and then predicting that prices could be raised a substantial amount without losing sufficient business to make the price rise unprofitable. In *Staples*, the Commission argued that there were differences in business format between office supply super stores and its rivals, and argued further that prices responded primarily to the presence of other office supply super stores. The Court accepted this view. In effect, it found that the various office supply super stores had raised prices a significant amount over a substantial period of time, in those cities where one chain faced no other super store competition, and had not lost sufficient business to other kinds of rivals to make those price increases unprofitable.

An interesting question for future debate is what to make of this difference in approach between predicting price effects, as opposed to using economic data to show what price effects were across markets. Some have suggested that a useful way to think about the case is to regard all sources of consumable office supplies as rivals but recognize, as a result of the price studies, that the three office supply super stores were the closest substitutes to each other. Proceeding along that line, any prediction that prices would increase as a result of the merger is a variation on a "unilateral effects theory." There surely will be cases in the future where that sort of analysis is the most illuminating. I do not believe, however, that it is essential or appropriate to the *Staples* case, and it is clear that the District Judge, in deciding the case, relied on a more conventional form of analysis.

In my view, the Court appropriately found that office

supply super stores do business in a sufficiently special way that they constitute a separate product market—not a submarket but a market. The econometric evidence showed that there was cross elasticity of demand among customers of the various super stores—hence prices were lowest when super stores met each other in the same geographic market—but there was relatively little cross elasticity between the super stores and other sources of consumable office supplies. In that view, the econometric evidence demonstrated the existence of a separate relevant market, and was not a technique whereby the government could avoid its obligation to demonstrate the existence of a market. And of course once that narrow market was established, market shares were extremely high, including HHI's of 10,000 in those cities where the merger resulted in two office supply super stores combining into one, with the result that the merger was illegal under the most conventional form of merger analysis.

Finally, while the District Court opinion cited the Supreme Court's *Brown Shoe* opinion at several critical points and even cited the *Brown Shoe* set of factors for determining relevant product market, it is clear from reading the entire opinion that the critical factor in the Court's view was high cross elasticity of demand between office supply super stores, and low cross elasticity of demand between super stores and other sources of consumable office supplies—not the factors cited in *Brown Shoe* and sometimes criticized as only marginally relevant. I believe the Court took what is best in *Brown Shoe* and applied it in a sensible way to a kind of data rarely available when *Brown Shoe* was decided.

Because of the vast increase in the availability of data as a result of the computerization of the business world, it almost certainly will be true that the kind of price comparisons across markets, both product and geographic, that was accomplished in the *Staples* case will be available to enforcement agencies in the future. Will parties in future litigation usually have such a rich source of economic data about prices and price elasticity as in *Staples*? Almost certainly not. When such data is available, however, it surely offers a more reliable description of the "competitive arena" in which rivalry occurs than we have sometimes seen in past merger cases.

b. Efficiency Analysis.
Staples contention throughout the litigation was that even if

prices might rise slightly as a result of the merger in some markets, those price increases resulting from market power would be overwhelmed by the substantial efficiencies that would be generated by the combination of firms. The Court could have disposed of that argument by concluding that the Supreme Court allows District Judges no authority to balance efficiency claims against market power effects, citing the 1967 decision in *FTC v. Procter & Gamble Co.* to the effect that "possible economies cannot be used as a defense to illegality in Section 7 merger bases."

The District Court instead noted that the revised DOJ-FTC Merger Guidelines now allow limited scope for efficiency claims, and examined the efficiency issue as several district court judges have done in recent years.

There is little question in my mind that debate over the existence and magnitude of efficiencies associated with a merger will become an important element of future merger review and merger enforcement.

Staples pointed to many efficiencies as a result of the combination of Staples and Office Depot stores, but the principal one was that the combined firm would have augmented purchasing power and could extract better prices from its various vendors. The District Court rejected the efficiency claims essentially on two grounds. First, it found that the claims were not based on "creditable evidence," and appeared to be grossly exaggerated. For example, it noted that the cost savings estimate submitted to the Court exceeded by almost 500% the figures presented to the Boards of Directors of the two firms when they approved the transaction less than a year earlier. More important, the Court noted that the efficiencies were not merger specific. Both parties to the merger were expanding rapidly by opening new stores, as many as 100 or 150 new stores per year for each, so that increased buying power, even assuming it could be used to extract better prices from vendors, would have occurred as a result of internal expansion in any event. If there was an efficiency, it involved moving to a larger enterprise immediately rather than over a period of 3 or 4 years, but those efficiencies would have been temporary and declining in significance. The merger, on the other hand, and its anticompetitive effects, would have been permanent.

I would have added two less significant points in addressing the efficiency issue. First, the anticompetitive effect was so great (13% at retail in many markets), and the creditable efficiencies so modest, that the efficiencies couldn't possibly lead overall to consumer benefits. Second, in cities where Staples and Office Depot operated, but OfficeMax was not present, the merger would have led to monopoly or near monopoly. In those circumstances, the view of the new merger guidelines, and the appropriate approach in my view, is that efficiencies cannot trump anticompetitive effects. Efficiencies should turn the tide in the marginal case, for example, where a merger reduces players in a properly defined relevant market from five to four, but except in extremely rare circumstances should not be a justification for monopoly.

2. Boeing

Despite the enormous amount of public attention paid to Boeing's acquisition of McDonnell Douglas, the FTC's decision not to challenge the transaction broke no new ground. As many have noted, the proposed merger on its face did appear to raise serious antitrust concerns in connection with the commercial aircraft sector because Boeing accounts for roughly 60% of the sales of large commercial aircraft and McDonnell Douglas, while its market share was slightly below 5%, was a non-failing direct competitor. Airbus Industrie was the only other significant rival and barriers to entry were exceptionally high.

The critical question under U.S. law was whether Douglas Aircraft, McDonnell Douglas' commercial arm, had prospects of playing a significant competitive role in the commercial aircraft market in the future. Had the Commission elected to challenge the transaction, it would have found itself in court facing the virtually unanimous testimony of about 40 purchasers of aircraft that Douglas' prospects for future aircraft sales were close to zero. In a sense the merger did not reduce existing players from three to two; rather the market already consisted of only two significant players. Moreover, the Commission staff's unusually extensive investigation failed to turn up any evidence that McDonnell Douglas could be expected rationally to invest the vast amounts necessary to create even the possibility that it could turn itself around, nor was there any other player in the market ready to purchase all or part of Douglas and compete in the future. Following the teaching of *General Dynamics*—that future market potential is a critical factor rather than past market shares—the Commission had little basis to mount a challenge.

The proposed merger attracted enormous worldwide attention because the European Commission, in interpreting its antitrust laws, took the view that the acquisition was anticompetitive in the commercial aircraft sector and extracted various concessions from Boeing before clearing the deal. Many factors contributed to this divergence of view between the U.S. and the EC, and I do not propose to discuss all of them here. I would offer one thought in connection with antitrust review of the transaction. Many do not appreciate that antitrust authorities in Brussels and in Washington are enforcing two different statutes with modestly different emphases. In Europe, the concern is with mergers that increase the leverage that can be exercised by a dominant firm and the possible impact of the merger on competitors. That is not an approach that was conjured up by the European Commission in order to block the Boeing transaction but rather was reflected in the *de Havilland* decision some 6 years ago. In that case, the European Commission challenged the combination of French, Italian and Canadian manufacturers of commuter aircraft whose market shares increased from 46 to 63%, and it was concluded the higher market shares would give the combined firms advantages in pricing flexibility (for example, the ability to offer a joint price on a wider range of models) and the ability to offer a wider range of product models with similar technology (which could make switches to other suppliers more expensive). Several of the "anticompetitive effects" identified by the EC in that case would not be given much weight in an American court; indeed, they might be regarded today as an efficiency rather than an anticompetitive effect.

But the precedent obviously would influence European enforcement. In the United States, the emphasis is less on competitors and "competitive leverage," and more on the effect of a merger on future prices. As a result, Douglas' future potential as a viable competitor is critical since the merger would only have a future substantial effect if Douglas, standing alone or in the hands of a different purchaser than Boeing, would be likely to be an effective competitor. That too is not a limit on enforcement dreamed up by the FTC in order to clear the Boeing transaction, but is rooted in many decisions, including *General Dynamics*, decided over 20 years ago.

This is not the place to explore all the differences in

European and U.S. merger enforcement that led to different attitudes in reviewing the Boeing transaction, but only to note that, to some extent, those differences might be explained by the different statutes, precedent and enforcement authority of the two jurisdictions.
[Footnotes omitted]

Directory of Agencies and Organizations

"Pecuniary Truth:
Truth is what sells.
Truth is what you want people to believe.
Truth is that which is not legally false."
—Henry Jules

The following agencies and organizations are involved in some way in consumer protection. They may be federal enforcement bodies, such as the Federal Bureau of Investigation or the Federal Trade Commission; state agencies, such as the Washington State Attorney General's Office; or local agencies, such as the City of Detroit's Department of Consumer Affairs. Most of the government bodies provide consumer information. Some investigate or mediate individual complaints.

Private organizations also provide information, mediate complaints, or advocate before Congress or federal agencies for consumer protections. These include Better Business Bureaus across the country, membership organizations like the American Association of Retired Persons (AARP), and groups like the National Fraud Information Center of the National Consumers League.

Although we have tried to prepare a comprehensive list of consumer protection agencies and organizations at all levels, this information changes rapidly. Wherever possible, fax, TDD (Telecommunications Device for the Deaf) numbers, and Website addresses have been included with mail addresses and telephone numbers.

Selected Federal Agencies

Federal laws (see Chapter 4 for more details) seek to protect consumers in the marketplace. There are both civil and criminal statutes, and different agencies may have primary jurisdiction over the distinct laws. Some agencies also serve as complaint handlers for goods and services purchased by consumers. Others solely investigate and enforce laws for the public at large. Many agencies, such as the Consumer Information Center, the Federal Trade Commission, and the Food and Drug Administration, provide alerts and information about consumer frauds and abuses. These may be in the form of fact sheets, booklets, or other printed and electronic formats.

Most federal agencies are now accessible on the Internet, with both Websites and/or e-mail addresses. In many cases, their consumer publications can be downloaded from the Internet. The Uniform Resource Locators (URLs) for these sites are listed along with agency telephone numbers and street addresses. If you need further help in contacting an agency, you may call the Federal Information Center (FIC) (800) 688-9889 (toll-free).

Commodity Futures Trading Commission (CFTC)
1155 21st Street, N.W.
Washington, DC 20581
(202) 418-5506 (complaints)
(202) 418-5080 (information)
TDD: (202) 418-5514 (complaints)
TDD: (202) 418-5515 (information)
Website: http://www.cftc.gov

The CFTC oversees the trading of futures (commodities like pork bellies, corn, and oil as well as stock indices and other items) and options on various exchanges across the country. The Division of Enforcement, the agency's law enforcement arm, investigates fraudulent solicitations, churning, selling illegal commodity options, price manipulation, and other violations of federal commodities laws.

Consumer Information Center (CIC)
Consumer Information Catalog
Pueblo, CO 81009

(719) 948-4000
Website: http://www.pueblo.gsa.gov
   (access to the catalog and full text of all publications)

Although the CIC is not a consumer protection agency, it publishes the Consumer Information Catalog listing more than 200 free and low-cost government booklets on a wide variety of topics, including consumer protection. For a free copy of the catalog, write to the address above or visit the CIC Website.

Consumer Product Safety Commission (CPSC)
Washington, DC 20207
(800) 638-2772 (toll-free hotline)
TDD: (800) 638-8270 (toll-free hotline)
E-mail: info@cpsc.gov
Website: http://www.cpsc.gov

Congress created the CPSC to "protect the public against unreasonable risks of injuries and deaths associated with consumer products." This agency has a hotline to report hazardous products and publishes consumer information on unsafe products.

Department of Agriculture (USDA)
Food Safety and Inspection Service (FSIS)
FSIS Food Safety Education and Communications Staff
Department of Agriculture
Room 1175–South Building
1400 Independence Avenue, S.W.
Washington, DC 20250
(202) 720-7943
(800) 535-4555 (toll-free hotline)
Fax: (202) 720-1843
Website: http://www.usda.gov/fsis

The FSIS enforces the Meat Inspection and Poultry Products Inspection Acts. It inspects meat and poultry slaughterhouses and tests for the presence of disease-causing microorganisms.

Department of Justice (DOJ)
Tenth & Constitution Avenue, N.W.
Washington, DC 20530
(202) 514-2000
Website: http://www.usdoj.gov

The Justice Department is the nation's law firm with thousands of lawyers, investigators, and agents spread throughout the country. This agency investigates and prosecutes crime, assures competition in the marketplace, and litigates on behalf of the federal government. One of the largest DOJ agencies is the Federal Bureau of Investigation (FBI).

Department of Transportation (DOT)
400 Seventh Street, S.W.
Washington, DC 20590
(202) 366-4000
(800) 322-7873 (toll-free hotline for
  Federal Aviation Administration)
(800) 424-9393 (toll-free auto safety hotline
  for National Highway Traffic Safety Administration)
Website: http://www.usdot.gov

The DOT is responsible for safety on the nation's airlines, and in automobiles, buses, trains, and other forms of transportation.

Federal Bureau of Investigation (FBI)
Department of Justice
Washington, DC 20535
(202) 324-3000
Website: http://www.fbi.gov

Federal Trade Commission (FTC)
Correspondence Branch
Sixth & Pennsylvania Avenue, N.W.
Washington, DC 20580

Written complaints only
Public Reference Section
Sixth & Pennsylvania Avenue, N.W., Room 130
Washington, DC 20580
(202) 326-2222 (publications)
Website: http://www.ftc.gov

Created in 1914, the FTC seeks to prevent consumer deception and abuse in the marketplace. It develops standards for consumer products and services ranging from advertising substantiation to Zoysia grass and enforces these through civil actions. The FTC does not represent individual consumers. It also publishes hundreds of consumer guides (see Chapter 6 for a partial listing). There are regional FTC offices listed in local telephone directories.

Food and Drug Administration (FDA)
Consumer Affairs

Food and Drug Administration (HFE-88)
Department of Health and Human Services
5600 Fishers Lane, Room 16–75
Rockville, MD 20857
(301) 443-3170 or
(800) 532-4440 (toll-free nationwide)
Website: http://www.fda.gov

The FDA, part of the Department of Health and Human Services (HHS), is the federal agency charged with setting safety and effectiveness standards for food, food additives, drugs, cosmetics, and medical devices. Congress created the FDA in the 1930s. To find the nearest FDA office, look in your telephone directory under "U.S. Government, Health and Human Services Department, Food and Drug Administration." If it does not appear there, call the Federal Information Center at (800) 688-9889.

Postal Inspection Service
Chief Postal Inspector
U.S. Postal Service
Washington, DC 20260-2100
(202) 268-2284
Website: http://www.usps.gov/websites/depart/inspect

The Postal Inspection Service is the law enforcement arm of the U.S. Postal Service. It investigates mail fraud and other crimes, and provides consumer information on mail fraud.

Securities and Exchange Commission (SEC)
Office of Investor Education and Assistance
450 Fifth Street, N.W.
Washington, DC 20549
(202) 942-7040
(800) 733-0330 (toll-free for information and
    to order publications)
Fax: (202) 942-9634
E-mail: help@sec.gov
Website: http://www.sec.gov

This agency administers federal laws designed to protect investors in stocks and bonds. Among other things, federal securities laws require the accurate disclosure of financial information by anyone selling securities. The SEC's Office of Investor Education and

Assistance handles individual investor complaints and provides consumer information (see Chapter 6).

National Consumer Organizations

These organizations advocate on behalf of consumers for a safer marketplace and/or provide consumer assistance. Agencies that assist individuals with marketplace problems are identified. Most, though not all, develop and distribute consumer information.

Alliance Against Fraud in Telemarketing (AAFT)
1701 K Street, N.W., Suite 1200
Washington, DC 20006
(202) 835-3323
Fax: (202) 835-3323

The alliance, coordinated by the National Consumers League, is an international coalition to alert potential victims to the threat of telemarketing fraud.

American Association of Retired Persons (AARP)
601 E Street, N.W.
Washington, DC 20049
(202) 434-6030
Website: http://www.aarp.org

AARP advocates on behalf of older consumers and has developed national educational campaigns on topics such as telemarketing and health care fraud.

Call for Action
5272 River Road, Suite 300
Bethesda, MD 20816
(301) 657-8260 (hotline for list of affiliated
    radio and television stations)
Fax: (301) 657-2914
TDD: (301) 657-9462

Call for Action assists consumers in mediating marketplace problems. It is a nonprofit hotline affiliated with radio and television stations across the country. A list of the affiliated radio and television stations is available by contacting the hotline.

Center for Auto Safety (CAS)
2001 S Street, N.W., Suite 410
Washington, DC 20009
(202) 328-7700

The CAS assists consumers with auto-related problems and advocates for auto safety and related issues.

Center for Science in the Public Interest (CSPI)
1875 Connecticut Avenue, N.W., Suite 300
Washington, DC 20009
(202) 332-9110
Fax: (202) 265-4954
E-mail: CSPI@cspinet.org

The CSPI is a nonprofit membership organization that conducts research and develops education and advocacy information on food safety and related issues. It also publishes a newsletter and other consumer information.

Consumers Union (CU)
101 Truman Avenue
Yonkers, NY 10703-1057
(914) 378-2000
Fax: (914) 378-2900

CU researches and tests consumer goods and services and publishes the results in its monthly magazine, Consumer Reports. It also advocates on behalf of consumers.

Council of Better Business Bureaus, Inc. (CBBB)
4200 Wilson Boulevard
Arlington, VA 22203
(703) 276-0100
Fax: (703) 525-8277
E-mail: bbb@bbb.org
Website: http://www.bbb.org

Sponsored by national businesses and local Better Business Bureaus, the Council of Better Business Bureaus coordinates BBB activity, offers a national advertising review program, dispute resolution services, and an advisory service reporting on national charities.

Health Research Group (HRG)
1600 20th Street, N.W.
Washington, DC 20009
(202) 588-1000

HRG advocates for protection against unsafe foods, drugs, and medical devices. It publishes the monthly, *Health Letter,* and other publications.

National Association of Consumer Agency Administrators (NACAA)
1010 Vermont Avenue, N.W., Suite 514
Washington, DC 20005
(202) 347-7395
Fax: (202) 347-2563

NACAA is an association of the administrators of local, state, and federal government consumer protection agencies. This agency provides training, research, and professional publications.

National Consumers League (NCL)
1701 K Street, N.W., Suite 1200
Washington, DC 20006
(202) 835-3323
Fax: (202) 835-0747

Founded in 1899, NCL is the nation's oldest consumer organization. The league is a nonprofit, membership organization working for health, safety, and fairness in the marketplace. Current issue focus includes consumer fraud and food and drug safety. The league also sponsors the National Fraud Information Center.

National Fraud Information Center (NFIC)
P.O. Box 65868
Washington, DC 20035
(800) 876-7060 (toll-free: 9:00 A.M.–5:00 P.M.; TDD available)
Fax: (202) 835-0767
Website: http://www.fraud.org

The NFIC is a national hotline to assist consumers with recognizing and filing complaints about telemarketing and Internet fraud.

State, County, and City Consumer Protection Offices and Local Better Business Bureaus

In addition to federal law, every state has its own consumer protection statute(s). Consumer lawyers frequently refer to these laws as Unfair and Deceptive Acts and Practices (UDAP) statutes. The Federal Trade Commission Act is the model, at least in part, for many of these laws. There are also separate state insurance and securities codes protecting consumers in these transactions.

To enforce these laws and regulations, states, counties, and cities have created a variety of consumer protection agencies. These agencies might do no more than mediate complaints. Most, however, conduct investigations, prosecute or refer offenders for enforcement, promote strong consumer protection, and provide consumer information.

At the state level, the office of the attorney general is normally the chief consumer protection agency. A number of states, including California, Connecticut, Florida, Georgia, Hawaii, Tennessee, and Utah, have created a separate state agency to investigate consumer complaints and provide information. These agencies refer investigations to the attorney general's office for enforcement.

There are also independent state boards that license and set standards for professions and businesses such as physicians, hearing aid sellers, home contractors, and many others. State legislatures created licensure boards to protect public health, safety, and welfare. Space does not permit the inclusion of these boards here.

At the county level, there may be a separate consumer protection office, or this activity could be headquartered in the county prosecutor's office (called a county, district, commonwealth, or state's attorney). Similarly, at the city level, there may be a separate consumer protection office, or the city attorney may have this responsibility.

All of these government agencies can usually be found in the blue pages or government listings in telephone directories. Please note that many city and county consumer agencies have closed their doors in the recent past as a result of budget cutting. Some of the agencies listed here may be closed in the future. Legislatures have also curtailed or closed consumer protection agencies or activities at the state level.

Consumer protection is not for consumers alone. Honest businesses are hurt when dishonest companies defraud consumers. To protect themselves, many local businesses join together to organize Better Business Bureaus (BBBs). These organizations promote ethical advertising and selling practices, resolve marketplace disputes, and publish business and consumer information. These not-for-profit agencies are also listed here. Please be aware that some BBBs serve multistate regions. For example, the Memphis BBB serves parts of both Arkansas and Mississippi, as well as Tennessee.

This list is arranged in alphabetical order by state. Each state listing lists state, county, and city consumer protection agencies with their respective telephone numbers and, where available, fax numbers and Websites. Local BBBs follow the governmental listings, where available.

Alabama

State Offices
Consumer Protection
Consumer Affairs Division
Office of Attorney General
11 South Union Street
Montgomery, AL 36130
(334) 242-7334
(800) 392-5658 (toll-free in Alabama)
Fax: (334) 242-2433
Website: http://www.e-pages.com/aag

Insurance
Department of Insurance
135 South Union Street, Suite 200
Montgomery, AL 36130
(334) 269-3550
Fax: (334) 241-4192

State Securities Agency
Securities Commission
770 Washington Street, Suite 570
Montgomery, AL 36130-4700
(334) 242-2984
(800) 222-1253 (toll-free in Alabama)
Fax: (334) 242-0240

Better Business Bureaus
BBB Birmingham
P.O. Box 55268
Birmingham, AL 35255
(205) 558-2222
Fax: (205) 558-2239
Website: http://www.birmingham-al.bbb.org

BBB Huntsville
P.O. Box 383
Huntsville, AL 35804
(205) 533-1640
Fax: (205) 553-1177
Website: http://www.northalabama.bbb.org

BBB Mobile
100 North Royal Street
Mobile, AL 36602-3295
(334) 433-5494
Fax: (334) 438-3191
Website: http://www.mobile.bbb.org

Alaska

State Offices
Consumer Protection
There is no consumer protection agency at the state level in Alaska.

Insurance
Department of Commerce and Economic Development
Division of Insurance
P.O. Box 110805
Juneau, AK 99811-0805
(907) 465-2515

Division of Insurance
3601 C Street, Suite 1324
Anchorage, AK 99503-5948
(907) 269-7900

State Securities Agency
Department of Commerce and Economic Development
Banking and Securities

P.O. Box 110807
Juneau, AK 99811-0807
(907) 465-2521
Fax: (907) 465-2549
Website: http://www.state.ak.us/local/akpages/Commerce/
bsc.htm

Better Business Bureaus
BBB of Alaska, Inc.
2805 Bering Street, Suite 5
Anchorage, AK 99503
(907) 562-0704
Fax: (907) 562-4061
Website: http://www.alaska.bbb.org

BBB Fairbanks Branch
P.O. Box 74675
Fairbanks, AK 99707
(907) 451-0222
Fax: (907) 451-0228

BBB Kenai Branch
P.O. Box 1229
Kenai, AK 99611
(907) 283-4880
Fax: (907) 283-9486
Website: http://www.kenai.net/bbbk

Arizona

State Offices
Consumer Protection
Office of the Attorney General
1275 West Washington Street, Room 259
Phoenix, AZ 85007
(602) 542-3702
(800) 352-8431 (toll-free in Arizona)
TDD: (602) 542-5002
Fax: (602) 542-4377

Office of the Attorney General
400 West Congress South Building, Suite 315

Tucson, AZ 85701
(602) 628-6504

Insurance
Department of Insurance
2910 North 44th Street
Suite 210
Phoenix, AZ 85018-7256
(602) 912-8444

State Securities Agency
Corporation Commission
Securities Division
1300 West Washington Street, 3rd Floor
Phoenix, AZ 85007
(602) 542-4242
Fax: (602) 594-7470
Website: http://www.state.ccsd.cc.state.az.us

County Offices
Apache County Attorney's Office
P.O. Box 637
St. Johns, AZ 85936
(520) 337-4364, ext. 240
Fax: (520) 337-2427

Cochise County Attorney's Office
P.O. Drawer CA
Bisbee, AZ 85603
(520) 432-9377
Fax: (520) 432-4208

Coconino County Attorney's Office
Coconino County Courthouse
100 East Birch
Flagstaff, AZ 86001
(520) 779-6518
Fax: (520) 779-5618

Gila County Attorney's Office
1400 East Ash Street
Globe, AZ 85501
(520) 425-3231
Fax: (520) 425-3720

Graham County Attorney's Office
Graham County Courthouse
800 West Main
Safford, AZ 85546
(520) 428-3620

Greenlee County Attorney's Office
P.O. Box 1717
Clifton, AZ 85533
(520) 865-4108
Fax: (520) 865-4665

La Paz County Attorney's Office
1320 Kofa Avenue
P.O. Box 709
Parker, AZ 85344
(520) 669-6118
Fax: (520) 669-2019

Mohave County Attorney's Office
315 North 4th Street
P.O. Box 7000
Kingman, AZ 86402-7000
(520) 753-0719
Fax: (520) 753-2669

Navajo County Attorney's Office
P.O. Box 668
Holbrook, AZ 86025
(520) 524-4026
Fax: (520) 524-4244

Pima County Attorney's Office
1400 Great American Tower
32 North Stone
Tucson, AZ 85701
(520) 740-5733
Fax: (520) 791-3946

Pinal County Attorney's Office
P.O. Box 887
Florence, AZ 85232
(520) 868-6271
Fax: (520) 868-6521

Santa Cruz County Attorney's Office
2100 North Congress Drive, Suite 201
Nogales, AZ 85621
(520) 287-2468

Yavapai County Attorney's Office
Yavapai County Courthouse
Prescott, AZ 86301
(520) 771-3344
Fax: (520) 771-3110

Yuma County Attorney's Office
168 South Second Avenue
Yuma, AZ 85364
(520) 329-2270
Fax: (520) 329-2284

City Office
Consumer Affairs Division
Tucson City Attorney's Office
P.O. Box 27210
Tucson, AZ 85726-7210
(520) 791-4886

Better Business Bureaus
BBB Phoenix
4428 North 12th Street
Phoenix, AZ 85014-4585
(900) 225-5222 ($3.80 first 4 minutes, $.95/minute
    thereafter, not to exceed $9.50)
Fax: (602) 263-0997
Website: http://www.phoenix.bbb.org

BBB Tucson
3620 North 1st Avenue, Suite 136
Tucson, AZ 85719
(520) 888-5353
Fax: (520) 888-6262
Website: http://www.tucson.bbb.org

Arkansas

State Offices
Consumer Protection
Office of Attorney General
200 Catlett Prien
323 Center Street
Little Rock, AR 72201
(501) 682-2341
Website: http://www.state.ar.us/ag/ag.html

Insurance
Department of Insurance
1200 West 3rd Street
Little Rock, AR 72201-1904
(501) 371-2600
(800) 852-5494 (toll-free in Arizona)

State Securities Agency
Securities Department
Heritage West Building
201 East Markham, 3rd Floor
Little Rock, AR 72201-1692
(501) 324-9260
Fax: (501) 324-9268

Better Business Bureau
BBB Arkansas
1415 South University
Little Rock, AR 72204
(501) 664-7274
Fax: (501) 664-0024
Website: http://www.arkansas.bbb.org

California

State Offices
Consumer Protection
California Department of Consumer Affairs
400 R Street, Suite 3000
Sacramento, CA 95814
(916) 445-4465

(800) 952-5200 (toll-free in California)
TDD: (916) 322-1700

Bureau of Automotive Repair
California Department of Consumer Affairs
10240 Systems Parkway
Sacramento, CA 95827
(916) 445-1254
(800) 952-5210 (toll-free in California, auto repair only)
TDD: (916) 322-1700

Office of Attorney General
Public Inquiry Unit
P.O. Box 944255
Sacramento, CA 94244-2550
(916) 322-3360
(800) 952-5225 (toll-free in California)
TDD: (916) 324-5564
Website: http://www.caag.state.ca.us

Insurance
Commissioner
Department of Insurance
300 Capitol Mall, Suite 1500
Sacramento, CA 95814
(916) 445-5544
(800) 927-4357 (toll-free in California)

State Securities Agency
Department of Corporations
3700 Wilshire Boulevard, Suite 600
Los Angeles, CA 90010-3001
(213) 736-2741
Fax: (213) 736-2117
Website: http://www.corp.ca.gov

County Offices
Alameda County Consumer Affairs Commission
4400 MacArthur Boulevard
Oakland, CA 94619
(510) 535-6444

Contra Costa County District Attorney's Office
725 Court Street, 4th Floor
P.O. Box 670
Martinez, CA 94553
(510) 646-4500
Fax: (510) 646-2116

Fresno County District Attorney's Office
Business Affairs Unit
1250 Van Ness Avenue, 2nd Floor
Fresno, CA 93721
(209) 488-3156
Fax: (209) 495-1315

Kern County District Attorney's Office
1215 Truxtun Avenue, 4th Floor
Bakersfield, CA 93301
(805) 861-2421
Fax: (805) 861-2797

Los Angeles County Department of Consumer Affairs
500 West Temple Street, Room B-96
Los Angeles, CA 90012
(213) 974-1452

Marin County District Attorney's Office
Consumer Protection Division
Hall of Justice
3501 Civic Center Drive, Room 183
San Rafael, CA 94903
(415) 499-6450
Fax: (415) 499-3719

Mendocino County District Attorney's Office
P.O. Box 1000
Ukiah, CA 95482
(707) 463-4211
Fax: (707) 463-4687

Monterey County District Attorney's Office
Consumer Protection Division
P.O. Box 1369
Salinas, CA 93902

(408) 755-5073
Fax: (408) 755-5608

Napa County District Attorney's Office
Consumer Affairs Division
P.O. Box 720
Napa, CA 94559
(707) 253-4211
Fax: (707) 253-4041

Orange County District Attorney's Office
Consumer/Environmental Protection Unit
405 West 5th Street, Suite 606
Santa Ana, CA 92701
(714) 568-1240
Fax: (714) 568-1250

Riverside County District Attorney's Office
Economic Crime Division
4075 Main Street
Riverside, CA 92501
(909) 275-5400
Fax: (909) 275-5470

Sacramento County District Attorney's Office
Consumer and Environmental Protection Division
P.O. Box 749
Sacramento, CA 95812-0749
(916) 440-6174

San Diego County District Attorney's Office
P.O. Box X-1011
San Diego, CA 92112–4192
(619) 531-3507 (fraud complaint message line)

San Francisco County District Attorney's Office
Consumer Protection Unit
732 Brannan Street
San Francisco, CA 94103
(415) 552-6400 (public inquiries)
(415) 553-1814 (complaints)
Fax: (415) 552-7038

San Joaquin County District Attorney's Office
P.O. Box 990
Stockton, CA 95202
(209) 468-2481
Fax: (209) 468-0314

San Luis Obispo County
Director, Economic Crime Unit
Consumer Fraud Department
County Government Center
1050 Monterey Street, Room 235
San Luis Obispo, CA 93408
(805) 781-5856

San Mateo County District Attorney's Office
Consumer Fraud and Environmental Protection Unit
401 Marshall Street, Hall of Justice and Records
Redwood City, CA 94063
(415) 363-4656
Fax: (415) 363-4873

Santa Barbara County District Attorney's Office
Consumer Protection Unit
1105 Santa Barbara Street
Santa Barbara, CA 93101
(805) 568-2300
Fax: (805) 568-2398

Santa Clara County Consumer Protection Unit
70 West Hedding Street
West Wing, Lower Level
San Jose, CA 95110-1705
(408) 299-4211

Santa Clara County District Attorney's Office
Consumer Fraud Unit
70 West Hedding Street, West Wing
San Jose, CA 95110
(408) 299-8478
Fax: (408) 279-8742

Santa Cruz County District Attorney's Office
Division of Consumer Affairs

701 Ocean Street, Room 200
Santa Cruz, CA 95060
(408) 454-2050
Fax: (408) 454-2227

Solano County District Attorney's Office
Consumer Affairs Unit
600 Union Avenue
Fairfield, CA 94533
(707) 421-6860
Fax: (707) 421-7986

Stanislaus County District Attorney's Office
Consumer Fraud Unit
P.O. Box 442
Modesto, CA 95353-0442
(209) 525-5550
Fax: (209) 525-5545

Ventura County District Attorney's Office
Consumer and Environmental Protection Division
800 South Victoria Avenue
Ventura, CA 93009
(805) 654-3110

Yolo County District Attorney's Office
Special Services Unit—Consumer and Environmental
P.O. Box 245
Woodland, CA 95776
(916) 666-8424
Fax: (916) 666-8423

City Offices
Los Angeles City Attorney's Office
Consumer Protection Division
200 North Main Street
Los Angeles, CA 90012
(213) 485-4515
Fax: (213) 237-0402

Consumer Protection, Fair Housing & Public Rights Unit
1685 Main Street, Room 310
Santa Monica, CA 90401

(310) 458-8336
(310) 458-8370 (Spanish hotline)
Fax: (310) 395-6727

Better Business Bureaus
BBB Bakersfield
705 18th Street
Bakersfield, CA 93301
(805) 322-2074
Fax: (805) 322-8318
Website: http://www.bakersfield.bbb.org

BBB Cypress
6101 Ball Road, Suite 309
Cypress, CA 90630
(900) 225-5222 ($3.80 first 4 minutes, $.95/minute thereafter, not
    to exceed $9.50)
(909) 426-0813 ($2.75 flat rate)
(714) 527-3208
Website: http://www.la.bbb.org

BBB Fresno
2519 West Shaw, #106
Fresno, CA 93711
(209) 222-8111
Fax: (209) 228-6518
Website: http://www.cencalbbb.org

BBB Los Angeles
3727 West Sixth Street, Suite 607
Los Angeles, CA 90020
(900) 225-5222 ($3.80 first 4 minutes, $.95/minute thereafter, not
    to exceed $9.50)
(909) 426-0813 ($2.75 flat rate)
Fax: (213) 251-9984
Website: http://www.la.bbb.org

BBB Oakland
510 16th Street, Suite 550
Oakland, CA 94612-1584
(510) 238-1000
Fax: (510) 238-1018
Website: http://www.oakland.bbb.org

BBB Sacramento
400 S Street
Sacramento, CA 95814-6997
(916) 443-6843
Fax: (916) 443-0376
Website: http://www.sacramento.bbb.org

BBB San Diego
5050 Murphy Canyon, Suite 110
San Diego, CA 92123
(619) 496-2131
Fax: (619) 496-2141
Website: http://www.sandiego.bbb.org

BBB San Mateo
400 South El Camino Real, Suite 350
San Mateo, CA 94402–1706
(650) 696-1240
Fax: (650) 696-1250
Website: http://www.sanmateo.bbb.org

BBB Santa Barbara
P.O. Box 129
Santa Barbara, CA 93101
(805) 963-8657
Fax: (805) 962-8557
Website: http://www.santabarbara.bbb.org

BBB of Southland
P.O. Box 970
Colton, CA 92324
(900) 225-5222 ($3.80 first 4 minutes, $.95/minute thereafter, not
    to exceed $9.50)
(909) 426-0813 ($3 flat rate)
Website: http://www.la.bbb.org

BBB Stockton
11 South San Joaquin Street
Stockton, CA 95202-3202
(209) 948-4880
Fax: (209) 465-6302
Website: http://www.stockton.bbb.org

Colorado

State Offices
Consumer Protection
Office of Attorney General
1525 Sherman Street, 5th Floor
Denver, CO 80203-1760
(303) 866-5189
Website: http://www.state.co.us/gov_dir/dol/index.hm

Insurance
Commissioner of Insurance
1560 Broadway, Suite 850
Denver, CO 80202
(303) 894-7499, ext. 400

State Securities Agency
Division of Securities
1580 Lincoln, Suite 420
Denver, CO 80203-1506
(303) 894-2320
Fax: (303) 861-2126
TDD: (303) 894-7880
Website: http://www.state.co.us/gov_dir/regulatory_dir/
securities_reg.html

County Offices
Archuleta, LaPlata, and San Juan Counties
District Attorney's Office
P.O. Drawer 3455
Durango, CO 81302
(970) 247-8850
Fax: (970) 259-0200

Boulder County District Attorney's Office
P.O. Box 471
Boulder, CO 80306
(303) 441-3700
Fax: (303) 441-4703

Denver District Attorney's Economic Crimes Division
Consumer Services
303 West Colfax Avenue, Suite 1300

Denver, CO 80204
(303) 640-3557 (complaints)
Fax: (303) 640-2592

El Paso and Teller Counties District Attorney's Office
Economic Crime Division
105 East Vermijo, Suite 205
Colorado Springs, CO 80903-2083
(719) 520-6002
Fax: (719) 520-6006

Jefferson and Gilpin Counties
Consumer Fraud Unit
1726 Cole Boulevard
Golden, CO 80401
(303) 271-6944

Pueblo County District Attorney's Office
201 West 8th Street, Suite 801
Pueblo, CO 81003
(719) 583-6030
Fax: (719) 583-6666

Weld County District Attorney's Office
P.O. Box 1167
Greeley, CO 80632
(970) 356-4010
Fax: (970) 352-8023

Better Business Bureaus
BBB Colorado Springs
P.O. Box 7970
Colorado Springs, CO 80933-7970
(719) 636-1155
Fax: (719) 636-5078

BBB Denver
1780 South Bellaire, Suite 700
Denver, CO 80222-4350
(303) 271-6944
Fax: (303) 271-6888
Website: http://www.denver.bbb.org

BBB Fort Collins
1730 South College Avenue, Suite 303
Fort Collins, CO 80525-1073
(970) 484-1348
Fax: (970) 221-1239
Website: http://www.rockymtn.bbb.org

BBB Pueblo
119 West 6th Street, Suite 203
Pueblo, CO 81003-3119
(719) 542-6464
Fax: (719) 542-5229
Website: http://www.pueblo.bbb.org

Connecticut

State Offices
Consumer Protection
Department of Consumer Protection
165 Capitol Avenue
Hartford, CT 06106
(860) 566-2534
(800) 842-2649 (toll-free in Connecticut)
Fax: (860) 566-1531

Antitrust/Consumer Protection
Office of Attorney General
110 Sherman Street
Hartford, CT 06105
(860) 566-5374
Fax: (860) 523-5536
Website: http://www.cslnet.ctstateu.edu/attygenl

Insurance
Department of Insurance
P.O. Box 816
Hartford, CT 06142-0816
(860) 297-3800

State Securities Agency
Department of Banking
260 Constitution Plaza

Hartford, CT 06103
(860) 240-8230
Fax: (860) 240-8295
Website: http://www.state.ct.us/dob/

City Office
Middletown Office of Consumer Protection
City Hall
245 DeKoven Drive
P.O. Box 1300
Middletown, CT 06457
(860) 344-3491
TDD: (860) 344-3521
Fax: (860) 344-0136

Better Business Bureau
BBB Connecticut
Parkside Building
821 North Main Street Ext.
Wallingford, CT 06492-2420
(203) 269-2700
Fax: (203) 269-3124
Website: http://www.connecticut.bbb.org

Delaware

State Offices
Consumer Protection
Consumer Protection Unit
Department of Justice
820 North French Street
Wilmington, DE 19801
(302) 577-3250
Fax: (302) 577-6499
Website: http://www.state.de.us/attgen/index.htm

Insurance
Department of Insurance
P.O. Box 7007
Dover, DE 19903-1507
(302) 739-4251
(800) 282-8611 (toll-free in Delaware)

State Securities Agency
Securities Division
Department of Justice
State Office Building
820 North French Street, 8th Floor
Wilmington, DE 19801
(302) 577-2515
Fax: (302) 655-0576

Better Business Bureau
BBB Wilmington
1010 Concord Avenue
Wilmington, DE 19802
(302) 594-9200
Fax: (302) 594-1052
Website: http://www.wilmington.bbb.org

District of Columbia

Consumer Protection
There is no consumer protection agency in the
District of Columbia at this time.

Insurance
Department of Insurance and Securities Regulation
P.O. Box 37378
Washington, DC 20001
(202) 727-8000, ext. 3007

State Securities Agency
Department of Insurance and Securities Regulation
P.O. Box 37378
Washington, DC 20001
(202) 727-8000
Fax: (202) 727-3351

Better Business Bureau
BBB Metropolitan Washington
1012 14th Street, N.W., 9th Floor
Washington, DC 20005-3410
(202) 393-8000
Fax: (202) 393-1198
Website: http://www.dc.bbb.org

Florida

State Offices
Consumer Protection
Consumer Litigation Section
Office of the Attorney General
110 S.E. 6th Street
Fort Lauderdale, FL 33301
(954) 712-4600
Fax: (954) 712-4658
Website: http://www.legal.firn.edu/

Economic Crimes Division
Office of Attorney General
110 S.E. 6th Street
Fort Lauderdale, FL 33301
(954) 712-4600
Fax: (954) 712-4658

Department of Agriculture and Consumer Services
Division of Consumer Services
407 South Calhoun Street
Mayo Building, 2nd Floor
Tallahassee, FL 32399-0800
(904) 488-2221
(800) 435-7352 (toll-free in Florida)
Fax: (904) 487-4177

Insurance
Department of Insurance
State Capitol
Plaza Level Eleven
Tallahassee, FL 32399-0300
(904) 922-3130
(800) 342-2762 (toll-free in Florida)

State Securities Agency
Comptroller
Division of Securities
The Capitol LL-22
Tallahassee, FL 32399-0350
(850) 488-9805
(800) 372-8792 (toll-free in Florida)
Fax: (850) 681-2428

County Offices
Broward County Consumer Affairs Division
115 South Andrews Avenue, Annex Room A460
Fort Lauderdale, FL 33301
(954) 765-5355
Fax: (954) 765-5199

Dade County Economic Crime Unit
Office of States Attorney
1350 N.W. 12th Avenue, 5th Floor
Graham Building
Miami, FL 33136-2111
(305) 547-0671

Hillsborough County Commerce Dept.
Consumer Protection Unit
P.O. Box 1110
Tampa, FL 33601
(813) 272-6750
Fax: (813) 276-2691

Metropolitan Dade County
Consumer Protection Division
140 West Flagler Street, Suite 902
Miami, FL 33130
(305) 375-4222
Fax: (305) 375-4120

Orange County Consumer Fraud Unit
P.O. Box 1673
Orlando, FL 32802
(407) 836-2490

Palm Beach County
Division of Consumer Affairs
50 South Military Trail, Suite 201
West Palm Beach, FL 33415
(561) 233-4820
Fax: (561) 233-4838

Palm Beach County Citizens Intake
Office of the State Attorney
401 North Dixie Highway, Suite 1600

West Palm Beach, FL 33401
(561) 355-7108
Fax: (561) 355-7192

Pasco County Consumer Affairs Division
Consumer Affairs/Code Compliance Manager
7530 Little Road, Suite 140
New Port Richey, FL 34654
(813) 847-8110
Fax: (813) 847-8969

Pinellas County Office of Consumer Protection
P.O. Box 17268
Clearwater, FL 34622-0268
(813) 464-6129
Fax: (813) 464-6200

City Offices
City of Jacksonville
Division of Consumer Affairs
421 West Church Street, Suite 404
Jacksonville, FL 32202
(904) 630-3667
Fax: (904) 630-3638
Website: http://www.itd.ci.jaxfl.us/consumer/consumer.htm

Lauderhill Consumer Protection Board
Department Secretary
1176 N.W. 42nd Way
Lauderhill, FL 33313
(954) 321-2456
TDD: (954) 321-2455

Better Business Bureaus
BBB Central Florida
1011 North Wymore Road, Suite 204
Winter Park, FL 32789
(407) 621-3300
Fax: (407) 629-9334
Website: http://www.orlando.bbb.org

BBB Clearwater
P.O. Box 7950

Clearwater, FL 34618
(813) 842-5522
Fax: (813) 530-5522
Website: http://www.clearwater.bbb.org

BBB Jacksonville
7820 Arlington Expressway, #147
Jacksonville, FL 32211
(904) 721-2288
Fax: (904) 721-7373
Website: http://www.jacksonville.bbb.org

BBB Pensacola
P.O. Box 1511
Pensacola, FL 32597
(805) 429-0002
Fax: (805) 429-0006
Website: http://www.pensacola.bbb.org

BBB South Florida
2710 Swamp Cabbage Court
Fort Myers, FL 33901-9333
(941) 275-4224
Fax: (941) 275-6710
Website: http://www.miami.bbb.org

BBB St. Lucie
1950 Port St. Lucie Blvd., Suite 211
Port St. Lucie, FL 34952
(561) 337-2083
Fax: (561) 337-2083
Website: http://www.westpalm.bbb.org

BBB West Palm Beach
580 Village Boulevard, Suite 340
West Palm Beach, FL 33409
(561) 686-2200
Fax: (561) 686-2775
Website: http://www.westpalm.bbb.org

Georgia

State Offices
Consumer Protection
Governor's Office of Consumer Affairs
2 Martin Luther King, Jr. Drive, S.E., Suite 356
Atlanta, GA 30334
(404) 656-3790
(800) 869-1123 (toll-free in Georgia)
Fax: (404) 651-9018

Insurance
Department of Insurance
2 Martin Luther King, Jr. Drive
Atlanta, GA 30334
(404) 656-2070

State Securities Agency
Office of the Secretary of State
Division of Securities and Business Regulation
2 Martin Luther King, Jr. Drive
Suite 802, West Tower
Atlanta, GA 30334
(404) 656-3920
Fax: (404) 657-8410
Website: http://www.SOS.State.Ga.US/Securities/

Better Business Bureaus
BBB Albany
204 North Jackson
Albany, GA 31706-3241
(912) 883-0744
Fax: (912) 438-8222

BBB Atlanta
P.O. Box 2707
Atlanta, GA 30301
(404) 688-4910
Fax: (404) 688-8901
Website: http://www.atlanta.bbb.org

BBB Augusta
301 7th Street

P.O. Box 2085
Augusta, GA 30903-2085
(706) 722-1574
Fax: (706) 724-0969
Website: http://www.augusta-ga.bbb.org

BBB Columbus
P.O. Box 2587
Columbus, GA 31901-2137
(706) 324-0712
Fax: (706) 324-2181
Website: http://www.columbus-ga.bbb.org

BBB Macon
277 Martin Luther King Jr. Boulevard, Suite 102
Macon, GA 31201
(912) 742-7999
Fax: (902) 742-8191
Website: http://www.macon.bbb.org

BBB Savannah
6606 Abercorn Street, Suite 108-C
Savannah, GA 31405-5817
(912) 354-7521
Fax: (912) 354-5068
Website: http://www.savannah.bbb.org

Hawaii

State Offices
Consumer Protection
Department of the Attorney General
425 Queen Street
Honolulu, HI 96813
(808) 586-1282

Office of Consumer Protection
Department of Commerce and Consumer Affairs
P.O. Box 3767
Honolulu, HI 96813-3767
(808) 586-2636
Fax: (808) 586-2640

Office of Consumer Protection
Department of Commerce and Consumer Affairs
75 Aupuni Street
Hilo, HI 96720
(808) 974-6230

Office of Consumer Protection
Department of Commerce and Consumer Affairs
P.O. Box 1098
Wailuku, HI 96793
(808) 984-8244

Insurance
Insurance Division
Department of Commerce and Consumer Affairs
250 South King Street, 5th Floor
Honolulu, HI 46813-3614
(808) 586-2790
(800) 586-2790 (toll-free in Hawaii)

State Securities Agency
Commissioner of Securities
Department of Commerce and Consumer Affairs
P.O. Box 40
Honolulu, HI 96810
(808) 586-2744
(808) 586-2740 (Securities Enforcement Unit)
(800) 468-4644 (toll-free in Hawaii)
Fax: (808) 586-2733
Website: http://www.hawaii.gov/icsd/lrb/ph_dcca.htm

Better Business Bureau
First Hawaiian Tower
1132 Bishop Street
Honolulu, HI 96813
(808) 536-6956
Fax: (808) 532-2335
Website: http://www.hawaii.bbb.org

Idaho

State Offices
Consumer Protection
Office of the Attorney General
Consumer Protection Unit
650 West State Street
Boise, ID 83720-0010
(208) 334-2424
(800) 432-3545 (toll-free in Idaho)
Fax: (208) 334-2830
Website: http://www2.state.id.us/ag/index.htm

Insurance
Department of Insurance
700 West State Street
Boise, ID 83720
(208) 334-4320
(800) 721-3272 (toll-free in Idaho)

State Securities Agency
Department of Finance
Securities Bureau
P.O. Box 83720
Boise, ID 83720-0031
(208) 332-8004
Fax: (208) 332-8099
Website: http://www.state.id.us./finance/dof.htm

Better Business Bureaus
BBB Boise
1333 West Jefferson
Boise, ID 83702-5320
(208) 342-4649
Website: http://www.boise.bbb.org

BBB Idaho Falls
1575 South Boulevard
Idaho Falls, ID 83404-5926
(208) 523-9754
Fax: (208) 524-6190
Website: http://www.idahofalls.bbb.org

Illinois

State Offices
Consumer Protection
Consumer Fraud Bureau
Office of the Attorney General
100 West Randolph, 13th Floor
Chicago, IL 60601
(312) 814-3580
(800) 386-5438 (toll-free in Illinois)
TDD: (312) 814-3374
Website: http://www.acsp.uic.edu/~ag/

Carbondale Regional Office
Office of Attorney General
1001 Main Professional Park East
Carbondale, IL 62901
(618) 457-3505
TDD: (618) 457-4421

Champaign Regional Office
Office of Attorney General
34 East Main Street
Champaign, IL 61820
(217) 333-7691 (Voice/TDD)
Fax: (217) 244-0022

Consumer Fraud Bureau
Office of Attorney General
500 South Second Street
Springfield, IL 62706
(217) 782-9020
(800) 252-8666 (toll-free in Illinois)

Insurance
Department of Insurance
320 West Washington Street
Springfield, IL 62767
(217) 782-4515

Department of Insurance
100 West Randolph Street, Suite 15-100
Chicago, IL 60601
(312) 814-2420

State Securities Agency
Illinois Securities Department
Office of Secretary of State
Lincoln Tower, Suite 200
520 South Second Street
Springfield, IL 62701
(217) 782-2256
(800) 628-7937 (toll-free in Illinois)
Website: http://www.sos.state.il.us/depts/securities/sec_
home.html

County Offices
Cook County Office of State's Attorney
Consumer Fraud Division–303
303 Daley Center
Chicago, IL 60602
(312) 345-2400

Madison County Office of State's Attorney
157 North Main, Suite 402
Edwardsville, IL 62025
(618) 692-6280
Fax: (618) 656-7312

City Offices
Chicago Department of Consumer Services
121 North LaSalle Street, Room 808
Chicago, IL 60602
(312) 744-4006
TDD: (312) 744-9385
Fax: (312) 744-9089

City of Des Plaines
Consumer Protection Office
1420 Miner Street
Des Plaines, IL 60016
(847) 391-5006
Fax: (847) 391-5378

Better Business Bureaus
BBB Chicago
330 North Wabash
Chicago, IL 60611

(312) 832-0500 ($3.80/call)
Fax: (312) 832-9985
Website: http://www.chicago.bbb.org

BBB Peoria
3024 West Lake
Peoria, IL 61615-3770
(309) 688-3741
Fax: (309) 681-7290
Website: http://www.peoria.bbb.org

BBB Rockford
810 East State Street, 3rd Floor
Rockford, IL 61104-1001
(815) 963-2222 ($3.80/call)
Fax: (815) 963-0329

Indiana

State Offices
Consumer Protection
Office of Attorney General
Indiana Government Center South, 5th Floor
402 West Washington Street
Indianapolis, IN 46204
(317) 232-6330
(800) 382-5516 (toll-free in Indiana)
Website: http://www.ai.org/hoosieradvocate/index.html

Insurance
Department of Insurance
311 West Washington Street, Suite 300
Indianapolis, IN 46204-2787
(317) 232-2395
(800) 622-4461 (toll-free in Indiana)

State Securities Agency
Office of the Secretary of State
Securities Division
302 West Washington, Room E-111
Indianapolis, IN 46204
(317) 232-6681
Fax: (317) 233-3675
(800) 223-8791 (toll-free in Indiana)

County Office
Marion County Prosecuting Attorney
560 City-County Building
200 East Washington Street
Indianapolis, IN 46204-3363
(317) 327-5338
Fax: (317) 327-5409

Better Business Bureaus
BBB Elkhart
P.O. Box 405
Elkhart, IN 46515-0405
(219) 262-8996
Fax: (219) 262-9884
Website: http://www.elkhart.bbb.org

BBB Evansville
4004 Morgan Avenue, Suite 201
Evansville, IN 47715-2265
(812) 473-0202
Fax: (812) 473-3080
Website: http://www.evansville.bbb.org

BBB Ft. Wayne
1203 Webster Street
Fort Wayne, IN 46802-3493
(219) 423-4433
Fax: (219) 423-3301
Website: http://www.fortwayne.bbb.org

BBB Indianapolis
22 East Washington Street, Suite 200
Indianapolis, IN 46204-3584
(317) 488-2222
Fax: (317) 488-2224
Website: http://www.indianapolis.bbb.org

BBB Merrillville
6111 Harrison Street, Suite 101
Merrillville, IN 46410
(219) 980-1511
Fax: (219) 884-2123
Website: http://www.gary.bbb.org

BBB of Michiana
207 Dixie Way North, Suite 130
South Bend, IN 46637-3360
(219) 277-9121
Fax: (219) 273-6666

Iowa

State Offices
Consumer Protection
Office of Attorney General
1300 East Walnut Street, 2nd Floor
Des Moines, IA 50319
(515) 281-5926
Fax: (515) 281-6771
Website: http://www.state.ia.us/government/ag/index.html

Insurance
Division of Insurance
Lucas State Office Building, 6th Floor
Des Moines, IA 50319
(515) 281-5705

State Securities Agency
Enforcement Section
Securities Bureau
340 East Maple
Des Moines, IA 50319
(515) 281-4441
Fax: (515) 281-6467
Website: http://www.state.ia.us/government/com/ins/
security/security.htm

Better Business Bureaus
BBB Des Moines
505 5th Avenue, Suite 615
Des Moines, IA 50309-2375
(515) 243-8137
Fax: (515) 243-2227
Website: http://www.desmoines.bbb.org

BBB Sioux City
505 6th Street, Suite 417

Sioux City, IA 51101
(712) 252-4501
Fax: (712) 252-0285
Website: http://www.siouxcity.bbb.org

BBB Quad Cities
852 Middle Road, Suite 290
Bettendorf, IA 52722-4100
(319) 355-6344
Fax: (319) 355-0306

Kansas

State Offices
Consumer Protection
Office of Attorney General
301 West 10th
Kansas Judicial Center
Topeka, KS 66612-1597
(913) 296-3751
(800) 432-2310 (toll-free in Kansas)
Fax: (913) 291-3699
Website: http://www.lawlib.wuacc.edu/ag/homepage.html

Insurance
Department of Insurance
420 S.W. 9th Street
Topeka, KS 66612
(913) 296-7829
(800) 432-2484 (toll-free in Kansas)

State Securities Agency
Office of the Securities Commissioner
618 South Kansas Avenue, 2nd Floor
Topeka, KA 66603-3804
(913) 296-3307
Fax: (913) 296-6872
Website: http://www.cjnetworks.com/~ksecom

County Offices
Johnson County District Attorney's Office
Consumer Fraud Division
Johnson County Courthouse

P.O. Box 728
Olathe, KS 66051
(913) 764-8484, ext. 5287
Fax: (913) 791-5011

Sedgewick County District Attorney's Office
Consumer Fraud & Economic Crime
535 Main Street
Wichita, KA 67203
(316) 383-7921
Fax: (316) 383-7266

City Office
City Attorney's Office
215 S.E. 7th Street
Topeka, KS 66603
(913) 368-3885
Fax: (913) 368-3901

Better Business Bureaus
BBB Topeka
501 S.E. Jefferson, Suite 24
Topeka, KS 66607-1190
(785) 232-0454
Fax: (785) 232-9677
Website: http://www.topeka.bbb.org

BBB Wichita
P.O. Box 11707–1190
Wichita, KS 67211
(316) 263-3146
Fax: (316) 263-3063
Website: http://www.wichita.bbb.org

Kentucky

State Offices
Consumer Protection
Office of Attorney General
P.O. Box 2000
Frankfort, KY 40601-2000
(502) 573-2200
Website: http://www.law.state.ky.us/

Consumer Protection Division
Office of Attorney General
107 South 4th Street
Louisville, KY 40202
(502) 595-3262
Fax: (502) 595-4627

Insurance
Department of Insurance
215 West Main Street
Frankfort, KY 40601
(502) 564-6088

State Securities Agency
Department of Financial Institutions
477 Versailles Road
Frankfort, KY 40601
(502) 573-3390
Fax: (502) 573-8787
Website: http://www.dfi.state.Ky.us

Better Business Bureaus
BBB Lexington
410 West Vine Street, Suite 280
Lexington, KY 40507-1616
(606) 259-1008
Fax: (606) 259-1639
Website: http://www.lexington.bbb.org

BBB Louisville
844 South Fourth Street
Louisville, KY 40203-2186
(502) 583-6546
Fax: (502) 589-9940
Website: http://www.ky-in.bbb.org

Louisiana

State Offices
Consumer Protection
Office of Attorney General
P.O. Box 94095
Baton Rouge, LA 70804-9095

(504) 342-9638
Fax: (504) 342-9637
Website: http://www.laag.com/home.cfm

Insurance
Department of Insurance
P.O. Box 94214
Baton Route, LA 70801-9214
(504) 342-1259

State Securities Agency
Securities Commission
Energy Centre
1100 Poydras Street, Suite 2250
New Orleans, LA 70163
(504) 846-6970

County Office
Jefferson Parish District Attorney's Office
Consumer Protection Division
Gretna Courthouse Annex, 5th Floor
Gretna, LA 70053
(504) 364-3644
Fax: (504) 364-3636

Better Business Bureaus
BBB Alexandria
1605 Murray Street, Suite 117
Alexandria, LA 71301-6875
(318) 473-4494
Fax: (318) 473-8906
Website: http://www.alexandria-la.bbb.org

BBB Baton Rouge
2055 Wooddale Boulevard
Baton Rouge, LA 70806–1546
(504) 926-3010
Fax: (504) 924-8040
Website: http://www.batonrouge.bbb.org

BBB Houma
3038 Park, N.E., Suite 204
Houma, LA 70360-6354

(504) 868-3456
Fax: (504) 876-7664

BBB Lafayette
P.O. Box 30297
Lafayette, LA 70593-0297
(318) 981-3497
Fax: (318) 981-7559
Website: http://www.lafayette.bbb.org

BBB Lake Charles
P.O. Box 7314
Lake Charles, LA 70606-7314
(318) 478-6253
Fax: (318) 474-8981
Website: http://www.lakecharles.bbb.org

BBB Monroe
141 Desiard Street, Suite 808
Monroe, LA 71201-7380
(318) 387-4600
Fax: (318) 361-0461
Website: http://www.monroe.bbb.org

BBB New Orleans
1539 Jackson Avenue, Suite 400
New Orleans, LA 70130-5843
(504) 581-6222
Fax: (504) 524-9110
Website: http://www.neworleans.bbb.org

BBB Shreveport
3612 Youree Drive
Shreveport, LA 71105-2122
(318) 861-6417
Fax: (318) 861-6426
Website: http://www.shreveport.bbb.org

Maine

State Offices
Consumer Protection
Consumer and Antitrust Division

Office of Attorney General
State House Station No. 6
Augusta, ME 04333
(207) 626-8849
Website: http://www.state.me.us/ag/homepage.htm

Insurance
Bureau of Insurance
State House Station No. 34
Augusta, ME 04333-0034
(207) 624-8475
(800) 300-5000 (toll-free in Maine)

State Securities Agency
Department of Professional & Financial Regulation
Bureau of Banking
Securities Division
State House Station No. 121
Augusta, ME 04333-0121
(207) 624-8551
Fax: (207) 624-8590
Website: www.state.me.us/pfr/sec/sechome2-htm

Better Business Bureau
BBB Portland
812 Stevens Avenue
Portland, ME 04103-2648
(207) 878-2715
Fax: (207) 797-5818
Website: http://www.bosbbb.org

Maryland

State Offices
Consumer Protection
Office of Attorney General
200 St. Paul Place, 16th Floor
Baltimore, MD 21202-2021
(410) 528-8662 (consumer hotline)
TDD: (410) 576-6372 (Baltimore area)
Fax: (410) 576-6566
Website: http://www.oag.state.md.us/

Eastern Shore Branch Office. Consumer Protection Division
Office of Attorney General
201 Baptist Street, Suite 30
Salisbury, MD 21801-4976
(410) 543-6642

Consumer Protection Division, Office of Attorney General
138 East Antietam Street, Suite 210
Hagerstown, MD 21740-5684
(301) 791-4780

Insurance
Insurance Administration
501 St. Paul Place, 7th Floor
Baltimore, MD 21202
(410) 333-1782
(800) 492-6116 (toll-free in Maryland)

State Securities Agency
Office of the Attorney General
Division of Securities
200 St. Paul Place, 20th Floor
Baltimore, MD 21202
(410) 576-6360
Fax: (410) 576-6532

County Offices
Howard County Office of Consumer Affairs
6751 Columbia Gateway Drive
Columbia, MD 21046
(410) 313-6420
Fax: (410) 313-6424
TDD: (410) 313-6401

Montgomery County Office of Consumer Affairs
100 Maryland Avenue, 3rd Floor
Rockville, MD 20850
(301) 217-7373
Fax: (301) 217-7367

Prince George's County Office of Business
and Regulatory Affairs
County Administration Building, Suite L15

Upper Marlboro, MD 20772
(301) 952-5323
Fax: (301) 952-4709
TDD: (301) 952-5167

Better Business Bureau
BBB Baltimore
2100 Huntingdon Avenue
Baltimore, MD 21211-3215
(900) 225-5222 ($.95/min.)
Fax: (410) 347-3936
Website: http://www.baltimore.bbb.org

Massachusetts

State Offices
Consumer Protection
Consumer and Antitrust Division
Department of Attorney General
One Ashburton Place
Boston, MA 02108
(617) 727-2200
Fax: (617) 727-5765
Website: http://www.magnet.state.ma.us/ag/

Western Massachusetts Consumer Protection Division
Department of Attorney General
436 Dwight Street
Springfield, MA 01103
(413) 784-1240
Fax: (413) 784-1244

Executive Office of Consumer Affairs and Business Regulation
One Ashburton Place
Boston, MA 02108
(617) 727-7755 (information and referral only)
Fax: (617) 227-6094

Insurance
Division of Insurance
470 Atlantic Avenue, 6th Floor
Boston, MA 02210-2223
(617) 521-7777

State Securities Agency
Secretary of the Commonwealth
Securities Division
One Ashburton Place, Room 1701
Boston, MA 02108
(617) 727-3548
(800) 269-5428 (toll-free in Massachusetts)
Fax: (617) 248-0177

County Offices
Consumer Council of Worcester County
484 Main Street, 2nd Floor
Worcester, MA 01608-1690
(508) 754-1176
Fax: (508) 754-0203

Hampshire County District Attorney's Office
Consumer Fraud Prevention
1 Court Square
Northampton, MA 01060
(413) 586-9225
Fax: (413) 584-3635

North Western District Attorney's Consumer Protection Division
238 Main Street
Greenfield, MA 01301
(413) 774-5102
Fax: (413) 773-3278

City Offices
Cambridge Consumers' Council
831 Massachusetts Avenue
Cambridge, MA 02139
(617) 349-6152
Fax: (617) 349-6148
Website: http://www.ci.cambridge.ma.us/city-hall/consume.
html

Mayor's Office of Consumer Affairs and Licensing
Boston City Hall, Room 817
Boston, MA 02201
(617) 635-3834
Fax: (617) 635-4174

Better Business Bureaus
BBB Boston
20 Park Plaza, Suite 820
Boston, MA 02116-4344
(617) 426-9000
Fax: (617) 426-7813
Website: http://www.bosbbb.org

BBB Springfield
293 Bridge Street, Suite 320
Springfield, MA 01103-1402
(413) 734-3114
Fax: (413) 734-2006
Website: http://www.springfield-ma.bbb.org

BBB Worcester
P.O. Box 16555
Worchester, MA 01608-1900
(508) 755-2548
Fax: (508) 754-4158
Website: http://www.worcester.bbb.org

Michigan

State Offices
Consumer Protection
Consumer Protection Division
Office of Attorney General
P.O. Box 30213
Lansing, MI 48909
(517) 373-1140
Fax: (517) 335-1935
Website: http://www.state.mi.us/

Insurance
Insurance Bureau
611 West Ottawa Street, 2nd Floor North
Lansing, MI 48933
(517) 373-0240

State Securities Agency
Department of Consumer and Industry Services
Corporation, Securities and Land Development Bureau

P.O. Box 30222
Lansing, MI 48909-7554
(517) 334-6212
Fax: (517) 334-6223
Website: http://www.cis.state.mi.us

County Offices
Bay County Consumer Protection Unit
Bay County Building
Bay City, MI 48708-5994
(517) 895-4139

Consumer Protection Department Macomb County
Office of the Prosecuting Attorney
Macomb Court Building, 6th Floor
Mt. Clemens, MI 48043
(810) 469-5350
Fax: (810) 469-5609
TDD: (810) 466-8714

City Office
City of Detroit
Department of Consumer Affairs
1600 Cadillac Tower
Detroit, MI 48226
(313) 224-3508
Fax: (313) 224-2796

Better Business Bureaus
BBB Grand Rapids
40 Pearl, N.W., Suite 354
Grand Rapids, MI 49503
(616) 774-8236
Fax: (616) 774-2014
Website: http://www.grandrapids.bbb.org

BBB Southfield
30555 Southfield Road
Southfield, MI 48076
(248) 644-9100
(248) 644-5026
Website: http://www.detroit.bbb.org

Minnesota

State Offices
Consumer Protection
Consumer Services Division
Office of Attorney General
1400 NCL Tower
445 Minnesota Street
St. Paul, MN 55101
(612) 296-3353
Fax: (612) 296-9663
Website: http://www.ag.state.mn.us

Insurance
Commissioner of Insurance
Department of Commerce
133 East Seventh Street
St. Paul, MN 55101
(612) 296-2488

State Securities Agency
Department of Commerce
133 East Seventh Street
St. Paul, MN 55101
(612) 296-4026
(800) 657-3602 (toll-free in Minnesota)
Fax: (612) 296-2284
Website: http://www.commerce.state.mn.us

County Office
Hennepin County Citizen Information Hotline
Office of the Hennepin County Attorney
C-2000 County Government Center
Minneapolis, MN 55487
(612) 348-4528
Fax: (612) 348-9712

City Office
Minneapolis Department of Licenses & Consumer Services
One C City Hall
Minneapolis, MN 55415
(612) 673-2080
Fax: (612) 673-3399

Better Business Bureau
BBB Minnesota
2706 Gannon Road
St. Paul, MN 55116-2600
(612) 699-1111
Fax: (612) 699-7665
Website: http://www.mnd.bbb.org

Mississippi

State Offices
Consumer Protection
Office of the Attorney General
P.O. Box 22947
Jackson, MS 39225-2947
(601) 359-4230
(800) 281-4418 (toll-free in Mississippi)
Fax: (601) 359-4231
Website: http://www.ago.state.ms.us/

Bureau of Regulatory Services
Department of Agriculture and Commerce
P.O. Box 1609
Jackson, MS 39201
(601) 354-7063
Fax: (601) 354-6502

Insurance
Department of Insurance
1804 Walter Sillers Building
Jackson, MS 39205
(601) 359-3569
(800) 562-2957 (toll-free in Mississippi)

State Securities Agency
Securities Division
P.O. Box 136
Jackson, MS 39205
(601) 359-6371
Fax: (601) 359-2894

Better Business Bureau
BBB Jackson

P.O. Box 12745
Jackson, MS 39236-2745
(601) 987-8282
Fax: (601) 987-8285
Website: http://www.jackson.bbb.org

Missouri

State Offices
Consumer Protection
Consumer Protection Division
Office of Attorney General
P.O. Box 899
Jefferson City, MO 65102
(573) 751-3321
(800) 392-8222 (toll-free in Missouri)
Fax: (314) 751-7948
Website: http://www.ago.state.mo.us/ago/homepg.htm

Insurance
Department of Insurance
301 West High Street
6 North
Jefferson City, MO 65102-0690
(573) 751-2640
(800) 726-7390 (toll-free in Missouri)

State Securities Agency
Commissioner of Securities
P.O. Box 1276
Jefferson City, MO 65102
(573) 751-4136
(800) 721-7996
Fax: (573) 526-3124
Website: http://www.mosl.sos.state.mo.us/

Better Business Bureaus
BBB Kansas City
306 East 12th Street, Suite 1024
Kansas City, MO 64106-2418
(816) 421-7800
Fax: (816) 472-5442
Website: http://www.kansascity.bbb.org

BBB Springfield
205 Park Central East, Suite 509
Springfield, MO 65806-1326
(417) 862-4222
Fax: (417) 869-5544
Website: http://www.springfield-mo.bbb.org

BBB St. Louis
12 Sunnen Drive, Suite 121
St. Louis, MO 63143-1400
(314) 645-3300
Fax: (314) 645-2666
Website: http://www.stlouis.bbb.org

Montana

State Offices
Consumer Protection
Attorney General, State of Montana
215 North Sanders, Justice Building
Helena, MT 59620
(406) 444-3553
Website: http://www.doj.mt/gov/

Consumer Affairs Unit
Department of Commerce
Box 200501
Helena, MT 59620-0501
(406) 444-4312
Fax: (406) 444-2903

Insurance
Department of Insurance
126 North Sanders, Mitchell Building
Room 270
Helena, MT 59601
(406) 444-2040
(800) 332-6148 (toll-free in Montana)

State Securities Agency
Office of the State Auditor
Securities Department
P.O. Box 4009

Helena, MT 59604
(406) 444-2040
(800) 332-6148 (toll-free in Montana)
Fax: (406) 444-3497

Nebraska

State Offices
Consumer Protection
Consumer Protection Division
Department of Justice
P.O. Box 98920
Lincoln, NE 68509
(402) 471-2682
Fax: (402) 471 3297

Insurance
Department of Insurance
941 O Street, Suite 400
Lincoln, NE 68508
(402) 471-2201

State Securities Agency
Department of Banking & Finance
Bureau of Securities
P.O. Box 95006
Lincoln, NE 68509-5006
(402) 471-3445
Website: http://www.ndbf.org

Better Business Bureaus
BBB Lincoln
3633 O Street, Suite 1
Lincoln, NE 68510-1670
(402) 436-2345
Fax: (402) 476-8221
Website: http://www.lincoln.bbb.org

BBB Omaha
2237 North 91st Court
Omaha, NE 68134-6022
(402) 391-7612
Fax: (402) 391-7535
Website: http://www.omaha.bbb.org

Nevada

State Offices
Consumer Protection
Office of the Attorney General
316 Bridger Avenue, Suite 200
Las Vegas, NV 89102
(702) 687-4170
Fax: (702) 687-5798
Website: http://www.state.nv.us/ag/

Commissioner of Consumer Affairs
Department of Business and Industry
1850 East Sahara, Suite 101
Las Vegas, NV 89158
(702) 486-7355
Fax: (702) 486-7371
(800) 326-5202 (toll-free in Nevada)
TDD: (702) 486-7901

Consumer Affairs
Department of Business and Industry
4600 Kietzke Lane, B-113
Reno, NV 89502
(702) 688-1800
(800) 326-5202 (toll-free in Nevada)
Fax: (702) 688-1803
TDD: (702) 486-7901

Insurance
Division of Insurance
1665 Hot Springs Road, #152
Carson City, NV 89710
(702) 687-4270
(800) 992-0900 (toll-free in Nevada)

State Securities Agency
Office of the Secretary of State
Securities Division
555 East Washington Avenue, Suite 5200
Las Vegas, NV 89101
(702) 486-2440
Fax: (702) 486-2452
Website: http://www.state.nv.us

Better Business Bureaus
BBB Las Vegas
5595 Spring Mountain Road
Las Vegas, NV 89102
(702) 320-4500
Fax: (702) 320-4560
Website: http://www.lasvegas.bbb.org

BBB Reno
991 Bible Way
Reno, NV 89502
(702) 322-0657
Fax: (702) 322-8163
Website: http://www.reno.bbb.org

New Hampshire

State Offices
Consumer Protection
Consumer Protection and Antitrust Bureau
Office of Attorney General
33 Capitol Street
Concord, NH 03301
(603) 271-3641
Fax: (603) 271-2110
Website: http://www.state.nh.us/oag/ag.html

Insurance
Department of Insurance
169 Manchester Street
Concord, NH 03301-5151
(603) 271-2261

State Securities Agency
Bureau of Securities Regulation
Department of State
State House, Room 204
Concord, NH 03301-4989
(603) 271-1463
Fax: (603) 271-7933

Better Business Bureau
BBB Concord
410 South Main Street, Suite 3
Concord, NH 03301–3483
(603) 224-1991
Fax: (603) 228-9035
Website: http://www.concord.bbb.org

New Jersey

State Offices
Consumer Protection
New Jersey Division of Law
P.O. Box 45029
124 Halsey Street, 5th Floor
Newark, NJ 07101
(201) 648-7579
Fax: (201) 648-3879
Website: http://www.state.nj.us/lps/

Division of Consumer Affairs
P.O. Box 45027
Newark, NJ 07101
(201) 504-6534
Fax: (201) 648-3538
Website: http://www.state.nj.us/lps/ca/home.htm

Insurance
Department of Insurance
20 West State Street, CN329
Trenton, NJ 08625
(609) 984-2444

State Securities Agency
Department of Law and Public Safety
Division of Consumer Affairs
Bureau of Securities
P.O. Box 47029
Newark, NJ 07101
(973) 504-3600
Fax: (973) 504-3601
Website: http://www.state.nj.us/lps/ca/bos.htm

County Offices
Atlantic County Consumer Affairs
1333 Atlantic Avenue, 8th Floor
Atlantic City, NJ 08401
(609) 345-6700
Fax: (609) 343-2164

Bergen County Office of Consumer Protection
21 Main Street, Room 101-E
Hackensack, NJ 07601-7000
(201) 646-2650
Fax: (201) 489-6095

Burlington County Office of Consumer Affairs
49 Rancocas Road
Mount Holly, NJ 08060
(609) 265-5098
Fax: (609) 265-5065

Camden County Consumer Protection/Weights and Measures
Jefferson House
Lakeland Road
Blackwood, NJ 08012
(609) 374-6161
Fax: (609) 232-0748

Cape May County Consumer Affairs
4 Moore Road
Cape May Court House, NJ 08210
(609) 463-6475
Fax: (609) 465-6189

Cumberland County Department of Weights and Measures
    and Consumer Protection
788 East Commerce Street
Bridgeton, NJ 08302
(609) 453-2203
Fax: (609) 453-2206

Essex County Consumer Services
15 South Munn Avenue, 2nd Floor
East Orange, NJ 07018
(201) 678-8071
Fax: (201) 678-8928

Gloucester County Department of Consumer Affairs
152 North Broad Street
Woodbury, NJ 08096
(609) 853-3349
Fax: (609) 853-6813
TDD: (609) 848-6616

Hudson County Consumer Protection
583 Newark Avenue
Jersey City, NJ 07306
(201) 795-6295
Fax: (201) 795-6462

Hunterdon County Consumer Affairs
P.O. Box 283
Lebanon, NJ 08833
(908) 236-2249

Mercer County Consumer Affairs
P.O. Box 8068
Trenton, NJ 08650-0068
(609) 989-6671
Fax: (609) 989-6670

Middlesex County Consumer Affairs
10 Corporate Place South
Piscataway, NJ 08854
(908) 463-6000
Fax: (908) 463-6008

Monmouth County Consumer Affairs
P.O. Box 1255
Freehold, NJ 07728-1255
(908) 431-7900
Fax: (908) 294-5965

Ocean County Department of Consumer Affairs
P.O. Box 2191
Toms River, NJ 08754
(908) 929-2105
Fax: (908) 506-5330

Passaic County Consumer Affairs
401 Grand, Room 532
Paterson, NJ 07505
(201) 881-4547
Fax: (201) 881-0012

Somerset County Consumer Affairs
P.O. Box 3000
Somerville, NJ 08876-1262
(908) 231-7000, ext. 7400
Fax: (908) 707-4127

Union County Consumer Affairs
P.O. Box 186
Westfield, NJ 07091
(908) 654-9840

City Offices
Cinnaminson Consumer Affairs
P.O. Box 2100
1621 Riverton Road
Cinnaminson, NJ 08077
(609) 829-6000
Fax: (609) 829-3361

Clark Consumer Affairs
430 Westfield Avenue
Clark, NJ 07066
(908) 388-3600
Fax: (908) 388-3839

Elizabeth Consumer Affairs
City Hall
50–60 Winfield Scott Plaza
Elizabeth, NJ 07201
(908) 820-4183
Fax: (908) 820-0112

Livingston Consumer Affairs
357 South Livingston Avenue
Livingston, NJ 07039
(201) 535-7976
Fax: (201) 740-9408

Maywood Consumer Affairs
459 Maywood Avenue
Maywood, NJ 07607
(201) 845-2900
(201) 845-5749
Fax: (201) 909-0673

Middlesex Borough Consumer Affairs
1200 Mountain Avenue
Middlesex, NJ 08846
(908) 356-8090

Mountainside Consumer Affairs
1455 Coles Avenue
Mountainside, NJ 07092
(908) 232-6600

North Bergen Consumer Affairs
Municipal Building
4233 Kennedy Boulevard
North Bergen, NJ 07047
(201) 392-2157

Nutley Consumer Affairs
Public Safety Building
228 Chestnut Street
Nutley, NJ 07110
(201) 284-4936

Perth Amboy Consumer Affairs
City Hall
1 Olive Street
Perth Amboy, NJ 08861
(908) 826-0290, ext. 72
Fax: (908) 826-8069

Plainfield Action Services
510 Watchung Avenue
Plainfield, NJ 07060
(908) 753-3519
Fax: (908) 753-3540

Secaucus Department of Consumer Affairs
Municipal Government Center
Secaucus, NJ 07094
(201) 330-2019

Union Township Consumer Affairs
Municipal Building
1976 Morris Avenue
Union, NJ 07083
(908) 688-6763
Fax: (908) 686-1633

Wayne Township Consumer Affairs
475 Valley Road
Wayne, NJ 07470
(201) 694-1800, ext. 3290

Weehawken Consumer Affairs
400 Park Avenue
Weehawken, NJ 07087
(201) 319-6005
Fax: (201) 319-0112

Woodbridge Consumer Affairs
Municipal Building
One Main Street
Woodbridge, NJ 07095
(908) 634-4500, ext. 6058
Fax: (908) 602-6016

Better Business Bureaus
BBB Parsippany
400 Lanidex Plaza
Parsippany, NJ 07054-2797
(201) 581-1313
Fax: (201) 581-7022
Website: http://www.parsippany.bbb.org

BBB Trenton
1700 Whitehorse-Hamilton Square, Suite D-5
Trenton, NJ 08690-3596
(609) 588-0808
Fax: (609) 588-0546
Website: http://www.trenton.bbb.org

BBB Westmont
16 Maple Avenue
Westmont, NJ 08108-0303
(609) 854-8467
Fax: (609) 854-1130
Website: http://www.westmont.bbb.org

New Mexico

State Offices
Consumer Protection
Consumer Protection Division
Office of Attorney General
P.O. Drawer 1508
Santa Fe, NM 87504
(505) 827-6060
(800) 678-1508 (toll-free in New Mexcio)
Fax: (505) 827-6685

Insurance
Department of Insurance
P.O. Drawer 1269
Santa Fe, NM 87504-1269
(505) 827-4698
(800) 947-4722 (toll-free in New Mexico)

State Securities Agency
Regulation & Licensing Department
Securities Division
725 St. Michaels Drive
Santa Fe, NM 87501
(505) 827-7140 (general information)
Fax: (505) 984-0617
Website: http://www.state.nm.us/rld/rld_sd.html

Better Business Bureaus
BBB Albuquerque
2625 Pennsylvania, N.E., Suite 2050
Albuquerque, NM 87110-3657
(505) 346-0110
Fax: (505) 346-0696
Website: http://www.bbbnm.com

BBB Farmington
308 North Locke
Farmington, NM 87401-5855
(505) 326-6501
Fax: (505) 327-7731
Website: http://www.farmington.bbb.org

New York

State Offices
Consumer Protection
Bureau of Consumer Frauds and Protection
Office of Attorney General
State Capitol
Albany, NY 12224
(518) 474-5481
(800) 771-7755 (toll-free in New York)
Fax: (518) 474-3618
Website: http://www.oag.state.ny.us/

Bureau of Consumer Frauds and Protection
Office of Attorney General
120 Broadway
New York, NY 10271
(212) 416-8345
(800) 771-7755 (toll-free in New York)
TDD: (212) 416-8940

Central New York Regional Office
Office of Attorney General
44 Hawley Street, 17th Floor
State Office Building
Binghamton, NY 13901
(607) 721-8779

Office of Attorney General
65 Court Street
Buffalo, NY 14202
(716) 847-7184

Poughkeepsie Regional Office
Office of Attorney General
235 Main Street

Poughkeepsie, NY 12601
(914) 485-3920

Rochester Regional Office
Office of Attorney General
144 Exchange Boulevard
Rochester, NY 14614
(716) 546-7430
TDD: (716) 327-3249

Suffolk Regional Office
Office of Attorney General
300 Motor Parkway
Hauppauge, NY 11788
(516) 231-2400

Syracuse Regional Office
Office of Attorney General
615 Erie Boulevard West, Suite 102
Syracuse, NY 13204-2465
(315) 448-4848

Utica Regional Office
Office of Attorney General
207 Genesee Street
Utica, NY 13501
(315) 793-2225

New York State Consumer Protection Board
5 Empire State Plaza, Suite 2101
Albany, NY 12223-1556
(518) 474-8583
Fax: (518) 474-2474

Insurance
Department of Insurance
160 West Broadway
New York, NY 10013-3393
(212) 602-2488
(800) 342-3736 (toll-free in New York)

Department of Insurance
Agency Building One

Empire State Plaza
Albany, NY 12257
(518) 474-6600

State Securities Agency
Department of Law
Bureau of Investor Protection and Securities
120 Broadway, 23rd Floor
New York, NY 10271
(212) 416-8200
Fax: (212) 416-8816
Website: http://www.oag.state.ny.us

County Offices
Dutchess County Department of Consumer Affairs
38-A Dutchess Turnpike
Poughkeepsie, NY 12603
(914) 486-2949
Fax: (914) 486-2947

Erie County District Attorney's Office
Consumer Fraud Bureau
25 Delaware Avenue
Buffalo, NY 14202
(716) 858-2424

Nassau County Office of Consumer Affairs
160 Old Country Road
Mineola, NY 11501
(516) 571-2600
Fax: (515) 571-3389

Orange County District Attorney's Office
County Government Center
255 Main Street
Goshen, NY 10924
(914) 294-5471

Putnam County Consumer Affairs
110 Old Route 6
Carmel, NY 10512
(914) 225-2039
Fax: (914) 225-1421

Rockland County Office of Consumer Protection
18 New Hempstead Road
New City, NY 10956
(914) 638-5280
Fax: (914) 638-5415

Steuben County Department of Weights, Measures
and Consumer Affairs
3 East Pulteney Square
Bath, NY 14810
(607) 776-9631
Voice/TDD: (607) 776-9631, ext. 2406

Suffolk County Consumer Affairs
North County Complex, Bldg. 340
Veterans Memorial Highway
Hauppauge, NY 11788
(516) 853-4600

Ulster County Consumer Fraud Bureau
P.O. Box 1800
Kingston, NY 12402
(914) 339-5680

Westchester County Department of Consumer Protection
112 East Post Road, 4th Floor
White Plains, NY 10601
(914) 285-2155
Fax: (914) 285-3115

Westchester County District Attorney's Office
111 Grove Street
White Plains, NY 10601
(914) 285-3414
Fax: (914) 285-3594

City Offices
Town of Colonie Consumer Protection
Memorial Town Hall
Newtonville, NY 12128
(518) 783-2790

Lindenhurst Office of Citizen Services
Babylon Town Hall
200 East Sunrise Highway
Lindenhurst, NY 11757
(516) 957-7474

Mt. Vernon Office of Consumer Protection
City Hall
Mt. Vernon, NY 10550
(914) 665-2433
Fax: (914) 665-2496

New York City Department of Consumer Affairs
42 Broadway
New York, NY 10004
(212) 487-4401
Fax: (212) 487-4497
TDD: (212) 487-4465

Queens Neighborhood Office
New York City Department of Consumer Affairs
120–55 Queens Boulevard, Room 301A
Kew Gardens, NY 11424
(718) 286-2990
Fax: (718) 286-2997

Schenectady Bureau of Consumer Protection
City Hall, Room 204
Jay Street
Schenectady, NY 12305
(518) 382-5061

Yonkers Office of Consumer Protection
201 Palisade Avenue
Yonkers, NY 10703
(914) 377-6807

Better Business Bureaus
BBB Buffalo
346 Delaware Avenue
Buffalo, NY 14202-1899
(900) 225-5222 ($3.80 first 4 minutes, $.95/minute
   thereafter, not to exceed $9.50)

Fax: (716) 856-7287
Website: http://www.buffalo.bbb.org

BBB New York
257 Park Avenue, South
New York, NY 10010-7384
(900) 225-5222 ($3.80 first 4 minutes, $.95/minute thereafter, not
    to exceed $9.50)
Fax: (212) 477-4912
Website: http://www.newyork.bbb.org

BBB Syracuse
847 James Street, Suite 200
Syracuse, NY 13202-2552
(900) 225-522 ($3.80 first 4 minutes, $.95/minute thereafter, not
    to exceed $9.50)
Fax: (315) 479-5754
Website: http://www.syracuse.bbb.org

North Carolina

State Offices
Consumer Protection
Office of Attorney General
P.O. Box 629
Raleigh, NC 27602
(919) 733-7741
Fax: (919) 715-0577
Website: http://www.jus.state.nc.us/Justice/

Insurance
Department of Insurance
Dobbs Building
P.O. Box 26387
Raleigh, NC 27611
(919) 733-2004
(800) 662-7777 (toll-free in North Carolina)

State Securities Agency
Department of the Secretary of State
Securities Division
300 North Salisbury Street, Suite 100

Raleigh, NC 27603-5909
(919) 733-3924
(800) 688-4507 (toll-free in North Carolina)
Fax: (919) 821-0818
Website: http://www.state.nc.us./secstate/sec.htm

Better Business Bureaus
BBB Asheville
1200 BB&T Building
Asheville, NC 28801-3418
(704) 253-2392
Fax: (704) 252-5039
Website: http://www.asheville.bbb.org

BBB Charlotte
5200 Park Road, Suite 202
Charlotte, NC 28209-3650
(704) 527-0012
Fax: (704) 525-7624
Website: http://www.charlotte.bbb.org

BBB Greensboro
3608 West Friendly Avenue
Greensboro, NC 27410-4895
(910) 852-4240
Fax: (910) 852-7540
Website: http://www.greensboro.bbb.org

BBB Raleigh
3125 Poplarwood Court Suite 308
Raleigh, NC 27604-1080
(919) 872-9240
Fax: (919) 954-0622
Website: http://www.raleigh-durham.bbb.org

BBB Winston-Salem
500 West 5th Street, Suite 202
Winston-Salem, NC 27101-2728
(336) 725-8384
Website: http://www.winstonsalem.bbb.org

North Dakota

State Offices
Consumer Protection
Office of Attorney General
600 East Boulevard
Bismarck, ND 58505
(701) 224-2210
(800) 472-2600 (toll-free in North Dakota)
Website: http://www.state.nd.us/ndag/

Office of Attorney General
600 East Boulevard
Bismarck, ND 58505
(701) 224-3404

Insurance
Department of Insurance
600 East Boulevard
Bismarck, ND 58505-0320
(701) 328-2440
(800) 247-0560 (toll-free in North Dakota)

State Securities Agency
Office of the Securities Commissioner
600 East Boulevard
Bismarck, ND 58505-0510
(701) 224-2910
(800) 297-5124 (toll-free in North Dakota)
Fax: (701) 255-3113

County Office
Community Action Agency
1013 North 5th Street
Grand Forks, ND 58201
(701) 746-5431

Ohio

State Offices
Consumer Protection
Office of Attorney General

Consumer Frauds and Crimes Section
30 East Broad Street
State Office Tower, 25th Floor
Columbus, OH 43266-0410
(614) 466-4986 (complaints)
(800) 282-0515 (toll-free in Ohio)
TDD: (614) 466-1393
Website: http://www.ag.ohio.gov

Insurance
Department of Insurance
2100 Stella Court
Columbus, OH 43215-1067
(614) 644-2658
(800) 522-0071 (toll-free in Ohio)

State Securities Agency
Division of Securities
77 South High Street, 22nd Floor
Columbus, OH 43215
(614) 644-7381
Fax: (614) 466-3316
Website: http://www.securities.state.oh.us

County Offices
Franklin County Office of Prosecuting Attorney
Corrupt Activities Prosecution Unit
369 South High Street
Columbus, OH 43215
(614) 462-3555
Fax: (614) 462-6103

Montgomery County Fraud 107 and Economic Crimes Division
301 West 3rd Street
Dayton Montgomery County Courts Building
Dayton, OH 45402
(513) 225-4747
Fax: (513) 225-3470

Portage County Office of Prosecuting Attorney
466 South Chestnut Street
Ravenna, OH 44266-3000
(330) 296-4593
Fax: (330) 297-3856

Summit County Office of Prosecuting Attorney
53 University Avenue
Akron, OH 44308-1680
(330) 643-2800
Fax: (330) 643-2137

City Offices
Cincinnati Consumer Services
City Hall, Room 126
801 Plum Street
Cincinnati, OH 45202
(513) 352-3971
Fax: (513) 352-5241

Youngstown Office of Consumer Affairs
City Hall
26 South Phelps Street
Youngstown, OH 44503-1318
(330) 742-8884
Fax: (330) 743-1335

Better Business Bureaus
BBB Akron
222 West Market Street
Akron, OH 44303-2111
(330) 253-4590
Fax: (330) 253-6249
Website: http://www.akron.bbb.org

BBB Canton
P.O. Box 8017
Canton, OH 44711-8017
(330) 454-9401
Fax: (330) 456-8957
Website: http://www.canton.bbb.org

BBB Cincinnati
898 Walnut Street
Cincinnati, OH 45202-2097
(513) 421-3015
Fax: (513) 621-0907
Website: http://www.cincinnati.bbb.org

BBB Cleveland
2217 East 9th Street, Suite 200
Cleveland, OH 44115-1299
(216) 241-7678
Fax: (216) 861-6365
Website: http://www.cleveland.bbb.org

BBB Columbus
1335 Dublin Street, #30-A
Columbus, OH 43215-1000
(614) 486-6336
Fax: (614) 486-6631
Website: http://www.columbus-oh.bbb.org

BBB Dayton
40 West 4th Street, Suite 1250
Dayton, OH 45402-1828
(937) 222-5825
Fax: (937) 222-3338
Website: http://www.dayton.bbb.org

BBB Lima
P.O. Box 269
Lima, OH 45802-0269
(419) 223-7010
Fax: (419) 229-2029
Website: http://www.wcohio.bbb.org

BBB Toledo
3103 Executive Parkway, Suite 200
Toledo, OH 43606-1310
(419) 531-3116
Fax: (419) 578-6001
Website: http://www.toledo.bbb.org

BBB Youngstown
P.O. Box 1495
Youngstown, OH 44501-1495
(216) 744-3111
Fax: (330) 744-7336
Website: http://www.youngstown.bbb.org

Oklahoma

State Offices
Consumer Protection
Office of Attorney General
4545 North Lincoln Boulevard, Suite 260
Oklahoma City, OK 73105
(405) 521-4274
(405) 521-2029 (consumer hotline)
Fax: (405) 528-1867

Insurance
Department of Insurance
P.O. Box 53408
Oklahoma City, OK 73118
(405) 521-2991
(800) 522-0071 (toll-free in Oklahoma)

State Securities Agency
Department of Securities
First National Center
120 North Robinson, Suite 860
Oklahoma City, OK 73102
(405) 280-7700
Fax: (405) 280-7742
Website: http://www.oklaosf.state.ok.us/~osc

Better Business Bureaus
BBB Oklahoma City
17 South Dewey
Oklahoma City, OK 73102-2400
(405) 239-6081
Fax: (405) 235-5891
Website: http://www.oklahomacity.bbb.org

BBB Tulsa
6711 South Yale, Suite 230
Tulsa, OK 74136-3327
(918) 492-1266
Fax: (918) 492-1276
Website: http://www.tulsa.bbb.org

Oregon

State Offices
Consumer Protection
Financial Fraud Section
Department of Justice
1162 Court Street, N.E.
Salem, OR 97310
(503) 378-4732
Fax: (503) 373-7067
Website: http://www.doj.state.or.us/

Insurance
Department of Consumer and Business Services
350 Winter Street, N.E., Room 200
Salem, OR 97310-0700
(503) 378-4636

State Securities Agency
Department of Consumer and Business Services
Division of Finance & Corporate Securities
350 Winter Street, N.E., Room 410
Salem, OR 97310
(503) 378-4387 (Corporate Securities Section)
Fax: (503) 378-4178
Website: http://www.cbs.state.or.us/external/dfcs

Better Business Bureau
BBB Portland
333 S.W. Fifth Avenue, Suite 300
Portland, OR 97204
(503) 226-3981
Fax: (503) 226-8200
Website: http://www.oregonandwesternwa.bbb.org

Pennsylvania

State Offices
Consumer Protection
Bureau of Consumer Protection
Office of Attorney General
Strawberry Square, 14th Floor
Harrisburg, PA 17120

(717) 787-9707
(800) 441-2555 (toll-free in Pennsylvania)
Website: http://www.attorneygeneral.gov/

Office of Attorney General
1251 South Cedar Crest Boulevard, Suite 309
Allentown, PA 18103
(610) 821-6690

Office of Attorney General
919 State Street, Room 203
Erie, PA 16501
(814) 871-4371
Fax: (814) 871-4848

Office of the Attorney General
171 Lovell Avenue, Suite 202
Ebensburg, PA 15931
(814) 949-7900
Fax: (814) 949-7942

Office of Attorney General
21 South 12th Street, 2nd Floor
Philadelphia, PA 19107
(215) 560-2414

Office of Attorney General
Manor Complex, 6th Floor
564 Forbes Avenue
Pittsburgh, PA 15219
(412) 565-5394

Office of Attorney General
214 Samters Building
101 Penn Avenue
Scranton, PA 18503-2025
(717) 963-4913
Fax: (717) 963-3418

Office of the Attorney General
132 Kline Village
Harrisburg, PA 17104
(717) 787-7109

Insurance
Commissioner
Insurance Department
1326 Strawberry Square, 13th Floor
Harrisburg, PA 17120
(717) 787-2317

State Securities Agency
Securities Commission
Eastgate Office Building
1010 North 7th Street, 2nd Floor
Harrisburg, PA 17102-1410
(717) 787-8061
Fax: (717) 783-5122
Website: http://www.state.pa.us/

County Offices
Beaver County Alliance for Consumer Protection
699 Fifth Street
Beaver, PA 15009-1997
(412) 728-7267

Bucks County Consumer Protection
50 North Main Street
Doylestown, PA 18901
(215) 348-7442
Fax: (215) 348-4570

Chester County Consumer Affairs
Government Services Center, Suite 390
601 Westtown Road
West Chester, PA 19382-4547
(610) 344-6150

Cumberland County Consumer Affairs
One Courthouse Square
Carlisle, PA 17013-3387
(717) 240-6180
Fax: (717) 240-6490

Delaware County Consumer Affairs
Government Center Building

Second and Olive Streets
Media, PA 19063
(610) 891-4865
Fax: (610) 566-3947

Montgomery County Consumer Affairs
County Courthouse
Norristown, PA 19404
(610) 278-3565
Fax: (610) 278-3556

City Office
Philadelphia District Attorney's Office
Economic Crime Unit
1421 Arch Street
Philadelphia, PA 19102
(215) 686-8750
Fax: (215) 686-8765

Better Business Bureaus
BBB Bethlehem
528 North New Street
Bethlehem, PA 18018-5789
(610) 866-8780
Fax: (610) 868-8668
Website: www.easternpa.bbb.org

BBB Lancaster
29 East King Street, Suite 322
Lancaster, PA 17602-2852
(900) 225-5222 ($3.80 first 4 minutes, $.95/minute thereafter, not
   to exceed $9.50)
Fax: (717) 291-3241
Website: http://www.easternpa.bbb.org

BBB Philadelphia
P.O. Box 2297
Philadelphia, PA 19103-0297
(215) 893-3870 (credit card)
(900) 225-5222 ($3.80 first 4 minutes, $.95/minute thereafter, not
   to exceed $9.50)
Fax: (215) 893-9312
Website: http://www.easternpa.bbb.org

BBB Pittsburgh
300 6th Avenue, Suite 100-UL
Pittsburgh, PA 15222-2511
(412) 456-2700
Fax: (412) 456-2739
Website: http://www.pittsburgh.bbb.org

BBB Scranton
P.O. Box 993
Scranton, PA 18501-0993
(717) 342-9129
Fax: (717) 342-1282
Website: http://www.nepa.bbb.org

Puerto Rico

State Offices
Consumer Protection
Department of Justice
P.O. Box 192
San Juan, PR 00902
(787) 721-2900

Department of Consumer Affairs (DACO)
Minillas Station, P.O. Box 41059
Santurce, PR 00940-1059
(787) 721-0940
Fax: (787) 726-6570

Insurance
Office of the Commissioner of Insurance
Fernandez Juncos Station
1607 Ponce de Leon Avenue
Santurce, PR 00910
(787) 722-8686

State Securities Agency
Office of the Commissioner of Financial Institutions
Securities Division
Centro Europa Building, Suite 600
1492 Ponce de Leon Avenue
San Juan, PR 00907-4127
(787) 723-3131
Fax: (787) 723-4042

Better Business Bureau
BBB Puerto Rico
P.O. Box 363488
San Juan, PR 00936
(787) 756-5400
Fax: (787) 758-0095
Website: http://www.sanjuan.bbb.org

Rhode Island

State Offices
Consumer Protection
Department of Attorney General
72 Pine Street
Providence, RI 02903
(401) 274-4400
Fax: (401) 277-1331
(800) 852-7776 (toll-free in Rhode Island)
TDD: (401) 453-0410
Website: http://www.riag.state.ri.US/

Insurance
Insurance Division
233 Richmond Street
Providence, RI 02903-4233
(401) 277-2223

State Securities Agency
Department of Business Regulation
233 Richmond Street, Suite 232
Providence, RI 02903-4232
(401) 277-3048
Fax: (401) 273-5202
TDD: (401) 277-2223

Better Business Bureau
BBB Rhode Island
120 Lavan Street
Warwick, RI 02888-1071
(401) 785-1212
Fax: (401) 785-3061
Website: www.rhodeisland.bbb.org

South Carolina

State Offices
Consumer Protection
Office of Attorney General
P.O. Box 11549
Columbia, SC 29211
(803) 734-3970
Fax: (803) 734-3677
Website: http://www.scattorney.general.org/

Department of Consumer Affairs
P.O. Box 5757
Columbia, SC 29250-5757
(803) 734-9452
Fax: (803) 734-9365
(800) 922-1594 (toll-free in South Carolina)
TDD: (803) 734-9455

Insurance
Department of Insurance
P.O. Box 100105
Columbia, SC 24201
(803) 737-6150
(800) 768-3467 (toll-free in South Carolina)

State Securities Agency
Securities Section
Office of the Attorney General
P.O. Box 11549
Columbia, SC 29211
(803) 734-9916
Fax: (803) 734-0032
Website: http://www.scfattorney.general.org

Better Business Bureaus
BBB Columbia
2330 Devine Street
Columbia, SC 29202-8326
(803) 254-2525
Fax: (803) 779-3117
Website: http://www.columbia.bbb.org

BBB Greenville
307-B Falls Street
Greenville, SC 29601-2829
(803) 242-5052
Fax: (803) 271-9802
Website: http://www.greenville.bbb.org

BBB Myrtle Beach
1601 North Oak Street, Suite 101
Myrtle Beach, SC 29577-1601
(803) 626-6881
Fax: (803) 626-7455
Website: http://www.mb.bbb.org

South Dakota

State Offices
Consumer Protection
Office of Attorney General
500 East Capitol
State Capitol Building
Pierre, SD 57501-5070
(605) 773-4400
(800) 300-1986 (toll-free in South Dakota)
Fax: (605) 773-4106
TDD: (605) 773-6585
Website: http://www.state.sd.us/state/executive/attorney/attorney.html

Insurance
Division of Insurance
Department of Commerce and Regulation
500 East Capitol
Pierre, SD 57501-3940
(605) 773-3563

State Securities Agency
Enforcement Director
Division of Securities
118 West Capitol Avenue
Pierre, SD 57501-2017
(605) 773-4823
Fax: (605) 773-5953

Tennessee

State Offices
Consumer Protection
Office of Attorney General
500 Charlotte Avenue
Nashville, TN 37243-0491
(615) 741-3491
Fax: (615) 532-2910

Division of Consumer Affairs
500 James Robertson Parkway, 5th Floor
Nashville, TN 37243-0600
(615) 741-4737
(800) 342-8385 (toll-free in Tennessee)
Fax: (615) 532-4994
Website: http://www.state.tn.us/consumer

Insurance
Department of Commerce and Insurance
500 James Robertson Parkway
Nashville, TN 37243-0565
(615) 741-2218
(800) 342-4029 (toll-free in Tennessee)

State Securities Agency
Department of Commerce and Insurance
Securities Division
Davy Crockett Tower, Suite 680
500 James Robertson Parkway
Nashville, TN 37243-0485
(615) 741-2947
(800) 863-9117 (toll-free in Tennessee)
Fax: (615) 532-8375
Website: http://www.state.tn.us/commerce/securdiv.html

Better Business Bureaus
BBB Chattanooga
1010 Market Street, Suite 200
Chattanooga, TN 37402-2614
(423) 266-6144
Fax: (423) 267-1924
Website: http://www.chattanooga.bbb.org

BBB Knoxville
P.O. Box 10327
Knoxville, TN 37939-0327
(423) 522-2552
Fax: (423) 637-8042
Website: http://www.knoxville.bbb.org

BBB Memphis
P.O. Box 17036
Memphis, TN 38178-0036
(901) 759-1300
Fax: (901) 757-2997
Website: http://www.memphis.bbb.org

BBB Nashville
P.O. Box 198436
Nashville, TN 37219
(615) 242-4222
Fax: (615) 254-8356
Website: http://www.nashville.bbb.org

Texas

State Offices
Consumer Protection
Office of Attorney General
P.O. Box 12548
Austin, TX 78711
(512) 463-2070
Website: http://www.oag.state.tx.us/

Office of Attorney General
714 Jackson Street, Suite 800
Dallas, TX 75202-4506
Tel; (214) 742-8944
Fax: (214) 939-3930

Office of Attorney General
6090 Surety Drive, Room 113
El Paso, TX 79905
(915) 772-9476
Fax: (915) 772-9046

Office of Attorney General
1019 Congress Street, Suite 1550
Houston, TX 77002-1702
(713) 223-5886

Office of Attorney General
916 Main Street, Suite 806
Lubbock, TX 79401-3997
(806) 747-5238
Fax: (806) 747-6307

Office of Attorney General
3201 North McColl Road, Suite B
McAllen, TX 78501
(210) 682-4547
Fax: (210) 682-1957

Office of Attorney General
115 East Travis Street, Suite 925
San Antonio, TX 78205-1615
(210) 224-1007

Insurance
Department of Insurance
333 Guadalupe Street
P.O. Box 149104
Austin, TX 78714-9104
(512) 463-6464
(800) 252-3439 (toll-free in Texas)

State Securities Agency
State Securities Board
P.O. Box 13167
Austin, TX 78711-3167
(512) 305-8300
Fax: (512) 305-8310
Website: http://www.ssb.state.tx.us

County Offices
Dallas County District Attorney's Office
Specialized Crime Division
133 North Industrial Boulevard, LB 19
Dallas, TX 75207-4399

(214) 653-3820
Fax: (214) 653-3845

Harris County Consumer Fraud Division
Office of District Attorney
201 Fannin, Suite 200
Houston, TX 77002-1901
(713) 755-5836

Better Business Bureaus
BBB Abilene
3300 South 14th Street, Suite 307
Abilene, TX 79605-5052
(915) 691-1533
Fax: (915) 691-0309
Website: http://www.abilene.bbb.org

BBB Amarillo
P.O. Box 1905
Amarillo, TX 79101-3408
(806) 379-6222
Fax: (806) 379-8206
Website: http://www.amarillo.bbb.org

BBB Austin
2101 South IH 35, Suite 302
Austin, TX 78741-3854
(512) 445-2911
Fax: (512) 445-2096
Website: http://www.centraltx.bbb.org

BBB Beaumont
P.O. Box 2988
Beaumont, TX 77701-2988
(409) 835-5348
Fax: (409) 838-6858
Website: http://www.beaumont.bbb.org

BBB Bryan
P.O. Box 3868
Bryan, TX 77805-3868
(409) 260-2222
Fax: (409) 846-0276
Website: http://www.bryan.bbb.org

BBB Corpus Christi
216 Park Avenue
Corpus Christi, TX 78401
(512) 887-4949
Fax: (512) 887-4931
Website: http://www.corpuschristi.bbb.org

BBB Dallas
2001 Bryan Street, Suite 850
Dallas, TX 75201-3093
(900) 225-5222 ($3.80 first 4 minutes, $.95/minute thereafter, not
    to exceed $9.50)
Fax: (214) 740-0321
Website: http://www.dallas.bbb.org

BBB El Paso
Norwest Plaza, Suite 1101
El Paso, TX 79901
(915) 577-0191
Fax: (915) 557-0209
Website: http://www.elpaso.bbb.org

BBB Fort Worth
1612 Summit Avenue, Suite 260
Fort Worth, TX 76102-5978
(817) 332-7585
Fax: (817) 882-0566
Website: http://www.fortworth.bbb.org

BBB Houston
5225 Katy Freeway, Suite 500
Houston, TX 77007
(900) 225-5222 ($3.80 first 4 minutes, $.95/minute thereafter, not
    to exceed $9.50)
Fax: (713) 867-4947
Website: http://www.bbbhou.org

BBB Lubbock
916 Main Street, Suite 800
Lubbock, TX 79401-3410
(806) 763-0459
Fax: (806) 744-9748
Website: http://www.lubbock.bbb.org

BBB Midland
P.O. Box 60206
Midland, TX 79711-0206
(915) 563-1880
Fax: (915) 561-9435
Website: http://www.midland.bbb.org

BBB San Angelo
P.O. Box 3366
San Angelo, TX 76902-3366
(915) 949-2986
Fax: (915) 949-3514
Website: http://www.sanangelo.bbb.org

BBB San Antonio
1800 Northeast Loop 410, Suite 400
San Antonio, TX 78217-5296
(210) 828-9441
Fax: (210) 828-3101
Website: http://www.sanantonio.bbb.org

BBB Tyler
P.O. Box 6652
Tyler, TX 75711-6652
(903) 581-5704
Fax: (903) 534-8644
Website: http://www.tyler.bbb.org

BBB Waco
2210 Washington Avenue
Waco, TX 76701-1019
(254) 755-7772
Fax: (254) 755-7774
Website: http://www.waco.bbb.org

BBB Weslaco
P.O. Box 69
Weslaco, TX 78599-0069
(956) 968-3678
Fax: (956) 968-7638
Website: http://www.weslaco.bbb.org

BBB Wichita Falls
4245 Kemp Boulevard, Suite 900
Wichita Falls, TX 76308-2830
(940) 691-1172
Fax: (940) 691-1175
Website: http://www.wichitafalls.bbb.org

Utah

State Offices
Consumer Protection
Office of Attorney General
State Office Building
Salt Lake City, UT 84114
(801) 538-1331
Website: http://www.at.state.ut.us/

Division of Consumer Protection
Department of Commerce
160 East 300 South
Box 146704
Salt Lake City, UT 84114-6704
(801) 530-6601
(800) 721-7233 (toll-free in Utah)
Fax: (801) 530-6001

Insurance
Department of Insurance
3110 State Office Building
Salt Lake City, UT 84114
(801) 538-3805
(800) 439-3805 (toll-free in Utah)

State Securities Agency
Director, Securities Division
Department of Commerce
P.O. Box 146760
Salt Lake City, UT 84114-6760
(801) 530-6600
Fax: (801) 530-6980
Website: http://www.commerce.state.ut.us

Better Business Bureau
BBB Salt Lake
1588 South Main Street
Salt Lake City, UT 84115-5382
(801) 487-4656
Fax: (801) 485-9397
Website: http://www.saltlakecity.bbb.org

Vermont

State Offices
Consumer Protection
Office of Attorney General
109 State Street
Montpelier, VT 05609-1001
(802) 828-3171
Fax: (802) 828-2154
Website: http://www.state.vt.us/atg/

Consumer Assurance Section
Department of Agriculture
120 State Street
Montpelier, VT 05620-2901
(802) 828-2436

Insurance
Department of Banking, Insurance and Securities
89 Main Street, Drawer 20
Montpelier, VT 05620-3101
(802) 828-4884

State Securities Agency
Department of Banking, Insurance & Securities
Securities Division
89 Main Street, Drawer 20
Montpelier, VT 05620-3101
(802) 828-3420
Fax: (802) 828-2896
Website: http://www.state.vt.us/bis

Virgin Islands

State Offices
Consumer Protection
Department of Licensing and Consumer Affairs
Golden Rock Shopping Center
Christianstead, VI 00820
(809) 773-2226
Fax: (809) 778-8250

Insurance
Division of Banking and Insurance
Lt. Governor's Office
Kongens Gade 18
St. Thomas, VI 00802
(809) 774-7166

Virginia

State Offices
Consumer Protection
Antitrust and Consumer Litigation Section
Office of Attorney General
900 East Main Street
Richmond, VA 23219
(804) 786-2116
Fax: (804) 371-2086/2087
Website: http://www.cns.state.va.us/oag

Department of Agriculture and Consumer Services
P.O. Box 1163
Richmond, VA 23219
(804) 786-2043
TDD: (804) 371-7479
(800) 552-9963 (toll-free in Virginia)
Fax: (804) 371-7479

Insurance
Bureau of Insurance
State Corporation Commission
1300 East Main Street
Richmond, VA 23219
(804) 371-9694
(800) 552-7945 (toll-free in Virginia)

State Securities Agency
State Corporation Commission
Division of Securities & Retail Franchising
P.O. Box 1197
Richmond, VA 23218
(804) 371-9051
(800) 552-7945 (toll-free in Virginia)
Fax: (804) 371-9911
TDD: (804) 371-9203

County Offices
Fairfax County Consumer Affairs
12000 Government Center Parkway, Suite 433
Fairfax, VA 22035
Fax: (703) 222-5921 (mail complaints only)

Office of Citizen and Consumer Affairs
#1 Court House Plaza, Suite 314
2100 Clarendon Boulevard
Arlington, VA 22201
(703) 358-3260
Fax: (703) 358-3295

City Offices
Alexandria Office of Consumer Affairs
301 King Street
Alexandria, VA 22314
(703) 838-4350
Fax: (703) 838-6426
TDD: (703) 838-5056

Consumer Affairs Division
Office of the Commonwealth's Attorney
2305 Judicial Boulevard
Virginia Beach, VA 23456-9050
(757) 426-5836
Fax: (757) 427-8779

Norfolk Division of Consumer Affairs
City Hall
Norfolk, VA 23510
(757) 664-4888
Fax: (757) 664-4405

Roanoke Assistant to the City Manager for Community Relations
364 Municipal Building
215 Church Avenue, S.W.
Roanoke, VA 24011
(540) 981-2583
Fax: (540) 224-3138

Better Business Bureaus
BBB Fredricksburg
11903 Main Street
Fredericksburg, VA 22408
(540) 373-9872
Fax: (540) 373-0097
Website: http://www.richmond.bbb.org

BBB Norfolk
586 Virginian Drive
Norfolk, VA 23505
(757) 531-1300
Fax: (757) 531-1388
Website: http://www.hamptonroads.bbb.org

BBB Richmond
701 East Franklin, Suite 712
Richmond, VA 23219-2332
(804) 648-0016
Fax: (804) 648-3115
Website: http://www.richmond.bbb.org

BBB Roanoke
31 West Campbell Avenue
Roanoke, VA 24011-1301
(540) 342-3455
Fax: (540) 345-2289
Website: http://www.roanoke.bbb.org

Washington

State Offices
Consumer Protection
Consumer and Business Fair Practices Division
Office of the Attorney General
900 Fourth Avenue, Suite 2000

Seattle, WA 98164
(206) 464-6684
(800) 551-4636 (toll-free in Washington)
TDD: (206) 464-7293
(800) 276-9883 (TDD toll-free in Washington)
Website: http://www.wa.gov/ago

Office of the Attorney General
103 East Holly Street, Suite 308
Bellingham, WA 98225
(360) 738-6185

Office of the Attorney General
500 North Morain Street, Suite 1250
Kennewick, WA 99336-2607
(509) 734-7140

Office of the Attorney General
P.O. Box 40118
Olympia, WA 98504-0118
(360) 753-6210

Office of the Attorney General
West 1116 Riverside Avenue
Spokane, WA 99201
(509) 456-3123

Office of the Attorney General
1019 Pacific Avenue, 3rd Floor
Tacoma, WA 98402–4411
(206) 593-2904

Office of the Attorney General
500 West 8th Street, Suite 55
Vancouver, WA 98660
(360) 690-4751
Fax: (360) 690-4762

Insurance
Insurance Commission
Insurance Building-Capitol Campus
P.O. Box 40255
Olympia, WA 98504-0255
(360) 753-3613

State Securities Agency
Department of Financial Institutions
Securities Division
P.O. Box 9033
Olympia, WA 98507-9033
(360) 902-8760
(800) 372-8303 (toll-free in Washington)
Fax: (360) 586-5068
TDD: (360) 664-8126
Website: http://www.wa.gov/dfi/securities

City Offices
Seattle Chief Deputy Prosecuting Attorney
Fraud Division
900 4th Avenue, #1002
Seattle, WA 98164
(206) 296-9010

Seattle Department of Finance,
    Revenue and Consumer Affairs
600 4th Avenue, #103
Seattle, WA 98104-1891
(206) 684-8484
Fax: (206) 684-8625

Better Business Bureaus
BBB Sea Tac
4800 South 188th Street, Suite 222
Sea Tac, WA 98188
(206) 431-2222
Fax: (206) 431-2211
Website: http://www.oregonandwesternwa.bbb.org

BBB Spokane
508 West Sixth Avenue, Suite 401
Spokane, WA 99204-2730
(509) 455-4200
Fax: (509) 838-1079
Website: http://www.spokane.bbb.org

BBB Tri-Cities
101 North Union, #105
Kennewick, WA 99336-3819

(509) 783-0892
Fax: (509) 783-2893

BBB Yakima
P.O. Box 1584
Yakima, WA 98901
(509) 248-1326
Fax: (509) 248-8026
Website: http://www.yakima.bbb.org

West Virginia

State Offices
Consumer Protection
Office of Attorney General
812 Quarrier Street, 6th Floor
Charleston, WV 25301
(304) 558-8986
(800) 368-8808 (toll-free in West Virginia)
Fax: (304) 558-0184
Website: http://www.statewv.us/wvag

Insurance
Department of Insurance
2019 Washington Street, East
P.O. Box 50540
Charleston, WV 25305-0540
(304) 558-3856
(800) 642-9004 (toll-free in West Virginia)

State Securities Agency
State Auditor's Office, Securities Division
State Capitol Building
Building 1, Room W-110
Charleston, WV 25305
(304) 558-2257
Fax: (304) 588-4211
Website: http://www.wvauditor.com

City Office
City of Charleston Consumer Protection
P.O. Box 2749
Charleston, WV 25330

(304) 348-6439
Fax: (304) 348-8157

Wisconsin

State Offices
Consumer Protection
Office of the Attorney General
Department of Justice
P.O. Box 7857
Madison, WI 54707-7857
(608) 267-8901
(800) 362-8189 (toll-free in Wisconsin)
Website: http://www.doj.state.wi.us/

Department of Agriculture, Trade and Consumer Protection
P.O. Box 8911
Madison, WI 53708
(608) 224-4950
(800) 422-7128 (toll-free in Wisconsin)
Fax: (608) 224-4939

Department of Agriculture, Trade and Consumer Protection
927 Loring Street
Altoona, WI 54720
(715) 839-3848
Fax: (715) 839-1645

Department of Agriculture, Trade and Consumer Protection
200 North Jefferson Street, Suite 146A
Green Bay, WI 54301
(414) 448-5111

Department of Agriculture, Trade and Consumer Protection
10930 West Potter Road, Suite C
Milwaukee, WI 53226-3450
(414) 266-1231

Insurance
Office of the Commissioner of Insurance
121 East Wilson
Madison, WI 53702
(608) 266-0103
(800) 236-8517 (toll-free in Wisconsin)

State Securities Agency
Department of Financial Institutions
Division of Securities
P.O. Box 1768
Madison, WI 53702-1768
(608) 261-9555
Fax: (608) 256-1259
Website: http://www.wdfi.org

County Offices
Milwaukee County District Attorney's Office
Consumer Fraud Unit
821 West State Street, Room 412
Milwaukee, WI 53233-1485
(414) 278-4585
Fax: (414) 223-1955

Racine County Sheriff's Department
Consumer Fraud Investigator
717 Wisconsin Avenue
Racine, WI 53403
(414) 636-3125
Fax: (414) 636-3346

Better Business Bureau
BBB Milwaukee
740 North Plankinton Avenue
Milwaukee, WI 53203-2478
(414) 273-1600
Fax: (414) 224-0881
Website: http://www.wisconsin.bbb.org

Wyoming

State Offices
Consumer Protection
Office of Attorney General
123 State Capitol Building
Cheyenne, WY 82002
(307) 777-7874
Fax: (307) 777-6869
Website: http://www.state.wy.us/~ag/index.html

Insurance
Department of Insurance
Herschler Building
122 West 25th Street
Cheyenne, WY 82002-0440
(307) 777-7402
(800) 438-5768 (toll-free in Wyoming)

State Securities Agency
Secretary of State & Securities
State Capitol Building
Cheyenne, WY 82002-0020
(307) 777-7370
Fax: (307) 777-5339
Website: http://www.state.wy.us

Print Resources 6

The books, articles, congressional documents, and reports and publications listed in this chapter represent a broad selection of the print resources available on consumer fraud. Wherever possible, a range of opinions is presented as well as works for different audiences.

The final section of this chapter includes various consumer brochures and guides available from federal agencies. A large assortment of consumer brochures is available. Federal, state, and local government offices, Better Business Bureaus, consumer groups, and businesses all publish consumer guides, and space does not permit the listing of more than a representative sampling of these publications. The brochures included here are representative of what federal agencies can provide. These publications can also be downloaded from the Internet. (Chapter 5 of this book lists the Websites for the federal agencies named in this chapter.) You can also write to the appropriate agency or the federal Consumer Information Center for a copy (also see Chapter 5 for the mailing addresses).

Books

Aaker, David A., and George S. Day, editors. *Consumerism: Search for the Consumer Interest.* New York: Free Press, 1971. 500 pp. ISBN 0-02900-150-1.

Basic text, useful to those involved in the issue of the exploitation of vulnerable consumers. Includes a discussion of misleading advertising, truth-in-lending, and deceptive packaging.

Albrecht, W. Steve, Gerald W. Wernz, and Timothy L. Williams. *Fraud: Bringing Light to the Dark Side of Business.* Burr Ridge, IL: Irwin Professional Publishing, 1995. 296 pp. ISBN 1-55623-760-X.

An overview on the nature of the perpetrators of consumer frauds, and information on how to detect, investigate, and prevent it.

Anderson, Oscar Edward. *The Health of a Nation: Harvey W. Wiley and the Fight for Pure Food.* Chicago: Published for the University of Cincinnati by the University of Chicago Press, 1958.

A biography of Wiley, the father of the Pure Food and Drugs Act of 1906.

Andreasen, Alan R. *The Disadvantaged Consumer: Life in the Ghetto Marketplace.* New York: Free Press, 1975. 366 pp. ISBN 0-02900-690-2.

Written by a marketing professor, this scholarly work documents the exploitation of vulnerable consumers.

Angevine, Erma, editor. *Consumer Activists: They Made a Difference.* Mount Vernon, NY: Consumers Union Foundation, 1982. 365 pp.

Articles on the history of the consumer movement, written by its leaders. Different sections focus on topics such as federal consumer protection, product standards and product testing, consumer education, and lobbying.

Armstrong, David, and Elizabeth Metzger Armstrong. *The Great American Medicine Show: Being an Illustrated History of Hucksters, Healers, Health Evangelists and Heroes from Plymouth Rock to the Present.* New York: Prentice-Hall, 1991. 292 pp. ISBN 0-13364-027-2.

An amusing review of the bizarre and the unique in herbalism, homeopathy, temperance, hydropathy, phrenology, patent medicine, and other cure-alls from America's past.

Asch, Peter. *Consumer Safety Regulation: Putting a Price on Life and Limb.* New York: Oxford University Press, 1988. 172 pp. ISBN 0-19504-972-1.

An economist's review of federal safety regulations.

Bailey, Fenton. *Fall from Grace: The Untold Story of Michael Milken.* Secaucus, NJ: Carol Publishing Group, 1992. 330 pp. ISBN 1-55972-135-9.

Examines corrupt practices in the securities industry with the sale of junk bonds.

Barrett, Stephen. *Health Schemes, Scams, and Frauds.* Mt. Vernon, NY: Consumers Union, 1990. 245 pp. ISBN 0-89043-330-5.

Based on articles originally published in Consumer Reports magazine, this book focuses on the most prevalent and persistent forms of health fraud, false claims, worthless remedies, and health scare campaigns.

Bequai, August. *Technocrimes.* Lexington, MA: Lexington Books, 1987. 192 pp. ISBN 0-66912-342-0.

From hackers to espionage to organized crime, the author explores the depth and breadth of the high-tech revolution and its use for criminal purposes.

Bettman, Otto L. *The Good Old Days—They were Terrible!* New York: Random House, 1974. 297 pp. ISBN 0-394-70941-1.

The period from the end of the Civil War to the early 1900s, known as the Gilded Age and the Gay Nineties, is often described as the good old days. This books seeks to put this myth to rest with contemporary graphics from the Bettman Archive. It focuses on the lives of those who suffered from poverty, unhealthy conditions, adulterated foods, and unsanitary conditions.

Binstein, Michael and Charles Bowden. *Trust Me: Charles Keating and the Missing Billions.* New York: Random House, 1993. 420 pp. ISBN 0-67941-699-4.

A biography of Charles Keating, a Phoenix businessman and one of the most notorious figures in the 1980s savings-and-loan scandals. Keating headed the California-based Lincoln Savings & Loan. When this savings and loan collapsed in 1989, taxpayers had to absorb losses of over $3 billion.

Blankenship, Michael B., editor. *Understanding Corporate Criminality.* New York: Garland Publishing, 1993. 266 pp. ISBN 0-81530-883-3.

A series of essays written by criminologists exploring corporate crime, its victims, public perceptions, and the regulation and prosecution of these criminal acts.

Bologna, G. Jack, and Robert J. Lindquist. *Fraud Auditing and Forensic Accounting: New tools and Techniques.* 2d ed. New York: John Wiley & Sons, 1995. 240 pp. ISBN 0-47185-412-3.

Written by an internal auditor and a management consultant, this book surveys, in outline form, a variety of economic frauds and suggests mechanisms for detecting and controlling them.

Brickey, Homer. *Master Manipulator.* New York: American Management Association, 1985. 161 pp. ISBN 0-81445-818-1.

A reporter's chronicle of the 1983 collapse of a major brokerage firm and one of the largest stock-brokerage frauds in the history of the Securities and Exchange Commission.

Brickey, Kathleen F. *Corporate and White-Collar Crime: Cases and Materials.* Boston: Little, Brown, 1990. 663 pp. ISBN 0-31610-820-0.

A technical examination of major federal statutes that are invoked in corporate white-collar prosecutions using actual cases as well as other materials to establish the context in which issues are framed.

Brobeck, Stephen, editor. *Encyclopedia of the Consumer Movement.* Santa Barbara, CA: ABC-CLIO, 1997. 659 pp. ISBN 0-87436-987-8

A reference work on consumerism with almost 200 entries including biographies, a history of the consumer movement, fraud and consumer protection laws, warranties, international consumer organizations and issues, and many others. The various entries were written by different experts in the field.

Burkholz, Herbert. *The FDA Follies.* New York: Basic Books, 1994. 228 pp. ISBN 0-46502-369-X.

A journalist's critique of the Food and Drug Administration in the 1980s.

Burt, Dan M. *Abuse of Trust: A Report on Ralph Nader's Network.* Chicago: Regnery Gateway, 1982. 269 pp. ISBN 0-89526-661-X.

A conservative appraisal of what has been called the Nader Network. The author is connected with the Capitol Legal Foundation, a conservative legal advocacy organization.

Campbell, A. E. *America Comes of Age: the Era of Theodore Roosevelt.* New York: American Heritage Press, 1971. 127 pp. ISBN 0-70096-878-3.

A review of the era of the presidency of Teddy Roosevelt, a trust buster who signed into law the Pure Food and Drug Act and the Meat Inspection Act.

Caplovitz, David. *The Poor Pay More: Consumer Practices of Low-Income Families.* New York: Free Press of Glencoe, 1963. 225 pp.

Classic study of the plight of the poor in the ghetto marketplace and the pervasiveness of illegal and unethical practices that affect them. It is based on a survey of 400 households in a New York City housing project.

Chase, Stuart, and F. J. Schlink. *Your Money's Worth: A Study in the Waste of the Consumer's Dollar.* New York: Macmillan, 1927. 285 pp.

A book that helped spark the consumer movement of the 1920s and 1930s, *Your Money's Worth* focused public attention on the exploitative nature of much advertising and many deceptions regarding pricing, quality, and safety. It also helped introduce product research.

Cialdini, Robert B. *Influence: The Psychology of Persuasion.* 2d ed. New York: William Morrow, 1993. 320 pp. ISBN 0-68812-816-5.

An important work, from a business and consumer protection perspective, that looks at the tools of influence used by marketers to sell. Although the author is a social-psychologist, and this work includes research findings, it is very readable and contains humorous anecdotes from the author's experience in attending various sales training courses.

Clinard, Marshall B. *Corporate Corruption: The Abuse of Power.* New York: Praeger, 1990. 215 pp. ISBN 0-27593-485-3.

An in-depth study of the ethical conduct of American *Fortune* 500 corporations, from price fixing to health and safety code violations that caused accidents and deaths, and the marketing of unsafe products.

Clinard, Marshall B., and Peter C. Yeager. *Corporate Crime.* New York: Free Press, 1980. 386 pp. ISBN 0-02905-710-8.

A comprehensive treatment of corporate crime and its control, including a discussion of major types of such crime with case examples.

Coate, Malcom B., and Andrew N. Kleit, editors. *The Economics of the Antitrust Process.* Boston: Kluwer Academic Publishers, 1996. 260 pp. ISBN 0-79239-731-2.

A series of essays examining the antitrust regulatory process and how it affects the efficiency of antimonopoly enforcement. This is a technical, economic approach authored by scholars in the field.

Coleman, James W. *The Criminal Elite: The Sociology of White Collar Crime.* New York: St. Martin's Press, 1985. 260 pp. ISBN 0-31217-209-5.

Coleman contrasts the public concern with street crime and the "much bigger and more damaging" crimes perpetrated by organizations and industries, and the individuals within these systems.

Comstock, Anthony. *Frauds Exposed: How the People Are Deceived and Robbed, and Youth Corrupted.* Montclair, NJ: Patterson Smith, 1969 (reprint of 1882). 576 pp. ISBN 0-87585-079-0.

One of the first books on consumer fraud, particularly mail fraud, with advice on how consumers could protect themselves. This work was authored by a former postal agent.

Croall, Hazel. *White Collar Crime: Criminal Justice and Criminality.* Buckingham, England: Open University Press, 1992. 195 pp. ISBN 0-33509-657-3.

Written by an English criminologist, this book introduces readers to the major issues in the study of white-collar crime.

Dunn, Donald H. *Ponzi! The Boston Swindler.* New York: McGraw-Hill, 1975. 254 pp. ISBN 0-07018-270-1.

A biography of Charles Ponzi, a practitioner of the investment fraud that bears his name, the Ponzi Scheme. Under this scheme, early investors are paid with the contributions of later investors. As long as new investors can be found, the scheme continues to work. When no new investors can be found, which is inevitable, the scheme collapses. When Ponzi went bankrupt in 1920, investors lost $10 million.

Eichenwald, Kurt. *Serpent on the Rock.* New York: Harper Business, 1995. 480 pp. ISBN 0-88730-720-5.

Written by a *New York Times* reporter, this is a novel-like narrative of the Prudential-Bache securities fraud scandal. It is based on 600 interviews, a review of personal diaries, internal correspondence, insolvency reports, public documents, and sworn statements.

Feldman, Laurence P. *Consumer Protection: Problems and Prospects.* 2d ed. St. Paul, MN: West Publishing, 1980. 299 pp. ISBN 0-82990-064-0.

Dated but thorough text on the various aspects of consumer protection with a thoughtful chapter on the difference between legitimate persuasion and deceptive advertising.

Ferrell, O. C., and Raymond LaGarce, editors. *Public Policy Issues in Marketing.* Lexington, MA: Lexington Books, 1975. 192 pp. ISBN 0-66998-038-2.

Diverse essays that attempt to describe public policy and marketing relationships, with a goal of correcting deceptive advertising and improving business responsibility.

Filler, Louis. *The Muckrakers: Crusaders for American Liberalism*. Chicago: Regnery Company, 1968. 422 pp.

A classic study of the muckraking era in U.S. history (1900–1914) and how its participants helped enact fundamental reforms such as meat inspection laws, the Pure Food and Drug Act, and many others. This work originally was published in 1939 as *Crusaders for American Liberalism* and was revised in 1968.

Foreman, Christopher H. *Plagues, Products and Politics: Emergent Public Health Hazards and National Policymaking*. Washington, DC: Brookings Institute, 1994. 210pp. ISBN 0-81572-876-X.

Broad discussion of recent public health hazards, such as tampon-induced toxic shock syndrome, infections caused by intrauterine contraceptive devices, chloride-deficient infant formulas, *E. coli* bacteria–infected hamburgers, and others, and the way government policy is shaped by technical and political restraints.

Friedman, Howard M. *Securities and Commodities Enforcement: Criminal Prosecutions and Civil Injunctions*. Lexington, MA: Lexington Books, 1981. 238 pp. ISBN 0-66903-617-X.

Dated but comprehensive review of the pertinent federal and state laws regulating the sale of stocks, bonds, commodities, and other investment vehicles.

Friedrichs, David O. *Trusted Criminals: White Collar Crime in Contemporary Society*. Belmont, WA: Wadsworth Publishing, 1996. 441 pp. ISBN 0-53450-517-1.

A detailed, systematic review of white-collar crime with definitions, cost estimates, examples of criminal activity, and discussions of policing, prosecuting, and regulating this criminal activity.

Fuller, John Grant. *200,000 Guinea Pigs: New Dangers in Everyday Foods, Drugs, and Cosmetics*. New York: Putnam, 1972. 320 pp. ISBN 0-39911-000-3.

Forty years after the ground-breaking study by Arthur Kallet and F. J. Schlink, entitled *100,000 Guinea Pigs*, exposed the dangers of everyday foods, drugs, and cosmetics, the author updates information and concludes that matters are worse rather than better. It focuses on areas viewed as imminent health dangers by the author. Somewhat out of date, but valuable for historical context.

Garman, E. Thomas. *Consumer Economic Issues in America.* 2d ed. Houston: DAME Publications, 1993. 880 pp. ISBN 0-87393-221-8.

A college text reviewing the economic issues of consumerism, including fraud, misrepresentation, and deceptive schemes and practices.

Geis, Gilbert. *On White-Collar Crime.* Lexington, MA: Lexington Books, 1982. 216 pp. ISBN 0-66904-568-3.

This collection of essays, spanning more than 30 years, provides an excellent background on the subject of white-collar crime. It also contains Gies's suggestions for the direction that investigation of white-collar crime should take. The essays illustrate the changes in Gies's thinking and the changes in this field of study.

Geis, Gilbert, and Paul Jesilow, editors. *White-Collar Crime.* Newbury Park, CA: Sage Periodicals Press, 1993. ISBN 0-80394-688-0.

A series of essays describing the various forms of white-collar crime such as insider trading, fraud in commodities trades, and environmental crimes. Also discusses recent federal sentencing guidelines for white-collar criminals.

Geis, Gilbert, Robert F. Meir, and Lawrence M. Salinger, editors. *White-Collar Crime: Classic and Contemporary Views.* 3d ed. New York: Free Press, 1995. 511 pp. ISBN 0-02911-601-5.

A recent collection of scholarly essays on white-collar crime by the leading authorities on the subject.

Green, Mark J., with Beverly C. Moore Jr. and Bruce Wasserstein. *The Closed Enterprise System: Ralph Nader's Study Group Report on Antitrust Enforcement.* New York: Grossman, 1972. 488 pp. ISBN 0-67022-555-X.

Described by consumer activist Ralph Nader as "a report on crime in the suites," this book examines the policies and procedures of antitrust enforcement and evaluates the results.

Harding, T. Swann. *The Popular Practice of Fraud.* New York: Arno Press, 1976. 376 pp. ISBN 0-40508-020-4.

A book originally printed in the 1930s that attacks the advertising claims made by big business for household products.

Harris, Leon. *Upton Sinclair, American Rebel.* New York: Crowell, 1975. 435 pp. ISBN 0-69000-671-3.

A biography of Upton Sinclair, author of *The Jungle*.

Herzog, Arthur. *Vesco: From Wall Street to Castro's Cuba, The Rise, Fall, and Exile of the King of White-Collar Crime.* New York: Doubleday, 1987. 380 pp. ISBN 0-38524-176-3.

A popular biography of Robert Vesco, alleged to be the perpetrator of what was the largest securities fraud in modern history at the time. Written by a noted journalist and novelist.

Hills, Stuart L., editor. *Corporate Violence: Injury and Death for Profit.* Totowa, NJ: Rowan & Littlefield, 1987. 213 pp. ISBN 0-84767-535-1.

An anthology of articles discussing actual harm or risk of harm to consumers as a result of corporate decision making or the negligence of executives and managers.

Holsworth, Robert D. *Public Interest Liberalism and the Crisis of Affluence: Reflections on Nader.* Boston: G. K. Hall, 1980. 158 pp. ISBN 0-81619-032-1.

A highly academic evaluation of "public-interest liberalism" as personified by Ralph Nader.

Hudson, Michael, editor. *Merchants of Misery.* Monroe, ME: Common Courage Press, 1996. 232 pp. ISBN 1-56751-083-3.

A review of banking, insurance, rent-to-own, and other industries, and the struggle between maintaining corporate profits and preventing consumer rip-offs, particularly as they affect the poor. Written by journalists from the *Wall Street Journal*, *Barrons*, *National Law Journal*, and other publications.

Jacob, Craig, as told to Phil Berger. *Twisted Genius: Confessions of a $10 Million Scam Man.* New York: Four Walls Eight Windows, 1995. 204 pp. ISBN 1-56858-044-4.

A first-person account of a con man's scams and the swindles that earned him $10 million.

Jamieson, Katherine M. *The Organization of Corporate Crime: Dynamics of Antitrust Violation.* Thousand Oaks, CA: Sage Publications, 1994. 113 pp. ISBN 0-80395-199-X.

Explores causation in the deviant behavior of those corporate executives who apply illegal and anticompetitive means to achieve corporate goals. A good review and update of this area of study.

Jesilow, Paul, Henry N. Pontell, and Gilbert Geis. *Prescription for Profit: How Doctors Defraud Medicaid.* Berkeley, CA: University of California Press, 1993. 247 pp. ISBN 0-52007-614-1.

An analysis of the changes in medical practice resulting from the introduction of Medicare and Medicaid, focusing on case studies and interviews with doctors who were convicted of, or pled guilty to, Medicaid fraud.

Kintner, Earl W. *A Primer on the Law of Deceptive Practices: A Guide for the Businessman.* New York: Macmillan, 1971. 593 pp.

A somewhat dated but excellent description of what constitutes deceptive practices in advertising and other product promotion.

Kornbluth, Jesse. *Highly Confident: The Crime and Punishment of Michael Milken.* New York: Morrow, 1992.

The rise and fall of Michael Milken, junk bond king and convicted felon.

Krohn, Lauren. *Consumer Protection and the Law: A Dictionary.* Santa Barbara, CA: ABC-CLIO, Inc. 1995. 358 pp. ISBN 0-87436-749-2.

A reference book discussing various aspects of consumer protection, including federal and state laws, court decisions, consumer organizations and advocates, and historical events.

Kwitny, Jonathan. *The Fountain Pen Conspiracy.* New York: Alfred A. Knopf, 1973. 328 pp. ISBN 0-39447-935-1.

Dated but interesting review of swindlers who fleeced both consumers and banks, written by a former *Wall Street Journal* reporter.

Leinwand, Gerald, compiler. *The Consumer.* New York: Washington Square Press, 1970. 190 pp. ISBN 0-67147-184-8.

A classic look at the significant dilemmas of the urban consumer, with particular attention to the urban poor and their vulnerability to fraud, usury, false pricing, and deceptive labeling.

Lester, David, editor. *The Elderly Victim of Crime.* Springfield, IL: C. C. Thomas, 1981. 134 pp. ISBN 0-39804-506-2.

A collection of essays on crimes against the elderly, one of which discusses consumer fraud and older Americans.

McCarry, Charles. *Citizen Nader.* New York: Saturday Review Press, 1972. 335 pp. ISBN 0-84150-163-7.

A personal and public biography of Ralph Nader based on interviews with 300 persons, including Nader. It covers his background and early life, and although somewhat laudatory, contains valuable information.

McChesney, Fred S., and William F. Shughart II, editors. *The Causes and Consequences of Antitrust: The Public-Choice Perspective.* Chicago: University of Chicago Press, 1995. 379 pp. ISBN 0-22655-634-4.

Essays challenging fundamental assumptions regarding antitrust laws, contrasting the public-choice model with that of public interest. The authors maintain that antitrust laws are susceptible to the influence of special-interest groups at the expense of consumers.

Magnuson, Warren G., and Jean Carper. *The Dark Side of the Marketplace; The Plight of the American Consumer.* Englewood Cliffs, NJ: Prentice-Hall, 1968. 240 pp.

An early and influential critique of marketplace abuses in the post–World War II era, written when Magnuson was chair of the Senate Commerce Committee.

Mayer, Robert N. *The Consumer Movement: Guardians of the Marketplace.* Boston: Twayne Publishers, 1989. 197 pp. ISBN 0-80597-181- .

A historical, economic, and structural review of the consumer movement and its various groups, written by a sociologist focusing on consumer behavior.

Maynes, E. Scott, editor. *The Frontier of Research in the Consumer*

Interest: Proceedings of the International Conference on Research in the Consumer Interest. Columbia, MO: American Council on Consumer Interests, 1988. 889 pp. ISBN 0-94585-700-4.

This collection of articles was designed to lay a foundation in research for consumer economics, education, and information organized around the Consumer Bill of Rights first articulated by President John F. Kennedy.

Meier, Kenneth J., E. Thomas Garman, and Lael R. Keiser. *Regulation and Consumer Protection.* 3d ed. Houston: DAME Publications, 1998. 515 pp. ISBN 0-87393-640-X.

Regulation is a frequently used governmental tool to protect consumers. This book reviews various regulatory systems such as occupation licensure, antitrust policy, and food safety. Part of the focus is the cost of regulation versus the benefit to consumers.

Mitford, Jessica. *The American Way of Death.* New York: Simon & Schuster, 1978. 324 pp. ISBN 0-67124-706-9.

The classic study of the funeral industry that exposed the hidden and unnecessary costs built into a system that found its consumers at a most vulnerable moment. Instrumental in passing a federal trade rule requiring price disclosures.

Mizell, Louis R., Jr. *Masters of Deception: The Worldwide White-Collar Crime Crisis and Ways to Protect Yourself.* New York: John Wiley & Sons, 1997. 253 pp. ISBN 0-47113-355-8.

Covers the scope of white-collar crimes connected with education, medical services, legal practices, charities, insurance, and banking.

Morse, Richard L. D., editor. *The Consumer Movement: Lectures by Colston E. Warne.* Manhattan, KS: Family Economics Trust Press, 1993. 346 pp. ISBN 1-88133-101-6.

Colston Warne, the first president of Consumers Union, publisher of Consumer Reports, was an early guiding force in the consumer movement. Here he reviews, among other issues, the history of the consumer movement, the origins of consumer testing, advertising issues, and the future of consumerism.

Mungo, Paul, and Bryan Clough. *Approaching Zero: The Extraordinary Underworld of Hackers, Phreakers, Virus Writers and*

Keyboard Criminals. New York: Random House, 1992. 247 pp. ISBN 0-67940-938-6.

A very readable, novel-like study of the history, growth, and methods of computer fraud.

Myers, Kenneth D. *False Security: Greed and Deception in America's Multibillion-Dollar Insurance Industry.* Amherst, NY: Prometheus Books, 1995. 288 pp. ISBN 0-87975-928-3.

A colorful narrative of insurance fraud schemes perpetrated by industry executives. The author focuses mainly on the reinsurance business. He also makes recommendations for regulatory reforms and provides a unique glossary of industry terms.

Nadel, Mark V. *The Politics of Consumer Protection.* Indianapolis: Bobbs-Merrill, 1971. 257 pp.

An excellent general study of the influence of consumer action groups in the passage of federal consumer legislation in the 1960s.

Nader, Ralph. *Unsafe at Any Speed.* New York: Grossman, 1965. 365 pp.

The premier exposé of an unsafe product, automobiles, of the post–World War II era. Here Nader attacked the failure of U.S. auto manufacturers' to build safer cars, with particular attention focused on General Motors' Chevrolet Corvair.

Nader, Ralph, editor. *The Consumer and Corporate Accountability.* New York: Harcourt Brace Jovanovich, 1973. 375 pp. ISBN 0-15513-461-2.

Essays by various consumer activists addressing the ways in which corporate irresponsibility affects consumers' everyday lives.

Nader, Ralph, Mark Green, and Joel Seligman. *Taming the Giant Corporation.* New York: Norton, 1976. 312 pp. ISBN 0-39308-753-0.

The authors argue that federal, rather than state, chartering of corporations is needed to control abuses from large corporations.

Okun, Mitchell. *Fair Play in the Marketplace: The First Battle for Pure Food and Drugs.* Dekalb, IL: Northern Illinois University Press, 1986. 345 pp. ISBN 0-87580-115-3.

A history of the post–Civil War battle for state legislation regulating the adulteration of food and drugs, particularly in New York. These events preceded the passage of the federal Pure Food and Drug Act of 1906.

Pertschuk, Michael. *Revolt against Regulation: The Rise and Pause of the Consumer Movement.* Berkeley, CA: University of California Press, 1982. 165 pp. ISBN 0-52004-824-5.

An entertaining analysis of consumer advocacy and its push for federal consumer protection legislation in the 1960s as well as the forces that converged to erode the movement in the 1970s.

Peterson, Esther, with Winfred Conklin. *Restless: The Memoirs of Labor and Consumer Activist Esther Peterson.* Washington, DC: Caring Publishing, 1995. 193 pp. ISBN 1-88645-002-1.

An intriguing and candid self-portrait of the first presidential advisor for consumer affairs. Peterson describes her personal and professional growth over most of the twentieth century.

Poveda, Tony G. *Rethinking White-Collar Crime.* Westport, CT: Praeger, 1994. 171 pp. ISBN 0-27594-586-3.

Updates the ongoing definitional controversy of exactly what constitutes white-collar crime, and reviews the double standard in connection with the different official responses to white-collar as compared to conventional crime. This book reviews the major relevant theories and provides a history and analysis of white-collar crime legislation and enforcement.

Preston, Ivan L. *The Tangled Web They Weave: Truth, Falsity, and Advertisers.* Madison, WI: University of Wisconsin Press, 1994. 225 pp. ISBN 0-29914-190-X.

An anecdotal look at how advertisers avoid illegal falsity (not all false claims are illegal), while at the same time avoiding a significant amount of truth.

———. *The Great American Blow-Up: Puffery in Advertising and Selling.* 2d ed. Madison, WI: University of Wisconsin Press, 1997. 368 pp. ISBN 0-29906-730-0.

This books seeks to answer the question, "How does advertising really work?" It cites examples of puffery, deception, and false claims and defines the role of the Federal Trade Commission in regulating advertising.

Pridgen, Dee. *Consumer Protection and the Law.* New York: Clark Boardman, 1986. 1 vol., loose-leaf. ISBN 0-87632-501-0.

An exhaustive review of the Federal Trade Commission Act and the various state consumer protection laws (Unfair and Deceptive Acts and Practices statutes) spawned by the federal law. This loose-leaf volume is a law book, written for attorneys in the field of consumer protection. It reviews current cases and standards for responding to practices that injure consumers.

Richards, Jef I. *Deceptive Advertising: Behavioral Study of a Legal Concept.* Hillsdale, NJ: L. Erlbaum Associates, 1990. 244 pp. ISBN 0-80580-649-0.

A highly technical review of what constitutes deceptive advertising from the perspective of a behavioral scientist.

Rosefsky, Robert S. *Frauds, Swindles, and Rackets; A Red Alert for Today's Consumers.* Chicago: Follett Publishing, 1973. 338 pp. ISBN 0-69580-384-0.

Although dated, this book is designed to acquaint the reader with a multitude of specific fraudulent schemes and the general pattern of consumer fraud.

Ross, Irwin. *Shady Business: Confronting Corporate Corruption.* New York: Twentieth Century Fund, 1992. 175 pp. ISBN 0-87078-340-8.

A contemporary look at the phenomenon of corporate crime, its causes, and perpetrators. It analyzes six major areas, including kickbacks, securities violations, criminal antitrust, tax evasion, fraud in defense procurement, and fraud in general. An excellent overview.

Schulte, Fred. *Fleeced! Telemarketing Rip-Offs and How to Avoid Them.* Amherst, NY: Prometheus Books, 1995. 361 pp. ISBN 0-87975-963-1.

An introduction to telemarketing fraud, written by an investigative reporter. Together with anecdotal stories of different schemes, this book includes sample sales pitches, customer objections, and law enforcement agencies that have jurisdiction over telemarketing fraud.

Seidler, Lee J., Frederick Andrews, and Marc J. Epstein, editors.

The Equity Funding Papers: The Anatomy of a Fraud. Santa Barbara, CA: John Wiley & Sons, 1977. 578 pp. ISBN 0-47102-275-X.

A documentary approach to explain the Equity Funding fraud and how employees systematically developed and maintained the scam for a decade.

Shadel, Douglas P., and "John T." *Schemes and Scams.* Van Nuys, CA: Newcastle Publishing, 1994. 239 pp. ISBN 0-87877-186-7.

An overview of consumer frauds perpetrated against older Americans. Written by a consumer fraud investigator (Shadel) and a convicted telemarketer ("John T.").

Shapiro, Howard S. *How to Keep Them Honest: Herbert Denenberg on Spotting the Professional Phonies, Unscrewing Insurance and Protecting Your Interests.* Emmaus, PA: Rodale Press, 1974. 238 pp. ISBN 0-87857-084-5.

A popular biography of Herbert Denenberg, consumer advocate, journalist, and former insurance commissioner of Pennsylvania.

Shapiro, Susan P. *Wayward Capitalists: Target of the Securities and Exchange Commission.* New Haven, CT: Yale University Press, 1984. 227 pp. ISBN 0-30003-116-5.

A detailed examination of the Securities and Exchange Commission's enforcement apparatus and how it works, using previously unavailable data.

Sharkey, Joe. *Bedlam: Greed, Profiteering, and Fraud in a Mental Health System Gone Crazy.* New York: St. Martin's Press, 1994. 294 pp. ISBN 0-31210-421-9.

The author, a journalist struggling with a drinking problem, learns firsthand about health care fraud in private mental health institutions. Here he reviews allegations against the nation's for-profit psychiatric hospitals.

Silber, Norman Isaac. *Test and Protest: The Influence of Consumers Union.* New York: Homes & Meier, 1983. 172 pp. ISBN 0-84190-877-X.

An evaluation of product testing at Consumers Union, publisher of *Consumer Reports.* A limited but useful study.

Sinclair, Upton. *The Jungle.* New York: Bantam Books, 1981 (reprint of 1906). 346 pp. ISBN 0-553-21245-1.

A novel designed to expose working conditions in Chicago's stockyard at the turn of the century. Instead, this book set off a wave of disgust over unsanitary conditions in meatpacking, which led to the passage of the federal Pure Food and Drug Act of 1906 and the Meat Inspection Act.

Sloan, Irving J. *The Law and Legislation of Credit Cards: Use and Misuse.* New York: Oceana Publications, 1987. 153 pp. ISBN 0-37911-158-6,

Written for the nonlawyer, this work reviews the history of federal and state laws on credit cards and relevant court cases.

Smith, Ralph Lee. *The Health Hucksters.* New York: Crowell, 1960. 248 pp.

Written prior to enactment of the 1962 Kefauver amendments to the Food, Drug and Cosmetic Act, this book attacks medical deceptions and product misrepresentations in the prescription drug trade.

Sobel, Lester A., editor. *Consumer Protection.* New York: Facts on File, 1976. 174 pp.

Encyclopedic compilation of government efforts and policy development aimed at curbing consumer abuse. Covers the period of the Kennedy administration through the mid-1970s.

Sparrow, Malcolm K. *License to Steal: Why Fraud Plagues America's Health Care System.* Boulder, CO: Westview Press, 1996. 240 pp. ISBN 0-81333-067-X.

Written by a researcher at the Kennedy School of Government, this book discusses the nature and volume of fraud in the nation's health care system.

Spencer, Margaret P., and Ronald R. Simms, editors. *Corporate Misconduct: The Legal, Societal, and Management Issues.* Westport, CT: Quorum Books, 1995. 215 pp. ISBN 0-89930-879-1.

An up-to-date examination of a broad scope of corporate misconduct, with particular emphasis on the ways in which technology spawns new forms of financial crimes, including investment fraud, software piracy, and deceptive marketing.

Sterling, Bruce. *The Hacker Crackdown: Law and Disorder on the Electronic Frontier.* New York: Bantam Books, 1992. 328 pp. ISBN 0-553-8-058-X.

Offbeat but very engaging examination of cyberspace crimes by a journalist and science-fiction writer. The book focuses on the 1990 efforts by law enforcement officials to break the electronic underground.

Sutherland, Edwin H., with an introduction by Gilbert Geis and Colin Goff. *White Collar Crime: The Uncut Version.* New Haven, CT: Yale University Press, 1983. 291 pp. ISBN 0-30002-921-7.

A reissue of the classic 1949 work, in which the criminologist Sutherland introduces and names the concept of white-collar crime. This edition includes material cut from the original and contains an update by Geis and Goff that assesses Sutherland's impact.

Suthers, John W., and Gary L. Shupp. *Fraud and Deceit: How to Stop Being Ripped Off.* New York: Arco, 1982. 144 pp. ISBN 0-66805-318-6.

A dated but still useful consumers' guide, written by prosecutors who specialize in the investigation of consumer fraud. This work describes various common schemes arranged in apt categories. Simple, direct, and useful.

Turner, James S. *The Chemical Feast.* New York: Grossman, 1970. 273 pp.

Written by the project director of the Ralph Nader Study Group, this work exposed the inadequacy of the Food and Drug Administration to provide truthful and complete information regarding food purity, quality, nutritional value, additives, and adulterants to consumers in the 1970s. Useful for background and comparison with today's standards.

Utton, M. A. *Market Dominance and Antitrust Policy.* Brookfield, VT: E. Elgar, 1995. 342 pp. ISBN 1-85278-358-3.

A technical and scholarly work for students interested in the theoretical aspects of antitrust policy. A sophisticated analysis, complete with tables and statistics.

Villa, John K. *Banking Crimes: Fraud, Money Laundering, and Embezzlement.* 2 vols., loose-leaf. New York: Clark Boardman, 1987. ISBN 0-87632-546-0.

A comprehensive analysis of relevant legal cases involving banking crimes.

Washburn, Robert Collyer. *The Life and Times of Lydia Pinkham.* New York: Arno Press, 1976. 221 pp. ISBN 0-40508-055-7.

A biography of Lydia Pinkham, nineteenth-century America's most successful patent medicine merchant. Her company sold a popular elixir to treat "female problems," whose main ingredient was alcohol. Federal investigators, using the new Pure Food and Drug Act, were instrumental in removing this product from the marketplace.

Weisburd, David. *Crimes of the Middle Classes: White-Collar Offenders in the Federal Courts.* New Haven, CT: Yale University Press, 1991. 211 pp. ISBN 0-30004-952-8.

An examination of the backgrounds of convicted white-collar offenders using presentencing investigation reports. The author is a federal probation officer.

Whiteside, Thomas. *The Investigation of Ralph Nader: General Motors vs. One Determined Man.* New York: Pocket Books, 1972. 255 pp. ISBN 0-87795-034-2.

An account of the surveillance of consumer advocate, Ralph Nader, by agents hired by General Motors after the publication of Nader's book *Unsafe at Any Speed.*

Wiley, Harvey Washington. *An Autobiography.* Indianapolis: Bobb-Merrill, 1930.

An autobiography by the father of the Pure Food and Drug Act of 1906.

Young, James Harvey. *The Medical Messiahs: A Social History of Health Quackery in Twentieth-Century America.* Princeton, NJ: Princeton University Press, 1967. 460 pp.

After the passage of the 1906 Pure Food and Drug Act, many believed harmful nostrums would disappear. This book chronicles the development of patent medicines, such as a "tuberculosis-curing liniment," nutrition nonsense, and cancer quackery in the twentieth century.

Periodical Articles

Albert, James A. **"A History of Attempts by the Department of Agriculture to Reduce Federal Inspection of Poultry Processing Plants—A Return to the Jungle."** *Louisiana Law Review* 51 (July 1991): 1183.

Chicken has emerged as the meat of choice for newly health-conscious Americans. Yet, according to the author, a law professor from Drake University, the USDA has bowed to industry pressure rather than protect consumers from unsafe meat.

Athineos, Doris. **"Buyers Beware."** *Forbes* 159, no. 5 (10 March 1997): 210–211.

Fancy art galleries and auction houses have sold fakes and stolen art. Tips for buyers to protect themselves.

"Avoid Swindles on the Information Highway." *USA Today: The Magazine of the American Scene* 124, no. 2603 (August 1995): 13–14.

Financial scams on the Internet and ways consumers can protect themselves against them.

Baer, William J. **"Surf's Up: Antitrust Enforcement and Consumer Interests in a Merger Wave."** *Journal of Consumer Affairs* 30, no. 2 (Winter 1996): 292–321.

An unprecedented wave of corporate mergers and acquisitions is taking place, yet the Federal Trade Commission and the U.S. Department of Justice challenge less than 2 percent of these actions. Baer, director of the Bureau of Competition at the Federal Trade Commission, reviews antitrust law and explores whether economic efficiency or protecting consumers from anticompetitive practices is the focus of federal actions.

Barrett, Stephen. **"Stronger Laws Needed to Stop Mail Fraud."** *Health Weight Journal* 9, no. 3 (May 1995): 55.

Mail-order diet aids fail to live up to their claims. Consumers need more protections under federal mail fraud statutes.

Bedard, Patrick. **"One Little Guy Lays Siege to a Big, and Shady, Operation."** *Car & Driver* 40, no. 12 (June 1995): 17–18.

One man's crusade to expose the business practices of a high-pressure, classic car kit telemarketer. Questionable business practices are discussed.

Belsky, Gary. **"Watch Out: Car-Repair Crooks Have Some New Tricks Up Their Grimy Sleeves."** *Money* 25, no. 6 (June 1996): 172–174.

An estimated 25–50 percent of the $90 billion Americans spend on auto repair is lost to fraud or incompetence. Major problems consumers should look for are described.

Bender, Steven W. **"Consumer Protection for Latinos: Overcoming Language Fraud and English-Only in the Marketplace."** *American University Law Review* 45 (April 1996): 1027.

There are 27 million Latinos in the United States, many of whom have difficulty speaking and understanding English. Frauds based on language misunderstandings are frequently perpetrated against this minority population. The author makes recommendations for increased consumer protections.

Blake, Kevin. **"Auto Leasing Settlement."** *Consumers' Research Magazine* 80, no. 1 (January 1997): 38.

More than 20 state attorneys general settled a lawsuit against car manufacturers alleging misleading advertising in auto leasing programs.

———. **"More Credit Repair Fraud."** *Consumers' Research Magazine* 79, no. 6 (June 1996): 38.

The Federal Trade Commission announces settlement with law firms advertising on the Internet regarding credit repair. The FTC had charged these firms with deceptive advertising.

———. **"Dial F for Fraud."** *Consumers' Research Magazine* 78, no. 11 (November 1995): 38.

Discusses threats to consumers being victimized by phony 900-number demand notices.

Davis, Joel J. **"Ethics in Advertising Decisionmaking: Implications for Reducing the Incidence of Deceptive Advertising."** *Journal of Consumer Affairs* 28, no. 2 (Winter 1994): 380–402.

The results of a survey of 206 advertising professionals assessing the impact of "ethics, legal considerations, business considerations, and approval of management/peers" on decision making. The survey indicates that ethics played but a small part in advertising decision making. Legal considerations were ranked highest

by experienced professionals. For the novice, "business considerations and approval by management/peers" was more important than either ethics or legal implications.

Edmondson, Brad. **"Beware the Phone Frauds!"** *New Choices:
Living Even Better After 50* 36, no. 5 (June 1996): 42–49.

Tips from a reformed criminal telemarketer on how consumers
can protect themselves against phone fraud.

Farley, Dixie. **"Unproven Medial Claims Land Men in Prison."**
FDA Consumer 30, no. 7 (September 1996): 33–34.

Claims for an electrical shock-producing medical device as a
cure-all lands felony convictions for three individuals.

"Fish Fraud." *Nutrition Action Healthletter* 23, no. 9 (November
1996): 5.

How consumers can protect themselves against consumer frauds
in the sale of seafood.

Fitzgerald, Kate. **"AT&T, MCI Settle Deceptive-Ad Suits."** *Advertising Age* 61, no. 52 (17 December 1990): 33.

AT&T and MCI settle deceptive advertising suits against each
other out of court.

Fox, Justin. **"What's New about Digital Cash."** *Fortune* 134, no. 6
(30 September 1996): 50–54.

Electronic banking is advancing, but fraud and consumer resis-
tance must be overcome before it becomes more widespread.

Frank, Judith A. **"Preneed Funeral Plans: The Case for Uniformity."** *Elder Law Journal* 4 (Spring 1996): 1.

The sale of preneed (in advance of need) funeral plans is now a
big business throughout the country. There is a significant gap in
state consumer protection laws that leaves the elderly vulnerable
to exploitation by the sellers of these products.

Friedman, Monroe. **"Confidence Swindles of Older Consumers."**
Journal of Consumer Affairs: 26, no. 1 (Summer 1992): 20–46.

A report on the findings of a nationwide mail survey of police
bunco investigators (specialists in white-collar crimes), looking
at confidence swindles and their effect on older consumers.

Giese, William. **"Dumber and Dumber."** *Kiplinger's Personal Finance Magazine* 49, no. 3 (March 1995): 89–92.

Old scams, get-rich-quick schemes and sure-win investments, are taking on new wrappings on the Internet. This article discusses ways consumers can protect themselves.

Godin, Martha Allen. **"An Informed Consumer Is the Best Defense: Charitable Solicitation Regulation."** *North Carolina Law Review* 73 (September 1995): 2303.

The U.S. Supreme Court recently ruled that state laws limiting the percentage of charitable contributions used for fund-raising costs violate the First Amendment rights of charities. This article discusses these decisions and why consumer education is now the best defense against fraudulent charitable solicitations.

Hadden, Susan G. **"Regulating Product Risks through Consumer Information."** *Journal of Social Issues* 47, no. 1 (Spring 1991): 93–105.

Since the passage of the Pure Food and Drug Act in 1906, information (disclosure) has been a widely used tool in consumer protection laws. The author questions this tactic: first, because of language barriers to understanding, and second, because consumers do not necessarily read, understand, or act upon the disclosed information.

Hoffman, David R. **The Role of the Federal Government in Ensuring Quality of Care in Long-Term Care Facilities.** *Annals of Health Law* 6 (1997):147–156.

What is the role of the government in ensuring quality of care for the more than 1 million residents of the nation's nursing homes? This article, written by an assistant U.S. attorney, describes how the federal False Claims Act (31 U.S.C. §§ 3729-3733 [1995]) can be used to secure quality care. If a nursing home is paid by the government to feed and care for patients and does not provided quality of care, it can be prosecuted.

"How to Avoid Repair Rip-Offs." *USA Today: The Magazine of the American Scene* 124, no. 2611 (April 1996): 3–5.

Tips for avoiding consumer fraud for homeowners hit by natural disasters.

Hudson, Michael. **"Driven a Ford Lately?"** *The Nation* 262, no. 20 (20 May 1996): 12.

It was not cars, but home mortgages and car and consumer loans, that put Ford near the top of the *Fortune* 500 list, yet a number of lawsuits charge this car company with cheating borrowers.

Hunt, H. Keith. **"Consumer Satisfaction, Dissatisfaction, and Complaining Behavior."** *Journal of Social Issues* 47, no. 1 (Spring 1991): 107–117.

Consumer satisfaction and dissatisfaction are increasingly used as measures for targeting consumer protection resources. This article traces the development and usage of this methodology.

Israel, Glenn. **"Taming the Green Marketing Monster: National Standards for Environmental Marketing Claims."** *Boston College Environmental Affairs Law Review* 20 (Winter 1993): 303.

As the level of environmental awareness increases, manufacturers are developing and advertising more "green" products. Here the author reviews problems associated with unregulated advertising claims and provides different approaches to regulating green marketing claims.

Kertz, Consuelo Laude, and Roobina Ohanian. **"Recent Tends in the Law of Endorsement Advertising: Infomercials, Celebrity Endorsers and Nontraditional Defendants in Deceptive Advertising Cases."** *Hofstra Law Review* 19 (Spring 1991): 603.

Celebrity endorsements, along with infomercials, are increasingly misleading consumers; however, the authors believe that recent court cases will provide greater consumer protection.

Khalaf, Roula. **"Beware Charity Scams."** *Redbook* 182, no. 2 (December 1993): 46–52.

Charitable fund-raising during the holiday season can lead to consumer fraud. Tips for consumers are provided.

Lee, Jinkook, and Horacio Soberon-Ferrer. **"Consumer Vulnerability to Fraud: Influencing Factors."** *Journal of Consumer Affairs* 31, no. 1 (Summer 1997): 70–89.

Investigative reports suggest that some groups, such as older adults, are more vulnerable to consumer fraud than others. This article investigates different factors that influence a consumer's susceptibility to fraud.

Longo, Tracey. **"Put a Lock on Your Bank Account."** *Kiplinger's Personal Finance Magazine* 50, no. 7 (July 1996): 84.

Illegal telemarketers are securing checking and savings account numbers by promising discount magazines or sweepstakes winnings. Consumers need to protect their account numbers.

Lord, Mary. **"The Scholarship Scam Game."** *U.S. News & World Report* 121, no. 12 (23 September 1996): 88–89.

Thousands of families are falling victim to scholarship offers every year. The Federal Trade Commission recently launched a new campaign to help families avoid such scams.

McDonald, Duff. **"You Don't Have to Fret about Using a Credit Card on the Net."** *Money* 25, no. 10 (October 1996): 15.

Some credit card companies now offer to reimburse customers for fraudulent charges when shopping the Internet. Protection is not really needed, according to the author, because federal law limits consumers' liability to $50 for fraudulent use of credit cards regardless of where it occurs.

McHugh, Cathleen. **"Public Information?"** *Consumer's Research Magazine* 79, no. 12 (December 1996): 38.

Under a new Virginia gun purchase registration law, personal financial information is now available to the public on new firearm purchases.

McMahon, Maryrose J. **"Computer Scammers."** *Consumers' Research Magazine* 75, no. 9 (September 1995): 38.

The Minnesota attorney general charges Internet advertisers with consumer fraud violations and false advertising.

Mayer, Robert N. **"Gone Yesterday, Here Today: Consumer Issues in the Agenda-Setting Process."** *Journal of Social Issues* 47, no. 1 (Spring 1991): 21–39.

A provocative article examining how consumer problems become consumer issues in the policy-making process.

Mendenhall, Deborah. **"They Rip Off Seniors."** *Family Circle* 109, no. 16 (19 November 1996): 104–108.

Con artists target older Americans through telemarketing and other sales methods.

Nehf, James P. **"A Legislative Framework for Reducing Fraud in the Credit Repair Industry."** *North Carolina Law Review* 70 (March 1992): 781.

Fraudulent credit repair services are springing up nationwide to "correct" information contained on credit reports. One answer to reducing fraud is to amend the federal Fair Credit Reporting Act, according to the author of this article.

Norrgard, Lee. **"Consumer Protection and New Technologies."** *Generations* 19, no. 1 (Spring 1995): 47–48.

High-tech assistive devices, such as personal emergency response systems and new hearing aids, can improve the lives of the elderly. At the same time, the marketing of these devices is also spawning new consumer frauds.

Pope, Daniel. **"Advertising as a Consumer Issue: An Historical View."** *Journal of Social Issues* 47, no. 1 (Spring 1991): 41–56.

Advertising was, and remains, a major concern of the consumer movement. This article traces the way popular pressure has changed advertising methods and messages during the Progressive Era, the 1930s, 1960s, and 1970s.

Quinn, Jane Bryant. **"Buyers Beware."** *Newsweek* 12, no. 2 (13 July 1992): 46–48.

This article explains how to recognize fair life insurance policies and not be victimized by coverage that lapses prematurely.

"Scams Target Elderly People." *News for You* 43, no. 40 (11 October 1995): 3.

Discusses types of fraud perpetrated against the older population.

Senn, Stephen. **"The Prosecution of Religious Fraud."** *Florida State Law Review* 17 (Winter 1990): 325.

Religion and the First Amendment are frequently invoked by some scam artists. The author argues that religious frauds can and should be prosecuted.

Simon, Ruth. **"You're Losing Your Consumer Rights."** *Money* 25, no. 3 (March 1996): 100–109.

Consumer protections Americans take for granted are under attack by Congress and state legislatures. A review of what's happening on the national and state levels.

Spencer, Peter L. **"Bait and Switch?"** *Consumers' Research Magazine* 77, no. 5 (May 1994): 43.

How consumers can protect themselves against bait-and-switch real estate sales tactics.

Starnes, Richard A. **"Consumer Fraud and the Elderly: The Need for a Uniform System of Enforcement and Increased Civil and Criminal Penalties."** *Elder Law Journal* 4 (Spring 1996): 201.

Fraudulent telemarketers, investment advisors, and home repair swindlers increasingly target the older population. In this article the author describes various schemes that defraud seniors, reviews existing consumer protection laws, and recommends reforms.

Stehlin, Isadora B. **"Pharmaceutical Executives Convicted."** *FDA Consumer* 30, no. 2 (March 1996): 32.

Executives from a pharmaceutical company are found guilty of violating the Food, Drug and Cosmetic Act.

"Symposium: Cyberspace and the Law." *St. John's Journal of Legal Commentary* 11 (Summer 1996): 683.

Comments by various speakers who participated in a symposium on cyberspace. Presentations include "Internet: A Safe Haven for Anonymous Information Thieves?," "Privacy Protection on the Information Superhighway," and "Advertising on the Internet: An Opportunity for Abuse."

Szwak, David A. **"Date Rape: High-Tech Theft of Credit Identities."** *National Law Journal* 17, no. 20 (16 January 1995): C18–C19.

Crooks on the Internet find it easy to steal individual credit reports and use this personal information to commit fraud.

"Telephone Service: Don't Fall Prey to the Slam Scam." *Consumer Reports* 61, no. 10 (October 1996): 62–63.

Slamming, the illegal practice of switching a consumer's long-distance carrier without permission, is discussed, along with tips for avoiding this scam.

Updegrave, Walter. **"Don't Be Suckered Into the Life Insurance Mess."** *Money* 24, no. 1 (January 1995): 114–126.

Scandals involving major insurers (for example, MetLife fined $20 million in 1994) raise questions about insurance sales. The author argues that a complete overhaul of the way insurance is sold is needed.

Wiener, Daniel P., and Laura R. Thomas. **"Behind Those Fast-Buck Ads."** *U.S. News & World Report* 106, no. 16 (24 April 1989): 70–71.

Analysis of the "instant wealth" ads on television, over the telephone, and in print.

Wolf, Christopher, and Scott Shorr. **"Cybercops Are Cracking Down on Internet Fraud."** *National Law Journal* 19, no. 20 (13 January 1997): 12–14.

This article discusses stepped-up efforts initiated by federal and state officials to fight Internet frauds.

Congressional Documents

United States. Congress. House of Representatives. Committee on Banking, Finance, and Urban Affairs. Subcommittee on Consumer Credit and Insurance. **H.R. 3153, The Home Equity Protection Act of 1993: Hearing before the Subcommittee on Consumer Credit and Insurance of the Committee on Banking, Finance, and Urban Affairs, House of Representatives, One Hundred Third Congress, second session, March 22, 1994.** Washington, DC: U.S. Government Printing Office, 1995.

A hearing discussing the nationwide increases in home lending fraud and ways to increase federal protections. The Committee sought to strike a balance between curbing fraud and abuse without restricting the ability of the credit marketplace to provide financing.

———. Committee on Commerce. Subcommittee on Commerce, Trade, and Hazardous Materials. **Insurance State's and**

Consumer's Rights Clarification and Fair Competition Act: Hearing before the Subcommittee on Commerce, Trade, and Hazardous Materials of the Committee on Commerce, House of Representatives, One Hundred Fourth Congress, first session, on H.R. 1317, May 22, 1995. Washington, DC: U.S. Government Printing Office, 1995.

States have traditionally regulated almost every aspect of insurance. This hearing discusses whether or not to make legislative changes in these existing practices, particularly when the goal is how best to protect consumers.

———. Committee on Commerce. Subcommittee on Health and the Environment. **Waste, Fraud, and Abuse in the Medicare Program: Joint Hearing before the Subcommittee on Health and Environment and the Subcommittee on Oversight and Investigations of the Committee on Commerce, House of Representatives, One Hundred Fourth Congress, first session, May 16, 1995.** Washington, DC: U.S. Government Printing Office, 1995.

A fact-finding hearing, reviewing evidence of fraud, waste, and abuse in the Medicare program and the impact of losses on the federal trust funds financing this program.

———. Committee on Energy and Commerce. Subcommittee on Transportation and Hazardous Materials. **Oversight of FTC's Shared Responsibilities: Hearing before the Subcommittee on Transportation and Hazardous Materials of the Committee on Energy and Commerce, House of Representatives, One Hundred Second Congress, first session, Concerning Advertising and Labeling Issues with the Bureau of Alcohol, Tobacco, and Firearms, the Environmental Protection Agency and the Food and Drug Administration, November 21, 1991.** Washington, DC: U.S. Government Printing Office, 1992.

While the Federal Trade Commission (FTC) has primary jurisdiction over the regulation of advertising claims, it shares that authority with several other federal agencies with regard to certain products. For example, the Food and Drug Administration (FDA) regulates food labeling, and the FTC regulates advertising claims for the same products. This hearing reviews how the FDA, as well as several other federal agencies, and the FTC coordinate their regulatory activities in regard to commercial advertising.

———. Committee on Government Operations. **FDA's Continu-**

ing Failure to Prevent Deceptive Health Claims for Food: Twenty-Seventh Report by the Committee on Government Operations, Together with Dissenting and Additional Views. Washington, DC: U.S. Government Printing Office, 1990.

In 1987, the Food and Drug Administration lifted its ban on food manufacturers making disease prevention claims for their products. As a result, cereal companies, for example, began touting the attributes of bran in reducing the risk of cancer, something that had never been done before. This report, with dissenting views, strongly criticizes the FDA's new policy.

————. Committee on Government Operations. Information, Justice, Transportation, and Agriculture Subcommittee. **Pearl Jam's Antitrust Complaint: Questions about Concert, Sports, and Theater Ticket Handling Charges and Other Practices: Hearing before the Information, Justice, Transportation, and Agriculture Subcommittee of the Committee on Government Operations, House of Representatives, One Hundred Third Congress, second session, June 30, 1994.** Washington, DC: U.S. Government Printing Office, 1995.

In 1994, Pearl Jam, a rock group, submitted a legal brief to the Department of Justice alleging monopolistic practices in rock concert ticket sales. These practices prevented the group from offering what they describe as a reasonable ticket price, $18 per ticket, to fans. This hearing reviews the facts surrounding Pearl Jam's complaint and ticket sales practices to other concerts and events.

————. Committee on Government Operations. Legislation and National Security Subcommittee. **The Fraud and Abuse Provisions in H.R. 3600, the "Health Security Act": Joint Hearing before the Legislation and National Security Subcommittee and the Human Resources and Intergovernmental Relations Subcommittee of the Committee on Government Operations, House of Representatives, One Hundred Second Congress, second session, on H.R. 3600, to Ensure Individual and Family Security through Health Care Coverage for All Americans in a Manner That Contains the Rate of Growth in Health Care Costs and Promotes Responsible Health Insurance Practices, to Promote Choice in Health Care, and to Ensure and Protect the Health Care of All Americans, March 17, 1994.** Washington, DC: U.S. Government Printing Office, 1995.

President Clinton's ill-fated national health care reform proposal was resoundingly defeated on Capitol Hill. Nonetheless, one element of his proposal spurred Congress to begin looking at ways to curb fraud and abuse in public and private health programs. This hearing looks at the Clinton proposal to strengthen and coordinate federal criminal laws regarding health care fraud and abuse.

————. Committee on Government Reform and Oversight. **Health Care Fraud: All Public and Private Payers Need Federal Criminal Anti-Fraud Protections: Eleventh Report.** Washington, DC: U.S. Government Printing Office, 1996.

A congressional report discussing the issues surrounding the drafting of a new federal criminal law defining the crime of health care fraud.

————. Committee on Government Reform and Oversight. Subcommittee on Human Resources and Intergovernmental Relations. **Screening Medicare Claims for Medical Necessity: Hearing before the Subcommittee on Human Resources and Intergovernmental Relations of the Committee on Government Reform and Oversight, House of Representatives, One Hundred Fourth Congress, second session, February 8, 1996.** Washington, DC: U.S. Government Printing Office, 1996.

Medicare, with 73 contractors using nine different, incompatible computer systems, pays far too many medically unnecessary claims, according to this subcommittee. This hearing was called to take testimony on why Medicare's contractors are not using state-of-the-art software to review the accuracy of and the necessity for Medicare claims.

————. Committee on Small Business. Subcommittee on Regulation, Business Opportunities, and Energy. **Deception and Fraud in the Diet Industry: Hearing before the Subcommittee on Regulation, Business Opportunities, and Energy of the Committee on Small Business, House of Representatives, One Hundred First Congress, second session, March 26, 1990.** Washington, DC: U.S. Government Printing Office, 1990.

A congressional inquiry into deception and fraud in the nation's $33 billion diet industry. This hearing looks at its questionable products, the use of medically untrained providers, and charges of its deceptive advertising claims.

———. Committee on Small Business. Subcommittee on Regulation, Business Opportunities, and Energy. **Innovative Telemarketing and Consumer Fraud in Oregon and the Northwest: Hearing before the Subcommittee on Regulation, Business Opportunities, and Energy of the Committee on Small Business, House of Representatives, One Hundred Second Congress, second session, February 24, 1992.** Washington, DC: U.S. Government Printing Office, 1992.

A hearing that discussed the state of the art in telemarketing and direct mail frauds, with particular emphasis on the impact of these frauds in the Pacific Northwest.

———. Committee on Small Business. Subcommittee on Regulation, Business Opportunities, and Technology. **Questionable Sales Practices in the Drug Industry: Hearing before the Subcommittee on Regulation, Business Opportunities, and Technology, of the Committee on Small Business, House of Representatives, One Hundred Third Congress, second session, October 12, 1994.** Washington, DC: U.S. Government Printing Office, 1995.

An examination of potentially illegal marketing and promotional activities by pharmaceutical companies. This hearing takes testimony about the various financial inducements offered by drug companies or their distributors to encourage doctors and clinics to prescribe certain drugs.

———. Committee on the Judiciary. Subcommittee on Crime and Criminal Justice. **Deceit That Sickens America: Health Care Fraud and Its Innocent Victims: Hearing before the Subcommittee on Crime and Criminal Justice of the Committee on the Judiciary, House of Representatives, One Hundred Third Congress, second session, July 19, 1994.** Washington, DC: U.S. Government Printing Office, 1995.

In this hearing, victims of health care fraud testify about their experience with false diagnoses, altered lab reports, unnecessary treatments, bribes, kickbacks, and phony billing. This hearing also discuses needed statutory reforms.

———. Committee on the Judiciary. Subcommittee on Criminal Justice. **Prosecuting Fraud in the Thrift Industry: Impact of the Financial Institutions Reform, Recovery, and Enforcement Act of 1989: Hearing before the Subcommittee on Criminal Justice** of the Committee on the Judiciary, House of Representatives, One Hundred First Congress, second session, May 11, 1990. Washington, DC: U.S. Government Printing Office, 1990.

An oversight hearing reviewing prosecutions conducted by the Department of Justice against fraudulent practices in the savings and loan industry. The Justice Department provides statistical information about convictions, expenditures, and cases.

————. Select Committee on Aging. Subcommittee on Health and Long-Term Care. **Quackery, a $10 Billion Scandal: A Report by the Chairman of the Subcommittee on Health and Long-Term Care of the Select Committee on Aging, House of Representatives, Ninety-eighth Congress, second session.** Washington, DC: U.S. Government Printing Office, 1984.

An investigative report on the wide range of medical products sold with no proven efficacy in curing disease or chronic conditions. This hearing, now dated, is an encyclopedia of health quackery devices. It looks at quackery from Laetrile, an unproved cancer cure, to the use of copper bracelets to cure arthritis.

————. Committee on the Judiciary. **White Collar Crime: Hearings before the Committee on the Judiciary, United States Senate, Ninety-ninth Congress, second session, 1986.** Washington, DC: U.S. Government Printing Office, 1987.

Business fraud amounts to an estimated $160 billion a year. In this three-part hearing, various issues surrounding white-collar crime are reviewed. One hearing discusses money laundering, the second an investigation of investment fraud, and the third, a review of the impact of various amendments to the Criminal Code to combat white-collar crime.

————. Special Committee on Aging. **Health Care Fraud: Milking Medicare and Medicaid: Hearing before the Special Committee on Aging, United States Senate, One Hundred Fourth Congress, first session, November 2, 1995.** Washington, DC: U.S. Government Printing Office, 1996.

The Medicare and Medicaid programs lose approximately $33 billion a year to health care fraud. This hearing features the testimony of three convicted criminals to discuss how easy it was to steal from these programs.

————. Special Committee on Aging. **How Secure Is Your Retirement: Investments, Planning, and Fraud?: Hearing before the Special Committee on Aging, United States Senate, One Hundred Third Congress, first session, May 25, 1993.** Washington, DC: U.S. Government Printing Office, 1993.

Losing retirement savings to investment fraud is devastating to the older population since they have no way to recover such losses. This hearing provides examples of how older adults are losing their retirement savings to fraud, particularly in a period of low returns on bank deposits.

Senate Committee on Commerce, Science, and Transportation. Subcommittee on the Consumer. **Charitable Solicitation Fraud: Hearing before the Subcommittee on the Consumer of the Committee on Commerce, Science, and Transportation, United States Senate, One Hundred Third Congress, first session, October 11, 1993.** Washington, DC: U.S. Government Printing Office, 1994.

Americans contribute some $67 billion dollars annually to various charities. This hearing reviews tactics of crooked charities to defraud generous consumers.

Reports and Special Publications

American Association of Retired Persons (AARP). *A Report on Hearing Aids.* Washington, DC: AARP, 1993.

An investigative study of the hearing aid marketplace based on a history of federal regulatory actions, a "mystery shop" (consumers recording their shopping experiences) at offices of hearing aid dispensers, and user experiences.

————. *A Report on the 1993 Survey of Older Consumer Behavior.* Washington, DC: AARP, 1994.

Law enforcement often views older Americans as a vulnerable consumer population that is disproportionately victimized by different forms of consumer fraud. This report, conducted for AARP by Princeton Research Associates, seeks to compare older and younger consumers' awareness, knowledge, and perceptions.

————. *Telemarketing Fraud and Older Americans: A Report on a Survey of Victims.* Washington, DC: AARP, 1996.

A report on a survey of telemarketing fraud victims that dispels the stereotype of victims as socially isolated, older women.

Federal Bureau of Investigation (FBI). *Senior Sentinel.* Washington, DC: FBI, 1996.

In 1995, FBI agents, together with other federal and state law enforcement agencies, arrested and charged more than 400 individuals with telemarketing fraud. This report summarizes the telemarketing crime problem, discusses the Sentinel investigation, and provides a glossary of common telemarketing fraud terms.

Federal Trade Commission. *Auto Service Contracts.* Washington, DC: Federal Trade Commission, May 1997.

A guide to help consumers decide whether or not to purchase an auto service contract. Includes valuable information on warranty protection and questions to ask about auto service contracts.

————. *Avoiding Credit and Charge Card Fraud.* Washington, DC: Federal Trade Commission, August 1997.

A description of different credit card frauds and tips on how to guard against these scams.

————. *Credit and Your Consumer Rights.* Washington, DC: Federal Trade Commission, June 1996.

Explains consumer rights under various federal credit laws, including the Fair Credit Reporting Act, Equal Credit Opportunity Act, and the Fair Credit Billing Act.

————. *Fighting Consumer Fraud: The Challenge and the Campaign.* Washington, DC: Federal Trade Commission, 1997.

A report on the Federal Trade Commission's recent consumer protection activities including investment fraud, telemarketing fraud, and consumer finance scams.

————. *Getting a Loan: Your Home as Security, fast facts.* Washington, DC: Federal Trade Commission, February 1992.

Home equity frauds have claimed the largest investment many consumers ever make, their homes. This guide explains consumer rights under the Federal Truth in Lending Act, which gives consumers the right to rescind a loan agreement within three business days.

———. *Home Equity Credit Lines: fast facts.* Washington, DC: Federal Trade Commission, June 1992.

Explains the risks of borrowing against a home.

———. *Home Financing Primer: fast facts.* Washington, DC: Federal Trade Commission, December 1993.

Basic information about home mortgages, including how to shop for the best rates and the different kinds of loans available.

———. *How to Right a Wrong.* Washington, DC: Federal Trade Commission, June 1997.

A guide to resolving problems with mail and telephone shopping, door-to-door sales, and unsolicited merchandise.

———. *Infomercials.* Washington, DC: Federal Trade Commission, August 1996.

Infomercials—advertisements that look and sound like television shows—are increasingly prevalent. This is a guide to protect consumers if they buy products pushed through such presentations.

———. *Look Before You Lease.* Washington, DC: Federal Trade Commission, November 1996.

Advertisements and contracts for auto leasing are often confusing and, at times, deceptive and misleading. This guide helps consumers make informed decisions by defining key leasing terms and providing questions to ask about leasing or buying.

———. *Telecommunications Scams Using FCC Licenses.* Washington, DC: Federal Trade Commission, January 1996.

Fraudulent investment schemes in Federal Trade Commission licenses are a fast-growing scam. Tips to protect yourself.

———. *Timeshare Tips.* Washington, DC: Federal Trade Commission, March 1997.

Buying a timeshare—the use of a vacation home for a pre-planned, limited time—involves consumer risks and benefits. An explanation of terms and tips to protect yourself.

———. *Toy Ads on Television.* Washington, DC: Federal Trade Commission, February 1996.

Many young children have difficulty separating fact from fantasy in toy advertisements seen on television. Parents can help prevent disappointments by explaining that advertising is designed to sell products and that not all information about the toy may be included.

————. *Warranties: fast facts.* Washington, DC: Federal Trade Commission, November 1992.

Warranties, or the manufacturers' or sellers' promise to stand behind their product, are an important part of any major purchase. This guide gives facts about warranties and consumer rights under federal and state laws.

————. *Wealth-Building Scams.* Washington, DC: Federal Trade Commission, November 1996.

Infomercials, classified ads, and Internet sites tout schemes to get rich quick. All that's required is buying a book, tapes, or other materials for hundreds or thousands of dollars. This guide provides tips on how to evaluate these schemes.

Louis Harris and Associates, Inc. *Telephone-Based Fraud: A Survey of the American Public.* New York: Louis Harris and Associates on behalf of National Consumers League, 1992.

A report on a survey of Americans' knowledge and experience with telemarketing fraud, credit cards scams, and 900 numbers. The report is based on a survey of 1,255 Americans aged 18 and over conducted in the spring of 1992.

National Association of Attorneys General. *Auto Repair Task Force Report.* Washington, DC: National Association of Attorneys General, October 1995.

Complaints about auto repairs consistently place this problem among the top ten consumer complaints. This report identifies the problems with auto repairs and recommends reforms.

Securities and Exchange Commission. *Ask Questions.* Washington, DC: Securities and Exchange Commission, 17 October 1996.

Questions to ask about investment products, their sellers, the progress of an investment over time, and how to handle problems that arise.

―――. *Invest Wisely: Advice from Your Securities Industry Regulators.* Washington, DC: Securities and Exchange Commission, undated.

A guide to making investments, selecting a broker, and being alert for any danger signs with investments.

―――. *Invest Wisely: An Introduction to Mutual Funds.* Washington, DC: Securities and Exchange Commission, undated.

A checklist on investing in mutual funds. Also explains the different kinds of funds and the terms used.

―――. *Investment Fraud and Abuse Travel to Cyberspace.* Washington, DC: Securities and Exchange Commission, June 1996.

Online services create new opportunities and new dangers for investors. A guide to investment frauds on the Internet and ways consumers can protect themselves.

―――. *The Work of the SEC.* Washington, DC: Securities and Exchange Commission, June 1997.

A detailed overview of the SEC, including the various federal acts that protect investors, the different divisions, and how to contact this protection agency.

Securities and Exchange Commission and National Association of State Securities Agencies. *Cold Calling.* Washington, DC: Securities and Exchange Commission, September 1997.

Information on rules that cold callers (telemarketers) must follow, signs of trouble, and ways to protect yourself against boiler room investment fraud.

U.S. Postal Inspection Service. *Charity Fraud.* Washington, DC: U.S. Postal Inspection Service, undated.

A fact sheet on charity frauds and how consumers can protect themselves.

―――. *Credit Card Schemes.* Washington, DC: U.S. Postal Inspection Service, undated.

Promoters of phony credit cards charge advance fees for worthless products.

———. *The Free Vacation Scam.* Washington, DC: U.S. Postal In-

———. *The Free Vacation Scam.* Washington, DC: U.S. Postal Inspection Service, undated.

Postcards hyping free vacations are frequently scams in which consumers pay several hundred dollars and receive substandard accommodations, or nothing, in return. A tip sheet on how to protect yourself.

———. *Hot Tips on Playing Foreign Lotteries by Mail. "Don't Do It!"* Washington, DC: U.S. Postal Inspection Service, undated.

Buying foreign lottery tickets by mail is illegal, and the contest may be a fraud. Tips on what lotteries not to play.

———. *The Mail Fraud and False Representation Statutes.* Washington, DC: U.S. Postal Inspection Service, undated.

The Mail Fraud Statute is the nation's oldest federal consumer protection law. This guide provides facts about this law and the False Representation law.

———. *900 Telephone Number Schemes.* Washington, DC: U.S. Postal Inspection Service, undated.

There are legitimate uses for 900 numbers, but criminals are also using these services. Consumer tips on how to protect yourself.

———. *Work-at-Home Schemes.* Washington, DC: U.S. Postal Inspection Service, undated.

Advertisements for work-at-home schemes (assembling products, raising earthworms, and many others) are frequently scams. Tips on how to protect yourself.

Nonprint Resources 7

"And he came on, that filthy effigy of fraud,
and landed with his head and torso but did not
draw his tail onto the bank.
    The face he wore was that of a just man, so
gracious was his features' outer semblance; and
all his trunk, the body of a serpent; he had two
paws, with hair up to the armpits; his back and
chest as well as both his flanks had been
adorned with twining knots and circlets. . . .
    And all his tail was quivering in the void
while twisting upward its envenomed fork,
which had a tip just like a scorpion's."
                                    —Dante Alighieri

The audiovisual resources listed here are available at some libraries or from the company directly. Much of the information formerly confined to libraries or special offices is now available in a readily searchable form on the Internet. If you do not have a computer, check with a public library; many provide Internet access. The Internet sites referenced here contain links to other sites and information that provide additional information.

Videotapes

Bait, Bite, and Switch
Type: Videotape
Length: 10 minutes
Date: 1976
Source: Pyramid Film & Video
P.O. Box 1048
Santa Monica, CA 90406
Website: http://www.pyramidmedia.com

Through advertising, a young shopper is baited into shopping at an electronics store. There a salesperson steers the consumer into buying a more expensive tape deck. Through the actions of a consumer protection office, the consumer is able to return the expensive purchase and buy the advertised, less expensive model.

Buyer Be Aware: Avoid Rip-Offs
Type: Videotape
Length: 24 minutes
Date: Not known
Source: The Learning Seed
330 Telser Road
Lake Zurich, IL 60047

A review of some common schemes to defraud unsuspecting customers.

Can Regulatory Agencies Protect Consumers?
Type: Videotape
Length: 58 minutes
Date: 1997
Source: American Enterprise Institute
1150 17th Street, N.W.
Washington, DC 20036

Two experts debate whether consumer protection regulations weaken competition, and further, whether such regulation weakens competitive markets operating in the public interest.

Con Games and Swindles
Type: Videotape
Length: 25 minutes
Date: 1982
Source: Bullfrog Films, Inc.

P.O. Box 149
Oley, PA 19547
Website: http://www.bullfrogfilms.com

A program illustrating ways to recognize the phony, high-pressure propositions of a con artist.

Consumer Behavior Part Two: Breaking the Clutter
Type: Videotape
Length: 30 minutes
Date: Not known
Source: RMI Media Productions, Inc.
            1365 North Winchester
            Olathe, KS 66061
            Website: http://www.rmimedia.com

An examination of how professional advertisers use consumer behavior theory to create advertising that sells.

The Consumer Experience: Consumerism
Type: Videotape
Length: 30 minutes
Date: 1974
Source: University of Wisconsin-Extension
            Wisconsin Public Television
            2420 Nicolet Drive
            Green Bay, WI 54311
            Website: http://www.wpt.org

Consumer fraud and consumer protection issues are discussed along with rights and responsibilities.

The Consumer Fraud Series
Type: Videotape
Length: 50 minutes
Date: 1976
Source: Pyramid Film & Video
            P.O. Box 1048
            Santa Monica, CA 90406
            Website: http://www.pyramidmedia.com

A series of sketches where a family corrects purchasing mistakes created by consumer fraud.

Consumerism: Let the Buyer Beware
Type: Videotape
Length: 20 minutes

Date: 1975
Source: The Cinema Guild
1697 Broadway
New York, NY 10019
Website: http://www.cinemaguild.com

A discussion of consumer rights advocate Ralph Nader and his efforts to protect consumers from fraud.

Psycho-Sell: Advertising and Persuasion
Type: Videotape
Length: 25 minutes
Date: Not known
Source: The Learning Seed
330 Tesler Road
Lake Zurich, IL 60047

An exploration of the techniques used by advertisers to sway purchase decisions by consumers.

Websites

Advertising Law Internet Site
Website: http://www.webcom.com/~lewrose/home.html

A law firm in Washington, D.C., sponsors this site. It provides basic information on topics such as ad substantiation, pertinent federal regulations, and a large index of articles, speeches, and other information on the topic.

Antitrust Case Summary Browser
Website: http://www.stolaf.edu/people/becker/antitrust/antitrust.html

A selection of U.S. Supreme Court case summaries involving antitrust law violations.

Antitrust Policy
Website: http://www.antitrust.org

A Website linking economic analysis, policy-making initiatives, and legal cases. Included are topics such as mergers, price fixing, and vertical restraints.

Association of Certified Fraud Examiners
Website: http://www.acfe.org

Homepage for professional association representing fraud investigators. Contains information on seminars and conferences on
fraud as well as white papers on this subject.

Cagey Consumer
Website: http://www.geocities.com/WallStreet/5395/
consumer.html

A collection of consumer alerts and information on various
frauds, together with user tips and links to other sites.

Center for Democracy and Technology
Website: http://www.13x.com/cgi-bin/cdt/snoop.pl

Information and tools to protect personal and financial information while surfing the Internet.

Certified Financial Planner: Board of Standards
Website: http://www.cfp-board.org

This site is sponsored by a nonprofit, self-regulatory, professional
association of certified financial planners. It provides information about selecting and using a financial planner, this association's code of ethics, how to file a complaint against a financial
planner, and additional consumer information.

Charles K. Ponzi Website
Website: http://www.usinternet.com/users/mcknutson

A history of the first Ponzi scheme and its perpetrator, Charles
Ponzi. A Ponzi scheme is described as "paying the early comers
out of the contributions of later comers."

Consumer Action and Information Center of Hawaii
Website: http://www.consumerlaw.com

Describing itself as the homepage for Hawaiian consumers, this
site provides basic consumer protection information on topics
such as unfair and deceptive practices, car problems, home purchases, and false claim actions.

Consumer Alert
Website: http://www.consumeralert.org

A conservative perspective on consumer protection issues. Articles include "Who Are the Food Police?," a critique of the Center for Science in the Public Interest, and "Abolish the Consumer Product Safety Commission?"

Consumer Attorneys of California
Website: http://www.seamless.com/consumer

Information designed primarily for California consumers, featuring alerts, forums, and the members of the Consumer Attorneys of California.

Consumer Credit Counseling Service
Website: http://www.cccsintl.org

How to secure and correct credit reports, protect credit identity, and obtain debt counseling.

Consumer Law Page of Alexander Law Firm
Website: http://www.alexanderlaw.com

An extensive site covering topics such as defective products, personal injury, insurance fraud, crime, consumer fraud, general legal principles, toxic torts, traumatic brain injuries, and other issues.

Consumer Project on Technology
Website: http://www.cptech.org

Created by Ralph Nader, this site addresses antitrust, privacy, and telecommunications issues.

Consumer World
Website: http://www.consumerworld.org

An award-winning site listing consumer protection agencies, consumer and professional groups, shopping information, travel tips, and other information to protect oneself from fraud.

Contests & Sweepstakes Law Internet Site
Website: http://www.arentfox.com/features/sweepstakes/news/home.html

Complements the Advertising Law Internet Site (see above) but concentrates on the direct marketing tools of contests and sweepstakes for promotions. Widely used, these tactics are also the tools of choice for illegal telemarketing and mail fraud.

Fraud Information Center
Website: http://www.echotech.com

A comprehensive site containing fraud alerts and hotlines, conferences and papers, investigative tools, and information on health care fraud, telecommunications fraud, and many other areas. There are many lengthy articles on topics such as investment swindles, identity theft, Internet fraud, credit card fraud, and so on. This site is sponsored by a security firm.

Individual Investors Services
Website: http://www.investor.nasd.com

Sponsored by the National Association of Securities Dealers, the largest securities self-regulatory organization, this site contains information on investing, market data, newsletters, and brochures. Investor complaints may also be filed here.

National Association of Attorneys General
Website: http://www.naag.org

The Website for the nation's state attorneys general. This gateway site includes consumer news such as enforcement actions by state attorneys general, legal filings, and an archive of "scams." In addition, links to every attorney general with a Website are provided.

National Association of State Securities
   Administrators Association
Website: http://www.nasaa.org

Sponsored by an international organization of state and provincial governmental agencies assigned to investor protection, this site highlights recent enforcement actions and includes policy statements by association leaders and a search engine for finding state securities administrators.

National Charities Information Bureau
Website: http://www.give.org

When the caller asks for a contribution, check here to find out if the charity meets this organization's standards for giving. Also provides information on giving and detailed reports on charities.

National Consumer Law Center
Website: http://www.consumerlaw.org/

This site for lawyers and nonlawyers includes policy analysis and legal answers to consumer protection issues. Consumer information includes how to protect yourself against frauds in mortgage lending, home repair, telemarketing, and door-to-door sales.

National Institute for Consumer Education
Website: http://www.emich.edu/public/coe/nice/mission.html

The National Institute for Consumer Education (NICE) is a clearinghouse and development center on consumer issues for educators. Teacher lesson plans include sessions on different consumer frauds.

Privacy Rights Clearinghouse
Website: http://www.privacyrights.org

Consumer information on protecting your personal privacy.

Private Citizen
Website: http://www.private-citizen.com/index.html

Private Citizen is a consumer organization that concentrates on personal privacy issues relating to direct marketing (direct mail or telemarketing). This site provides information on how consumers can get off a direct marketer's call or direct mail list.

Quackwatch
Website: http://www.quackwatch.com

A guide to quackery and health frauds. Contains a search engine to find quack products, fraud discussion groups, tips on consumer protection, lists of consumer organizations, and misleading advertisements.

Scam Alerts and Information
Website: http://www.nsi.org/Tips/scams.html

A laundry list of current scams ranging from home improvements to car repairs, and credit card fraud to charity scams. Site is sponsored by a security firm.

Synopses of Major Government Fraud Statutes
Website: http://www.cottoncpa.com/laws.htm

A summary of the key federal fraud statutes together with a description of the key elements needed to prosecute, for example, mail and wire fraud and antitrust. Site is maintained by Cotton & Company, Certified Public Accountants.

U.S. Consumer Gateway
Website: http://www.consumer.gov

A gateway site connecting to all federal government consumer sites such as the Federal Trade Commission, the Food and Drug Administration, Consumer Product Safety Commission, and many others. It also includes consumer alerts, reports of recent enforcement actions, and other information.

Glossary

"A false balance is abomination to the Lord:
but a just weight is his delight."

—Proverbs 11:1

adulteration The intentional or accidental introduction of foreign matter into a product or substance. Foreign matter could include pesticides, additives, or product spoilage.

advance fee loans A scheme whereby promoters promise to process a loan, arrange financing, or secure sources of credit to cure a consumer's financial problems, such as a negative credit history. The consumer pays an advance fee to secure the credit but the promoters neither deliver the credit nor refund the fee.

advertising Promotional material designed to sell products, opinions, or causes by means of radio or television broadcasts, newspapers, magazines, or other printed matter, direct mail, telephone, or via the Internet. Advertising is also a form of speech protected by the First Amendment to the U.S. Constitution.

advertorial A print advertisement that has the appearance of a news story or editorial.

anticompetitive merger A merger of companies that reduces or eliminates competition. Under federal and state antitrust laws, such mergers are considered illegal.

antitrust laws Federal and state laws promoting competition and preventing monopoly powers. The core federal statutes are the Sherman and Clayton Antitrust Acts and the Federal Trade Commission Act.

attorney general The chief law officer of each state or the federal government. Most state attorneys general enforce their state's consumer protection laws.

bait-and-switch A deceptive advertising technique in which consumers are lured with false claims of discounts, low interest rates, or other misleading statements by a seller who does not intend to sell at that price, interest rate, etc. Once the consumer takes the "bait," by visiting the store, the seller tries to "switch" the consumer to a more expensive product.

blue sky laws State laws regulating the sale of securities such as stocks and bonds. Every state legislature has approved such laws to protect consumers from investments that are, in the words of a state judge, as economically valuable as "so many feet of blue sky."

boiler room A rudimentary office with multiple phone lines used for high-pressure, usually illegal, telemarketing sales. Boiler rooms are routinely fly-by-night operations that pick up and move as needed in order to evade the law.

caveat emptor A legal term meaning "buyer beware" in Latin. It stands for the philosophy that a seller assumes no responsibility for defective products and the buyer alone is responsible for making a wise purchase.

caveat venditor A legal term meaning "seller beware," or the opposite of *caveat emptor*. Under this legal theory, the seller bears responsibility for defective and unsafe products.

cease-and-desist order An order by a court or other body to prohibit a particular behavior or course of action. In consumer protection, the Federal Trade Commission or an attorney general may order a seller to cease an unfair or deceptive practice.

charitable solicitation fraud The practice of soliciting contributions for nonexistent charities. A questionable, but not an illegal, practice is the payment of excessive fund-raising costs by a charity. In some cases, charities receive only 5 cents per dollar raised. The other 95 cents goes to telemarketers or direct mail firms.

check debit or sight draft A direct electronic transfer of funds from a consumer's checking or savings account to a seller. Some legitimate sellers use this form of payment with consumers who do not have credit cards. Consumers are asked to provide their account numbers to the seller. Illegal telemarketers encourage their victims to pay electronically as a means to quickly secure payment. Some telemarketers secure bank account numbers through guile—"Please write void on your check and tell me the account number. I need to verify this information for our records."

churning The repeated trading of customers' accounts by stock and commodity brokers with the purpose of generating commissions. Churning is illegal but difficult to prove.

clickstream data Electronic markers, including consumer e-mail addresses and other personal data, captured by Websites visited by users. Sellers use this data to match products with potential customers on the Internet. Collecting such data is not illegal, although privacy is being debated by the Congress and at the Federal Trade Commission. Clickstream data can be used, however, to facilitate fraudulent activity.

closer A telemarketing sales representative who specializes in "closing" or finalizing a sale. Prospective buyers are referred to closers by cold callers because they are more skilled at persuasive tactics.

cold calling Unsolicited, outbound telemarketing or door-to-door sales to potential customers. Cold callers use lead lists (see below) to make their contacts.

consumer behavior How consumers behave in the marketplace. Increasingly, research in this area is used to determine the need for additional consumer protections and whether or not to take enforcement actions.

consumer fraud Fraud is a deliberate deception using false claims to persuade someone to take or not take an action. In popular usage, consumer fraud includes any unlawful or unfair scheme aimed at consumers.

Consumer Product Safety Act A federal act designed to protect consumers from unreasonable risks with consumer products.

Consumer Products Safety Commission An independent regulatory agency created by Congress in 1962 to administer the Consumer Product Safety Act, the Hazardous Substances Act, and other federal statutes.

consumer protection laws Laws protecting consumers against fraud, false claims, unsafe products, and anticompetitive pricing.

Consumers Union (CU) A nonprofit organization founded in 1936 to provide consumers with product ratings based on objective tests. Consumers Union publishes the magazine *Consumer Reports* and advocates on behalf of consumers in federal and state policy making.

contests, sweepstakes, and puzzles A direct marketing tool to promote sales through prize offerings. Such tactics are widely employed by marketers and are coming under scrutiny by state and federal agencies. Illegal telemarketers employ sweepstakes as their scam of choice in defrauding consumers. Victims pay administrative and handling charges for nonexistent or worthless prizes.

cookies Electronic tags recording visits to Internet sites by individual consumers. Sellers use this information to market products on the Internet. *See also* clickstream data.

cost-benefit analysis One means of evaluating an existing or proposed regulation. How much will it cost a business to be subject to regulation and how many benefits will consumers derive.

credit cards A card authorizing consumers to purchase goods and services on credit. Credit card fraud, including identity theft and telemarketing fraud, is a multibillion-dollar scam.

credit reports Data on individual consumers' outstanding lines of credit, their bill-paying history, income, employment history, and other financial information. Credit bureaus collect this data for credit granting agencies, which then use the information in approving or denying consumer credit applications.

deregulation Scaling back or removing regulations and the regulatory activity of government. For example, many states are deregulating the public monopoly status enjoyed by gas and electric utilities.

direct marketing Marketing directly to individual consumers through telemarketing, direct mail, e-mail, or in person rather than communicating through broad-based mediums such as television or newspapers.

division of markets When two or more companies divide the market for the sale of their product. This practice is similar to price fixing and violates federal antitrust laws.

door-to-door sales Direct selling, often employing high-pressure sales tactics, that takes place at a consumer's home.

economic concentration A condition where one or a handful of companies constitutes a large percentage of sales, production, or other economic activity in a particular industry. Economic concentration can lead to limited consumer choices and excessive costs. These practices may violate antitrust laws.

equity or **home equity** The value of a property, such as a house, minus the amount owed (mortgaged). Because of increased real estate values, many homeowners have built up a large equity in their homes. Fraud artists want to confiscate (*see* equity skimming) this equity.

equity skimming or **equity stripping** The often fraudulent practice whereby lenders profit from the equity, built up over time, in an individual's home. Lenders make high-cost, unaffordable loans secured by a vulnerable consumer's home. When the inevitable default occurs, the lender quickly forecloses.

exclusive dealing   A business agreement whereby one seller agrees to buy products from only one vendor (*see also* price fixing and division of markets). This practice is illegal under federal antitrust laws.

express warranty   A warranty created when a seller makes explicit claims (whether or not in writing) about the quality of the products he/she is selling.

false advertising   Any deceptive, misleading, or untruthful advertisement. Under federal law, the Federal Trade Commission retains broad powers to prohibit unfair and deceptive advertising. At the state level, many attorneys general have similar authority.

fiduciary responsibility   A legal obligation to carry out a duty by a financial advisor or other individual on behalf of someone else.

flipping   A practice employed by some sellers to change the financing mechanism for a major purchase such as an automobile. Sellers may *flip* a consumer into a more expensive loan or a lease with or without the consumer's knowledge or consent.

fruggers   Telemarketers who sell under the guise of conducting an opinion survey.

green advertising   Advertising that claims that certain products will help the environment. For example, sellers have claimed that certain diapers are biodegradable.

health care fraud   The practice of fraudulently obtaining money from private health insurance companies, government health programs (Medicare and Medicaid), or individual consumers for health care. Such practices include extracting payments for services not rendered, payments for unnecessary services or products, or paying more than necessary for products or services. Government and private authorities estimate that health care fraud costs consumers, taxpayers, and employers as much as $100 billion a year.

home improvement fraud   The practice of defrauding homeowners through the use of high-pressure sales and misrepresentations to sell poor-quality and incomplete work.

horizontal merger   The merger of two or more companies in the same industry at the same level of production or sales.

identity theft   The theft of credit card numbers, social security numbers, and other key pieces of an individual's personal identity. Criminals use such information to fraudulently impersonate another and spend and borrow from that individual's credit.

implied warranty of fitness for a particular purpose   A warranty that goods are suitable for a particular use, not a fitness for general purposes.

implied warranty of merchantability A warranty that is based on the sale of a product, not a specific written guarantee. Under the Uniform Commercial Code, applicable in all states, any product sold by a merchant comes with such a warranty, and unless the seller issues a disclaimer, the product must perform to certain minimum standards of quality.

infomercial A program-length television or radio advertisement that appears to be a news or talk show.

insider trading The practice of buying or selling securities (stocks and bonds) based on confidential information known only to insiders, not the general public. This is an illegal practice under federal and state securities laws.

Internet fraud Fraudulent sales practices on the new medium of the Internet. These include deceptive advertising, selling health quackery, bogus investments, and perpetrating credit card fraud. Many schemes are simply adapted to this medium from more traditional methods.

investment fraud The sale of securities based on false claims, usually by unregistered companies.

laissez-faire **capitalism** An economic system characterized by minimal governmental interference or regulation with business. *Laissez-faire* capitalism is often tied to the concept of *caveat emptor,* or buyer beware.

lead list A list of potential customers based on past purchasing habits, credit card ownership, zip codes, age, income, sex, or other characteristics. The buying and selling of names is a multibillion-dollar industry in this country.

lemon laws State laws providing extra warranty protection for new automobile purchasers. Typically, lemon laws require sellers to correct defects covered by an express warranty (see above) and if, after a reasonable number of attempts, they cannot make the needed repairs, to replace the automobile with a new one or refund the purchase price.

mail drop Mailing large volumes of award notifications and solicitations to entice consumers to call a telemarketing operation or respond in some other way.

market failure The inability of the marketplace to provide the intended benefits of competition, such as product safety or false advertising. Market failure is a powerful argument for government regulation.

material claim A seller's claim for a product that influences a consumer's purchase. Under the Federal Trade Commission Act and many state laws, legal action to correct unfair and deceptive practices can only be taken when there is a material claim.

misbranding Misbranding is the use of false or misleading labeling information in violation of federal or state laws. Labeling requirements for foods, drugs, medical devices, and cosmetics are set by the Food and Drug Administration. The Consumer Product Safety Commission sets labeling standards for hazardous substances.

misrepresentations A seller's false or exaggerated statements or impressions, made to consumers in an advertisement, direct marketing, or in person.

monopoly The exclusive control of an industry by a single seller.

monopoly power When a seller or group of sellers holds the power to set prices or exclude competition.

mooch A derisive term, commonly used by illegal telemarketers, ridiculing naive and easily manipulated consumers. A mooch is the victim of a telemarketing fraud scheme.

mooch list A list of names of past victims of telemarketing fraud. Because such victims are frequently scammed multiple times, such lists are valuable to illegal telemarketers. They buy and sell from one another, paying as much as $200 each per name.

mouse type The small or fine print in advertising disclaimers that is almost impossible to read, particularly during a 30-second television spot.

muckrakers Investigative journalists, such as Upton Sinclair and others, who specialized in exposing corruption, marketplace abuses, and unsafe products during the Progressive Era. Muckrakers, so titled by President Theodore Roosevelt because they were always "raking muck," are responsible for many of the nation's first consumer protection laws.

occupational licensure laws State laws licensing professionals to practice medicine, sell hearing aids, install electric lines, build houses, and other activities. These laws set minimum qualification standards for entry and establish norms for practice. It is illegal to practice a regulated profession without a license. Similarly, many boards set protocols for selling certain products. For example, with hearing aids, some states set minimum standards for all hearing evaluations. To provide less than the minimum testing violates state laws or regulations.

oligopoly Market power held by a group of sellers, as opposed to a monopoly, in which market power is held by a single entity.

one in four (five or six) A sweepstakes promotion frequently used by illegal telemarketers. Telemarketers tell victims they are guaranteed winners of one of four (five or six) lucrative prizes. To win, all they must do is pay taxes, accounting fees, or some other such fee in advance for their "free" winnings, which are never actually awarded.

opticals The visual images used to elicit interest or set a mood in advertising. Opticals alone can be false and misleading, regardless of what is said or written in the advertisement.

packing an auto loan   Loading up an automobile purchase agreement with credit insurance, service agreements, special undercoating, and other unnecessary items.

penny stocks   Stocks sold for under $5 per share. Historically, brokers have manipulated these securities in investment fraud schemes.

persuasion process   The rational and emotional process used by advertisers to influence consumer purchasing behavior.

Ponzi schemes   A form of financial fraud whereby investors are paid gains from money put up by later investors. Early investors can walk away with quick gains, but eventually no more participants can be found and the scheme collapses. A Ponzi scheme is similar to a pyramid scheme and chain letters.

predatory pricing   The business practice of selling at a loss (below production or wholesale costs) to drive out the competition. This practice is illegal under federal antitrust laws.

price discrimination   Selling the same product at different prices to different buyers. This is illegal if it limits competition under federal antitrust laws.

price fixing   An illegal arrangement between two or more sellers to set prices for a product.

product liability   The legal responsibility of manufacturers to compensate consumers for injuries or losses sustained as a result of unsafe or defective products.

puffery   An advertiser's exaggerated claims about the quality of his/her products that are based on opinion, not fact. Puffery claims include statements such as "feels good," or "tastes like it should." Because these are opinions, such claims cannot be considered deceptive.

pump and dump   A sales tactic frequently used with the sale of securities to pump up (increase) the price of a stock through e-mails, Websites, or other means of advertising. There may be claims of insider information or other crucial data. Only the promoters of the security stand to gain by pumping up the supposed value and then dumping their shares on the market before the price collapses.

pyramid schemes   Investors buy the right to become a sales representative and sell the same franchise to others. Sales representatives may sell products, but this is secondary to the recruitment of new investors.

quackery   Anything involving overpromotion in the field of health.

This could include false or unproven remedies, untested dietary supplements, misleading advertising, and other questionable products.

recovery room   A form of telemarketing fraud whereby a telemarketer promises to recover a victim's funds lost to past illegal misrepresentations. The victim, however, must pay a fee up front and nothing is ever recovered.

regulation   An attempt by government to control the behavior of individuals or corporations. Marketplace regulations set standards for consumer protection, promote competition, and limit predatory pricing.

reloading   A telemarketing term to describe the reuse of consumer names, particularly for fraudulent sales. When a telemarketer successfully closes a sale, the company may then reload or reuse the name of the buyer for another sale.

rent-to-own   A lease to purchase goods such as appliances, furniture, and automobiles offering low monthly payments. Payments for rent-to-own products, however, usually cost two, three, or four times more than either a cash purchase price or most time-payment plans for the same products.

restraint of trade   An agreement by sellers in an industry to restrict or limit competition. This practice is illegal under federal antitrust laws.

right to privacy   An individual's protection against the invasion of his/her private life by sellers, government, and others.

rip and tear   An illegal telemarketing operation that seeks to victimize as many people as possible and to quickly move on.

self-regulation   Businesses willing to regulate themselves by adopting codes of conduct or standard setting. Self-regulation is an alternative to government regulation.

slamming   The practice of switching a consumer's long-distance telephone carrier without his/her authorization.

spam, spamming   Unsolicited e-mail, or the sending of unsolicited e-mail.

spiff   A cash bonus paid to car salespeople for loading up a consumer's automobile purchase contract with credit life insurance, service contracts, and/or special options.

state securities agencies   State agencies created to protect investors purchasing securities.

suggers   Telemarketers who sell under the guise of conducting a survey.

target audience   A specific group of consumers targeted by advertisers, direct marketers, or other sellers.

telemarketing A form of direct marketing using the telephone to sell products.

telemarketing fraud The use of telemarketing for fraudulent sales. Frauds could include contests and sweepstakes, fake charities, investment frauds, or other schemes. It is estimated that telemarketing fraud costs consumers $40 billion a year.

tying A practice by which a seller refuses to sell a product unless it includes another good or service. Such practices frequently limit competition and may be illegal under federal antitrust laws.

unfair and deceptive acts or practices An oral or written factual claim, a practice, or the withholding of information that has the capacity or tendency to mislead consumers. Examples of such acts or practices are bait-and-switch advertising, Ponzi schemes, shoddy home repairs, and telemarketing fraud.

usury An interest rate in excess of the percentage allowed by federal or state laws.

vertical merger The combination of two or more companies in the same industry that are at different stages of production or sales.

warranty A seller's promise or assurance that a product will perform as indicated.

weights and measures The U.S. Constitution authorizes Congress to "fix" or standardize national weights and measures to improve commerce. State and local consumer protection agencies, however, are the agencies responsible for ensuring that gas pumps actually pump a gallon of gas or supermarket scales do not short weigh a pound of meat.

white-collar crime Illegal activities such as insider trading, fraud, or price fixing, committed by corporate managers.

wire fraud A scheme to defraud, transmitted by means of a wire (telephone), radio, or television.

work at home A scheme in which promoters offer to help find lucrative and stable employment that consumers can perform at home. All consumers need to do is pay the start-up fee. In turn they receive a business plan showing them how to operate vending machines, service pay phones, stuff envelops, or similar jobs. Invariably the business plans provide almost no useful information, but the promoter keeps the start-up fee.

Index

L ee E. Norrgard is investigative analyst and acting manager of the Consumer Affairs Division of the American Association of Retired Persons. Mr. Norrgard's publications include ABC-CLIO's *Final Choices: Making End of Life Decisions.*

J ulia M. Norrgard is a senior legal assistant at Aschcraft & Gerel in Alexandria, Virginia. She has an M.A. in history from George Mason University.